1975 May

Thur Fri Sat **Sun** Mon Tue Wed Thur Fri Sat **Sun** Mon Tue Wed Thur Fri Sat **Sun** Mon Tue Wed Thur Fri Sat **Sun** Mon Tue Wed Thur Fri Sat

22 23 24 **25** 26 27 28 29 30 31

26 Monday

Week 22 (146-219)

HOLIDAY IN ENGLAND, N. IR

...morning Paul and Lamel

...did some gardening an... ...and unsatisfactory

...for Petals for Thur... ...reach of dawn on Thursday

...around 1:00 for b... ...very melancholy about

...leaving Pig behind – she... ...which seen below Deluxe

...our Village Hall. ...giv... chinless wayne or something

...and drove them back in... ...ker and to the uproar roundabout. Rather less traffic than I'd

imagined and I reached London around 3:15. Sat in the car for a bit and then went and sat

in Petals office and made phone calls. The whole place quite deserted because it was a bank holiday

and I was feeling very lonely and very forlorn. Ambled over to the studio and the monitor

screen in the control room was showing Evel Knievel's attempt at Wembley Stadium to jump

a motor-cycle over 13 single-decker buses. Incredible American hokum with Evel telling us

that he is still kinda proud of that old red, white and blue, cheer-leaders high-stepping round

the ground, well out of time and dropping their batons as they went. Then Evel did a few ratther

nuttony wheelies and then stood on top of the buses to tell us, in his home-spun way, that are,

it's no kind of a politician but he reckons, y'all, that our wunnerful country sure should stay

the Common Market and that Amyurica would be real happy if we did. Unfortunately Bill

humo ex-Beefheart man, arrived with the tape of the LP of Madand which is the band which

was the Magic Band. I was a bit disappointed with their new vocalist though but the first half of

LP, which was all I had a chance to hear, sounded pretty good. Then Greg Nash arrived

and stayed for the first thirty minutes of the fa... ...e and really distressed me with a series

of silly questions while I was trying to get... ...the programme. Eventually chased him

off and tried to salvage something of the... ...hate doing these golden hit holiday shows

when it was over I ruled out and drove for... ...ih... round to Hadleigh and the White Lion.

arrived exactly at the same time as Pig and... ...then had a drink there – as usual the place

was almost empty. Had another drink at a... ...red pub outside Hadleigh and a third at one in

...derton. Looked fab from the outside but ch... ...filled w. scruffs around a duff jukebox.

Margrave of the Marshes

Margrave of the Marshes

JOHN PEEL
AND SHEILA RAVENSCROFT

BANTAM PRESS

LONDON · TORONTO · SYDNEY · AUCKLAND · JOHANNESBURG

TRANSWORLD PUBLISHERS
61–63 Uxbridge Road, London W5 5SA
a division of The Random House Group Ltd

RANDOM HOUSE AUSTRALIA (PTY) LTD
20 Alfred Street, Milsons Point, Sydney,
New South Wales 2061, Australia

RANDOM HOUSE NEW ZEALAND LTD
18 Poland Road, Glenfield, Auckland 10, New Zealand

RANDOM HOUSE SOUTH AFRICA (PTY) LTD
Isle of Houghton, Corner of Boundary Road and Carse O'Gowrie,
Houghton 2198, South Africa

Published 2005 by Bantam Press
a division of Transworld Publishers

A catalogue record for this book is available from the British Library.
ISBN 0593 052528

Typeset in 11/16pt Berling by
Falcon Oast Graphic Art Ltd.

Printed in Great Britain by
Clays Ltd, Bungay, Suffolk

1 3 5 7 9 10 8 6 4 2

Papers used by Transworld Publishers are natural, recyclable products made from wood grown in
sustainable forests. The manufacturing processes conform to the environmental regulations
of the country of origin.

It was John's wish that this book should be dedicated to the Revd R. H. J. Brooke.

And we would like to dedicate this book to John, with our love.

Contents

Acknowledgements

We would like to thank Chris Berthoud, Lawrence Blackall, Big Bob, Billy Bragg, Richard Clark, Fiona Couper, John Darin, Paul Gambaccini, David Gedge, Peter Griffiths, Stewart Henderson, Claire Hillier, Tracey Holmyard, Alison Howe, Kid Jensen, Anita Kamath, Louise Kattenhorn, Andy Kershaw, Phil Knappett, Chris Lycett, Mike McCartney, The Misunderstood, Tom Robinson, Mike Sampey, Shurley and Clive Selwood, Feargal Sharkey, Bridget St John, Mike Stax, Dave Tate, Helen Walters, all the staff at Transworld and all those friends we have almost certainly forgotten to mention.

An extra special thank you to Frank, Alan, Gabs, John, Angela, Paul, Carmel, Zahra, Ashley, Hermeet and Archie.

Also thank you to Ryan Gilbey and Cat Ledger for helping to make this as enjoyable an experience as it could have been.

Picture Credits

The line drawings in the text are by Sheila Ravenscroft, from books she wrote and illustrated for John many years ago, which he cherished.

Most of the images used in the illustration sections have been kindly supplied by the Ravenscroft family. Where credits exist we have listed them here, but we have not always been able to trace the copyright holders. Those who have not been contacted are invited to get in touch with the publishers.

First section
John Peel receives his honorary doctorate: *Eastern Daily Press*; K-Men publicity shot: *Richard Fowler*; JP with Captain Beefheart: *O. C. Hill*; JP signing autographs outside the BBC: *Peter Sanders*.

Second section
Hollywood festival (main picture and bottom left): *Barry Plummer*; Reading Festival 1976 (centre left): *Nando Val Verde*; line-up of DJs 1974 and JP with Alan Freeman: *BBC*; JP in the studio: *Denis Jones*; JP falling off a donkey: *Kevin Simpson*; JP with Woggle: *Richard Wallis*.

Third section
JP in Nan True's Hole: *Brian Moody/Rex Features*; JP at Wembley, 1976: *Joseph Coomber*; JP playing football, 1996: *Rex Features/Hayley Madden*; JP in the fountain: *Phil Knappett*; JP on *Top of the Pops*: *Daily Mirror*; JP with Franco Rossi: *Fin Costello*; family photo: © *Adrian Boot*.

Fourth section
JP at Reading with Thomas: *Jayne Houghton*; JP in Leningrad, Bulgaria and at the Victoria Falls: *Dave Tate*; JP at home with recording tape: *East Anglian Daily Times*; JP with Archie: *Paul Gilhooly*; family together at JP's sixty-fifth birthday party: *Mike McCartney*.

Introduction

This has been for our family an unexpected and daunting launch into the literary world and in the circumstances somewhat unwelcome. Dad got as far as writing half of this book. Although we had the option of publishing this alone, we thought it important that his story should be finished, if only to make clear that he didn't meet our mother in the establishment in which he ended his half. He got as far as his adventures in America but stopped just short of his first radio appearance. There are no first-hand accounts of the seven years between that radio début and his meeting Mum, and frankly, even after that details can be a little shaky, but we pieced together what we could until Mum's steadfast memory could be relied upon.

Various people had been on at Dad to write an autobiography and he had been promising to do so for the past thirty years. We even went so far as to have a room built for the purpose of his writing, which he promptly filled with records. Eventually, after the collapse of numerous pension schemes he realised it might be a good time to get started. At one point he wanted to begin with the line 'The junior officers exchanged glances. Mrs Bradshaw was on board again.' Not sure why. Once he'd developed a routine he was very productive, although cruelly all of his early progress was accidentally deleted one careless Monday morning. He wasn't terrifically good with computers. He would sit in his place at the kitchen table tapping away on his laptop under the watchful gaze of the Bill Shankly photo on the wall. To be honest, we were terrified when we learnt that Dad was writing a book. It's not that he made things up, but he had, in the past, exaggerated stories about us, misread situations and, well yes, he had also just made things up. We're fairly sure he hasn't done that here. We would like to have seen what, if he had got the chance, he would have concocted.

The title of the book had not, so far as we are aware, been decided upon. He enjoyed coming up with amusing if slightly puzzling titles: *How's Your Flow?*, *Wet Echo*, *Flying Cream Shots*, *Goatman Codds*, *If He Ever Hits Puberty*, *Buckskins and Buggery*, *The Wotters Won the Wace*, *A History of the Iodine Trade 1847–1902*, *An ABC of High-Jumping*, *The Questing of Stempel Garamond: How He Overcame the Gelks and Punished the Dwellers within the Well* and *Jesus Wasn't Made of Fish*. We found the titles in his suitcase from Peru alongside a note to self: 'Lay in bed composing powerfully vulgar Wayne Rooney chants. I've got a gem but this is not the forum for it,' evidence that he wasn't concentrating fully on the task in hand. Contained within this notebook were also various quotes, reminders and observations:

Woke at three,
people being woken at five,
American shouting at 5.30,
Man farting so loudly in adjoining cabin,

Then silence,
Has there been a coup?
6.45 complete silence.

The major difference between their political situation and ours
is that we are better – more subtle perhaps – at corruption and
cronyism. There is no Peter Mandelson in Peruvian politics.

Incorporate book on Finnish sheds into autobiography.

We put off making any decisions regarding the book, as we
had no idea what Dad had planned, if anything. We are fairly
sure, though, that he would have approved of Mum's silly
drawings of the both of them being used as chapter headings.
Dad always said they would be the first thing he would save
in the event of a house fire, but then he said that about
everything.

The research we have all done for the second part of the
book has, of course, been strange, but also an opportunity to
read Dad's many newspaper and magazine articles. Some of
these are really good, some fairly daft. Hidden away amongst
all the obscene badges, German thrash magazines and old
Radio 1 postcards, we found his old diaries that have been our
staple diet over the last six months. These cover, sporadically,
the years 1967 to 1983. They demonstrate just how hard Dad
worked, traipsing up and down the country gigging and sleeping in motorway service areas. We came across a few details we
would rather have missed, frankly, and plenty of stories about
us growing up that we found very amusing but won't bore you
with. Apparently, Thomas ate a mouse.

Later in the book you will come across Dad's account of his

close relationships with US presidents. The photographs to which he refers, the evidence of this bond, were not, as he believed, destroyed. His first wife's brother had been carrying the slides around for nearly forty years and offered to send them from America. When, after so long, he got them in his grubby hands, pleasure danced across his pretty face. He could hardly believe that he finally had proof that his stories were true.

There is no physical evidence that Dad isn't still with us here at home. The records in his to-listen-to pile are still stacked by the turntable, a smaller selection waiting to be allocated a place in a running order. The machinery of his long-established system is still in place, but unused. We don't know what to do with the piles of demo CDs that fill every corner. 'There could be another Elvis in there,' we can hear him say. We all feel as guilty as Dad used to at the thought of getting rid of these. Obviously we can't continue his work, listening to these demos and promoting these bands, but we felt that we could at least try to complete this book.

We can't pretend that *Margrave of the Marshes* will be the read that Dad would have provided, though in plagiarising enough of his work hopefully his voice remains throughout. There are many stories that he didn't tell us enough times for us to remember, but we have tried to include all the things we think were important to him. We hope the effort Mum and ourselves have put into making this a worthy chronicle of his life has gone some way to showing how much he meant to us all.

William, Alexandra, Thomas and Florence

Part One

It is obvious that disc-jockeys, as a class, are essentially parasitic. We are, with lamentably few exceptions, neither creative nor productive. We have, however, manipulated the creations of others (records) to provide ourselves with reputations as arbiters of public taste. There is no more reason (nor no less) why I should be writing this column than you – however I am in this unmerited position and you're not. I believe very much in radio as a medium of tragically unrealised possibilities and also in the music I play. Therefore accepting the falseness of my own precarious position I will do what I can, wherever I can, to publicise these good things I hear around me. These musicians have made you aware of, and appreciative of, their music – not J. Peel.

John Peel, *Disc and Music Echo*, 1969

Chapter One

Sheila and I are babysitting today and our grandson, Archie, isn't happy. He doesn't like the tomato, yam and basil mixture his mother, Alexandra, our daughter, sent over with him this morning. I'm not sure I would either. He also seems un-enthusiastic about the harness that secures him in place in his highchair. I'm with him most of the way on that one too. Do I really remember the pressure, the chafing, even the smell of the various harnesses that held the infant John Robert Parker Ravenscroft in place? There was, I know for a fact, a brown leather lead that Nanny used when she took me walking and I can remember the smell, even the taste, of that. It may have had bells on it.

I was born, I have always told people, at the age of four in a woodcutter's cottage in the Black Forest, but the disappointing truth is that I was born in Heswall Cottage Hospital a few days before the outbreak of the Second World War. The Cottage Hospital is a private home now and the family living there has been in touch with me twice. Once when the father sent me a brick from a wall they had removed, and more recently when I was playing Chibuku in Liverpool – it's a club, not a board game – and his sons invited me to stay in the building in which I was born. If we hadn't already been booked into the Racquets Club and I hadn't recognised that a lot of red wine would have to be taken to get me through the night, I'd have accepted too. You'd be amazed at the number of people who've suggested some sort of link between my birth and the outbreak of war. 'So it was your fault,' they've chortled, but I've never laughed – any more than I have at the people who have greeted me in more recent years with the words, 'D'yer ken John Peel, then?' Several of these are buried in shallow graves on B roads off the A505. The police have confessed themselves baffled.

Naturally I don't remember much about the war. Father was away, eyeball to eyeball with the Germans in North Africa. Mother was in her bedroom. Sometimes I'd be carried to the air-raid shelter at the top of the garden, out of the French windows from the sitting-room, across the crazy paving and up the former tennis court we called the Big Lawn. Later, I would be joined by Francis Houghton Leslie Ravenscroft; conceived, it was explained to me years later, in London, when Father was halfway home on leave. On the big blue radio in the air-raid shelter we heard, without understanding what it meant, of the war in Europe. Somehow, though, we understood that the words on the radio were linked to the aircraft-recognition books we were shown from time to time, with the barrage balloon that came down in the field across the road, with the strange powdered foods we ate and with the fact that Father wasn't there. Father, I decided, probably didn't exist at all, remaining, for the first six years of my life, a figure as remote and improbable as the characters in *The Blue Fairy Book*, less real to me than Dame Washalot, Moonface and the other folk of Enid Blyton's Faraway Tree.

The aircraft-recognition books were useful though. I knew to look for black crosses on the wings and had been warned that under no circumstances was I to venture into the top half of a garden that was about the size and shape of a football pitch, with a path running along, as it were, the halfway line between the sandstone wall and what would become, when Father came home, the hen run. One afternoon, I had toddled up the path from the kitchen door, past the tool shed, the greenhouse, the cesspit, the gooseberries, the rows of peas and beans, the rhubarb and the rubbish dump, with Francis, intriguingly yellow as a child and rarely awake, tottering unsteadily at my side. When we reached the path that divided the garden in two, I indicated to my brother that it was my intention to venture into the forbidden half. He demurred, in as much as an eighteen-month-old child can do serious demurring, as I took my first step as a free thinker. As I did, a plane – a German plane – hurtled low over the garden. Several years of peace had passed before I crossed the halfway line again.

I, it has already been established, was a child that liked to keep itself to itself. At home, if the weather was fine, I climbed trees and read. Thanks to Nanny, christened Florence Horne but re-christened Trader, in honour of the famous sea captain, by our father, I could read before I went to kindergarten. My favourite reading tree, a sappy, flaky pine, overlooked the field that separated our house from our neighbour's, a field in which, at appropriate times of the year, German prisoners of war worked. These prisoners worked unsupervised, showing as they did, I suppose, little enthusiasm for deserting the relative safety of a Cheshire farm for a profoundly uncertain future on, say, the Russian Front. In halting but rather charming English, they would warn me of the dangers of climbing pine trees. I have since claimed that on feast days they would give Francis and me presents carved from scrap wood, but an inner voice tells me that I have made this up.

Apart from the Whittimores, who farmed the fields across the lane that led to the Behrends' house some distance away in the trees, and Mr Hughes, who farmed across the main road, we had few visitors. Colin and Martin Whittimore were about the same ages as Francis and myself, and in the absence of any other children we could play with, we spent a lot of time with them. Francis even went through a form of marriage with Colin Whittimore, a marriage unrecognised, alas, by any of the major religions, but one that the Church of England might nowadays look upon in a friendlier spirit. (Note to self: check Church's position on same-sex marriages between consenting three-year-olds.)

When we were not with the Whittimores, Francis and I were pretty much left to our own devices. As Francis was usually asleep, this effectively meant that I was alone to wander the garden and commune with Boo Boo, my imaginary friend. Boo Boo lived in somewhat inhospitable quarters beneath a shrub in the rockery, only a stone's throw from the flagpole and just around the corner from where a temporary gardener, a lad in his late teens who cycled up from Burton to plough the fields and scatter, offered to let me see his penis. I remember being impressed by the size of this and by the lad's ability to make it grow bigger or smaller, seemingly at will. I declined his subsequent invitations to gaze upon it again. It was big though.

Apart from climbing trees, talking to Boo Boo, inspecting the private parts of junior members of staff and helping Mother hoist the Union Jack that flew over the garden throughout the war, the only real excitement in our lives came from our regular walks into Burton with Nanny. Depending on her whim, Francis, asleep in the pram, his yellow hue exciting comment from everyone we encountered (NB, Francis is not yellow now nor has he been for a number of years), and I, skipping, were led either down Denhall Lane towards Burton Point station and the marshes beyond or left along Burton Road towards the village. If Nanny had opted for the former – and longer – route, she was compelled to make a second decision when we reached the railway bridge two thirds of the way to the river. Here we could either go left through a gate and along the footpath that led to and beyond the station, or carry on down the hill to the marshes.

On the corner at the bottom of the hill lay the entrance to the home of the Summers family. The Summers were clearly several cuts above us socially. As we understood it, they owned the steelworks we could see through the blue haze on the far bank of the Dee. More importantly, they seemed to have dozens of gardeners of the type that vanished, deer-like, into the under-growth at the approach of visitors – and they had a swimming pool. From time to time, we were authorised to use the pool and to grow deeply envious of its changing rooms, wooden boats and implausibly blue waters. We were occasionally joined by a Summers, the only one we ever saw and who was at Shrewsbury when I turned up there years later. This Summers – I don't think we ever knew his name – looked the very model of the spookily good-looking boys drawn with care bordering on lust by the artists who illustrated the stories of schoolboy derring-do to which I was later to turn when I wearied of the Folk of the Faraway Tree. He had what would have been described in these stories as a frank and open face, and silver hair of the type now apparently considered essential for anyone running for high office in the US.

Whichever way Nanny, Francis and I walked, we ended up in Burton village. Here, at Mrs Boyle's or Jackson's the Grocers, Nanny would fall into conversation with other nannies. Jackson's the Grocers was a shop so breathtakingly exciting that I believed that a life in the grocery trade would bring me all of the thrills in life it was possible for one person to experience. Mrs Boyle's was run, reason insists, by a Mrs Boyle and sold, I think, newspapers. Both these shops ceased trading at some time lost in the mists of pre-history and Burton is now a dormitory village that you can drive through during working hours without seeing a living soul. I know this because I've done it on more than one occasion.

It was outside Jackson's that Nanny told a gathering of rival nannies the details of an event that was to shape the next twenty or so years of my life. I would be deceiving you if I were to attempt to persuade you that I was already, at the age of five, striving to establish some sort of identity for myself, something that set me apart from the rest of humankind, but I was aware, on some level, that whereas Francis was yellow and asleep, the Summers boy had silver hair and the gardener an enormous penis, I had nothing very interesting to commend me to the passer-by.

The day dawned, as all days seemed to then, with the sun shining, butterflies swarming outside the dining-room window and song-birds making idle conversation almost impossible. So it was that looking out on the morning and finding it fair, I elected to take my tricycle for a spin about the garden. The high point of this would be the wild dash through the vegetable garden from the rubbish dump, down a long straight which ended with a slight swerve past the greenhouse before the tricyclist changed down, as it were, for the tricky ride past the tool shed and the back door and through the gate into the driveway. Unfortunately for me, fate intervened at the slight-swerve stage, the steering on the tricycle failed and I plunged through the side of the greenhouse. Upon realising that I was out of control and headed for what was effectively a wall of glass, I had instinctively put my left arm up to protect myself and thus it was that Nanny found me lying in the wreckage, the left rear wheel of the tricycle probably still spinning lazily in the swooning air, with a deep gash on the inside of my elbow and another on the inside of my wrist. Looking at the scars now, it is hard to imagine how I avoided slashing open a major blood vessel and bleeding to death. If the opportunity ever presents itself, I'd be very happy to show you my wounds. Suffering from shock but curiously feeling no pain whatever, I was led into the house so that Mother could assess the damage and decide upon appropriate action. She chose to call Dr Gunn.

Dr Gunn I remember only for the case filled with surgical instruments and bottles of amusingly coloured liquids that he carried with him and for the fact that he drove a seriously strange car of a type I've not been able to identify to the present day. So strange was it, in fact, that throughout my childhood I treasured an early Dinky car that I never saw replicated in any-one else's collection which would now be worth, I like to think, thousands of your pounds, a car known to all the family as Dr Gunn's car. I waited for the doctor sitting on the dining-room table, the table favoured by Mother as the location for my many beatings, passing the time by gazing at my wounds. I remember thinking how like the inside of a tomato the inside of the human arm looked. I was still too shocked to cry, and continued tear-free when the doctor sewed up my arm – without anaesthetic, of course – before discharging me into the community.

That afternoon, outside Jackson's, I heard Nanny tell the massed nannies of Burton village that I had gone through all the above without a single tear. The nannies were impressed. So impressed, in fact, that I decided then and there that from now on I was to be The Boy That Never Cried. To be honest, I probably did cry on occasions after that: upon going to boarding school for the first time, perhaps, and when the puppy I had wanted from the womb and which I was given at Christmas 1947 was taken from me in the first week of 1948 and given to Mr Hughes the farmer instead. But by and large I rarely cried again until I met Sheila. Since then – and I don't know what an analyst would make of this – I have cried almost without cessation, at everything from *The Little House on the Prairie* to Liverpool's triumphs in Europe.

At the time of my accident I was already a pupil at Miss Jones's kindergarten, located in the badlands along the Neston/Parkgate border. Not for Miss Jones and her valkyries the reckless modern notion that a year or two should be spent in action-painting, plasticine work and drawing pictures of Mummy and Daddy. On the first day at her establishment we were taught the days of the week in French – I know some of these to the present day – and a Miss Laxton introduced us to the realities of contemporary education by throwing board rubbers at us. She had a sturdy throwing arm and a good eye, did Miss Laxton. Despite my accomplishments re. the days of the week in French, I failed to impress at Miss Jones's. So much so, in fact, that the Headmistress's report at the end of my first term read, in its entirety, 'Robin has failed to make much impression at school.' Wounding, I felt.

It was at Miss Jones's that I fell in love for the first time, with a dark-haired girl named Helen Maddox. Our love never took physical form – something to do with the poor wartime diet on which we'd both been raised, I expect – but I can still close my eyes and picture Helen and her home up a pathway near the Wheatsheaf pub in Ness. Or was that Jane Barker's house? She was kinda cute too. Either way, Francis and I walked past the end of the pathway on an unforgettable walk we had with Father.

Father rarely spoke to us on matters of moment, preferring to leave health and welfare issues to Mother – who didn't speak to us about them either. However, on this occasion we had travelled from Birkenhead to Neston on the bus and had missed the connecting bus to Burton so had no choice but to walk the three or four miles instead. Every step of the way Father spoke to Francis and I on the paramount importance of regular bowel movements and the damage that could be done to us both physically and spiritually if we failed to adhere to an appropriately rigorous regime in this area. I feel now that much of the wickedness that has emerged in me since that walk has been the result of my failure to follow Father's advice. 'Go when you want to go' has summed up my attitude to the whole untidy business and has been the advice I have given to our children when they have in turn sidled into my room, as sidle bewildered young persons will, to ask, 'Father dear, tell us about, you know, going to the lavatory.'

The above account will have alerted you to the fact that Father, unlike so many other fathers and grandfathers, mothers and grandmothers, had returned undamaged from the war. In common with almost everyone I've ever met who saw service in the Second World War, he never really spoke about his experiences. When he came home, Father came home as Captain Robert Ravenscroft, Royal Artillery, but settled almost immediately back into civilian life and had little time for other men who had signed up for the duration but insisted on being addressed by their military ranks after the war had ended.

Francis and I first set sight on our father when we were on holiday in Tre-Arddur Bay, Anglesey, where the then-unborn Alan was to go to school years later. It's hard to imagine now, but the unavailability of motor transport to all but a relatively well-heeled few, allied with petrol rationing, meant that there was little traffic on the roads, so whenever Francis or I heard a distant engine we would run to the end of the drive to watch whatever was passing pass. One afternoon – I think we can afford now to take the sun and blue skies as read, although you can add wheeling gulls to the equation if you like – we were playing in the garden when we heard a motorcycle engine at the top of the road and ran to the gateway to watch the bike pass by. To our surprise and, I think, mild alarm, instead of passing by, the bike slowed and turned into the driveway. This was of gravel and circled a small lawn, and as the rider carefully picked his way along this, I ran ahead across the lawn and into the house. Mother was washing her hair in a sink overlooking the driveway and I ran in shouting, 'Mummy! Mummy! There's a funny-looking man at the door.' She looked out of the window, burst into tears and said, 'That's your father.' Seconds later I stood with Francis looking up at the man we now thought of as our motorcyclist. So this was what a father looked like.

Years later I found myself standing in the same spot retelling this story for a television crew. As I told it, I could feel something ungovernable rising within me and fancied that I would have some sort of seizure at the completion of my account. In the event, I gave a rather theatrical low moan and slumped to the ground in tears. The television people mercifully edited this collapse from their film. I can only assume that their thoughtfulness was due to their lack of experience in the ways of television.

Chapter Two

Barbara from Radio Flora, Hannover, will ring shortly. When I spoke to her last week, she seemed a little vague about the programme I record each month, when I remember, for FSK in Hamburg. This, these days, is my only radio link with Germany. My friend Sebastian Cording copies the DAT tape I send to FSK and it is distributed to, I have been told, a dozen or more German-speaking radio stations. The bulk of these, unsurprisingly, are in Germany, although there have been subscribers in the past in both Austria and Switzerland. Quite what becomes of the programmes, two hours of matchless fun for all the family, after they have left the village post office, is something of a mystery. I'll go further: it's a complete mystery. Despite having recorded for FSK for four or five years at least, I have yet to receive my first letter or email from a listener – unless you count the note I got from a woman working for an unnamed community station somewhere near the coast of northern Germany. The highlight of her month, she told me, was when it fell to her to play out my programme and she could sit alone in the station with a glass of wine, staring out to sea, and listen to the music. It is for this woman and for her alone that I continue recording.

But Barbara is not sure that Radio Flora still transmits my work – 'Call that work?' The Voice of the Critic – and I wonder whether the station ever did. She will call soon on behalf of Kai who doesn't much English speak and Kai will want to know about David Bowie.

All Europeans want to know about David Bowie. Only a few weeks ago a film crew arrived from Denmark and wanted to know about David Bowie. 'Tell us about David Bowie,' they cried in their attractive, lilting voices. 'How did you react when you first heard "Aladdin Sane"?' In vain I explained that I really couldn't remember how I had reacted to the release of the LP. 'I expect I liked it and played tracks on the radio,' I smiled. 'But your deeper feelings, John, tell us of those,' they insisted. So, instead of explaining that I have no deeper feelings really, I told them about touring with Bowie and Tyrannosaurus Rex. This story gives me the chance to do a little mime I've worked up – nothing complex, just that man-in-a-phonebox business – that usually goes down well.

I only recall one of the gigs on the tour, the one in Brighton. It was Marc Bolan/Tyrannosaurus Rex's tour and Bowie, despite having had a huge hit with 'Space Oddity', was down on his luck and bottom of the bill; billed below, if you can believe it, that lowliest of God's creatures, an Australian sitar player. I was sitting backstage talking to Marc when I realised that it had gone eight thirty and that the show should have started, so went to the door and shouted down the corridor, 'David, you're on.' That was about the only direct contact I had with 'the chameleon of pop' (copyright: just about everyone who's ever written about Bowie) on the tour. I mean, what's the point in talking to a mime artist? D'ya know what I mean?

Anyway, cut forward a few years to the point at which David has become a star, has lived in Berlin and New York and is big, Big, BIG. His record company is hosting a reception for him somewhere dark and red and plush and I'm lurking in a corner musing on life and what little I remember of the Tyrannosaurus Rex tour and thinking of the letter Bowie wrote to me once asking if I would consider helping fund an Arts Lab he had in mind for Beckenham and District, and decided I'd go and have a word with my old mate. With this modest purpose in mind, I left my corner and moved towards where the star stood surrounded by impossibly glamorous courtiers. When I was but a few feet away, a very large black guy – a karate expert, I told everyone later – interposed his substantial body between me and my objective. 'Hey, asshole! Where the fuck you think you're going?' he wanted to know. 'Just going to have a word with David,' I replied with that quick, nervous smile I do. 'Like fuck ya gonna have a word with David,' he insisted. Since then, and surely way beyond the New York karate expert's intention, I've not had a single word with David. However, he did appear, on film, when I was the subject of *This Is Your Life*, and although I don't remember what he said about me, I imagine it was something pretty nice. As – was it Capt. W. E. Johns? – said, life's a funny business.

So I'll tell Barbara from Radio Flora this story and hope she'll be satisfied. People usually are.

*

At the age of seven, I left Miss Jones's, having served there with little distinction – although I like to think that by the time I left they had recognised that I was called John, not Robin – to spend the summer at home before being packed off to Woodlands School, Deganwy. I can recall little of that summer – you can build your own paragraph here but don't forget to include endless sunshine, butterflies, food shortages and a few thoughts on the amusingly primitive techniques involved in bringing in the harvest in those days, with, if you're up for it, a sidelong glance at the laughing land-girls and what can only be described as their sauciness – but probably spent much of it trying to imagine what life would be like at Woodlands and trying to avoid spending time with local children that my parents believed I would benefit from knowing. These boys would be startlingly good at everything, and I remember one in particular who was a classic example of a child hugely admired by adults but loathed and mistrusted by other children. In moments of despair, Father would ask me why I couldn't be more like him, and wouldn't listen when I tried to explain that I would rather be eaten alive than be like him. He excelled at cricket and tennis and probably at squash and fives and hockey and – oh, I don't know – everything, but on one of the rare occasions on which my defences were breached and he appeared in our garden, he had the impudence to attempt time and again, and on my bike, to beat the world-record time I had set for the track Francis and I had developed around the garden. As he left the start line, shouting with excitement, Francis and I watched gloomily as he disappeared from view, hoping against hope that as he reached the difficult right-then-left-hander through the gate by the kitchen door, he'd get it wrong and we would hear the satisfying sound of skull on gatepost followed by the crash of bike and rider hitting the concrete outside the garage.

As the summer – endless sunshine, butterflies, where have they all gone? – drew to an end, the household started to prepare for the trauma of sending the young master away to boarding school. A trunk big enough to house a couple of average-sized adults was bought and Mother took me to Browns of Chester to obtain the uniform, in a giddy combination of red and grey, with which to fill it. Although I have always striven to give the impression that, regardless of what I may look like as of even date, I was a comely child, Mother was convinced that in one respect at least I was seriously malformed. Arriving in the Boys' Uniform sector of Browns she sought assurances, in a booming voice, from the staff members who scurried obsequiously forward to offer assistance, that clothing could be found that would adequately cover what she characterised as an excessively large backside. As she shouted these her thoughts, the centre of Chester came to a standstill. Like something from an H. M. Bateman cartoon, I would shrivel almost to nothingness as other customers and members of staff craned to see the malformed body part and its unfortunate owner, doors to Accounts Departments and Managers' Offices would open and people would peer out, careworn faces eager with anticipation for what was likely to prove the day's only laugh. When I got home, I would, in the privacy of my own room, inspect, as best I could, my bottom and could see nothing abnormal in its dimensions whatsoever. I was never able to tell Mother when, a few years later, at Shrewsbury, my pert little rear was somewhat admired by a fair number of older boys. There are some things you cannot sensibly share with a parent.

Eventually the time came when, the trunk having been sent ahead by rail, I was taken to Chester Station to meet my new schoolmates and undertake the slow train journey through Prestatyn and Colwyn Bay to Llandudno Junction. To help the time pass I had been bought, from the station bookstall, a slim volume of jokes and cartoons devoted to and derived from the restaurant trade. One of the cartoons has remained with me ever since and seems to me to contain within it one of the universal truths, although I'm not sure which one. A diner is addressing a waiter whilst indicating his disapproval of the meal placed in front of him with a fork and a disdainful expression. 'Waiter,' he is saying. 'This is too big. It's not an omelette, it's an om.'

Upon our arrival at Llandudno Junction, we were formed into twos and marched the mile or so to the school. I was paired with a boy named Warburton who had been assigned the task of introducing the infant Ravenscroft to the many conventions and curiosities of life at boarding school. The first thing Warburton told me chilled me to the bone. The French, he revealed, had a word they used in everyday conversation that we regarded as effectively unsayable in a decently ordered society. When I pressed him for details, he said, 'Wee-wee' and looked away. I admired him for his refinement of feeling and we continued our walk to the school in silence.

Woodlands School, Deganwy, had a history dating back over fifty years and was one of a number of similar establishments in the area. I could equally well have been dispatched to Rydal, Epworth, Heronwater or Tre-Arddur Bay and never bothered to ask anyone why Woodlands. The headmaster was a Capt. Lloyd and chief amongst the teachers were a Mr Brooke – related, I was told, to the late Rupert Brooke – and Mr Gibson, who smelt of a heady mix of fruit and pencil shavings. There was a Mr Lloyd (no relation) as well, a man who owned a rather wonderful Daimler with an external water temperature gauge mounted on the bonnet.

Of far greater significance to me than the staff, obviously, were my fellow inmates. The only other new boy that term, and the only person outside my immediate family that I knew before my mid-twenties with whom I am still in contact, was Sparrow Harrison. Despite the fact that no-one was ever known by their first names and, indeed, I never even knew the first names of the boys I considered my best pals – Sparrow was always Sparrow. Until the summer of 2004, I had always believed that Sparrow was the name my friend was given at birth and rather gloried in this. Somehow I have discovered that he does, in fact, have another name, less glorious than but similar to Sparrow, but to me he remains and always will remain Sparrow.

Sparrow has a past that embraces rather grand origins, a very severe stammer and the setting up of an organisation to help people overcome, as he has, this disability, and a friend-ship with the Krays. This latter derives from Sparrow's enthusiasm for boxing – he boxed into his sixties – rather than any link to organised crime, and it was his boxing that made him such a useful friend at Woodlands. Bullying was pretty much endemic in the school, and in some of its more macabre forms rather sophisticated. In our first term, Sparrow and I stood and watched as a boy believed worthy of punishment by his peers was tied to the iron railings that ran the length of the rough area of land in which boys tunnelled and dug and built trenches that were covered over with sticks and turf and mud to form 'huts' that Health and Safety would not permit at any school today. Once the unfortunate youth had been secured to the fence, a curved length of corrugated iron, possibly a relic of a wartime air-raid shelter, was then placed against him and in its turn secured before being pelted with lumps of earth and stones. Happily I never did anything to have this punishment visited on me, but it must have been agonising and terrifying for those who were so punished.

Another popular form of bullying was called, for reasons I never identified, 'puto'. In this, the victim was placed on his back on a small table with his hands and feet tied to its legs, and then someone skilled in the art would drum and drum and drum on his stomach. At first, the luckless boy would be able to tense his stomach muscles against the assault, but would eventually give in to the relentless although not particularly violent drumming. Again I never experienced this, either as drummer or drummee, but was assured that it was extremely unpleasant by those that did.

But in the main, the bullying was pretty conventional stuff: kicking, punching and hair-pulling being its most common forms of expression. My principal tormentor – and that of most of my friends – was an oafish boy named Bardsley. Bardsley's family, rumour had it, were in the construction business in the Manchester area. In fact, it seemed that most of the boys at Woodlands came from the Manchester area and most of them were Manchester United supporters, so it was not surprising that I made the necessary leap of the imagination and assumed that Bardsley was himself a United supporter. In this assumption probably lies my continuing lack of enthusiasm for what has become less a local football team than a global business located in Manchester.

Before I further enrage Manchester United supporters, I should tell you about our friends Charlie and Alison.

In the early days of Radio 1, it was suggested to me that it would be somewhat inappropriate for me to become too well acquainted with any listener who might get in touch by mail. Quite what the thinking behind this was, I never really ascertained, but assumed that it was in line with traditional BBC thinking and possibly was the result of fears that too close a relationship with listeners might result in hand-holding before marriage or even, in extreme cases, kissing. Either way, it was a suggestion I completely ignored, with the result that many of the people Sheila and I regard as our closest friends I met in this way. There were others, I have to admit, with whom I did hold hands but will publish details of these relationships in a sealed section towards the end of the book.

Needless to say, most of the incoming mail addressed to me at Radio 1 concerned records I had played on air and was written, in the main, by people who had waited anything up to ten years before being driven to get in touch. 'What,' correspondents would want to know, 'was the name of the reggae track you played, possibly in the autumn of 1971, that had the word "Jah" in it? You played it just before a long record with a lot of guitaring in it.' But one day, amid letters and cards of this sort, there was a letter postmarked Marazion in Cornwall. The handwriting was generously proportioned and exuberantly well-rounded and seemed to me to indicate an optimistic and extrovert personality. It was from a fifteen-year-old girl named Alison Martin who was more interested in telling me about her life in Cornwall than in asking about old reggae records with the word 'Jah' in them, so I wrote back, thus initiating a correspondence that continued until one night when the so-called John Peel Roadshow was frustrating students at what was then Manchester Polytechnic by not having any of the records they wanted to hear. As I apologised for my inadequacies to the dissatisfied customers, a hand reached out and grabbed my arm and its owner shouted, 'Hello, I'm Alison from Marazion.' I looked down and identified a woman who looked to me very much as I thought someone from Marazion should look. She was short and dark, with more hair than seemed sensible, and fast became a family friend and a regular visitor to our home in the East Anglian badlands.

At some point in the 1990s, I took a phone call from Alison in which she confided that she had met someone she suspected might turn out to be The One for her, that his name was Charlie, but that – and, oh God, she was dreading how I might react to this – he was a Manchester United supporter. I told her that she must end the relationship forthwith or risk being cast into that outer darkness where all is sweeping and gnashing of teeth.

Alison ignored me, of course. Eventually she and Charlie married and now have three children (all of her pregnancy tests, she confided recently, were conducted in our downstairs bathroom), and I have come to terms with the United business through the realisation that all of Charlie's brothers, his father and ancestors dating back to the mists of pre-history have supported the club. He is not, therefore, one of those poor inadequates who support United solely because their own lives are so untainted by success that they need somewhere, some-how to forge a link with conspicuous success. Charlie also has the good manners not to mention it when United beat Liverpool and I try hard to reciprocate – although this has not been much of a problem in recent seasons.

Chapter Three

All letters home from Woodlands were read by someone on the staff before being posted, so it was not possible to alert my parents to the fact that I was being bullied. Sometimes it was possible though to slip a tightly rolled cry for help into the sealed envelope, and Mother remembered crying when she read one of these possibly tear-stained notes and begging Father to do something about it. In retrospect, it's difficult to imagine what this something might have been and Father contented himself with advising me to punch the boy Bardsley firmly on the nose. Although the literature of the time was awash with flaxen-haired lads named Jack who did this sort of thing at the drop of a hat, one sight of the brooding hulk that was Bardsley confirmed for me that sticking one on him was not a reasonable option. However, one afternoon I went into the upper changing-room, where both Francis and I had our lockers (76 and 54), and found my brother in tears as Bardsley practised one or other of his primitive techniques upon Frank's diminutive person. Remembering Father's words and thinking of all the Jacks who would have heartily endorsed my policy, I whacked the bully as hard as I could in the face. I'd like to record that he sat down on the cold stone floor and sobbed before turning to Jesus and devoting the rest of his life to good works, but he just looked startled and left the room. Amazingly, he never came near either of us again.

By the time Francis joined me at Woodlands, Capt. Lloyd had retired and his place had been taken by a duo, Colonel Sinker and a Revd Brooke. By some distance the more interesting of these was Revd Brooke. He was a portly soul whose outer garments invariably bore generous evidence of meals he had recently consumed, to the point at which reason insisted that a nourishing broth could be obtained from his clerical bib alone. Since reaching the age of sixty myself, I have come to understand that the wanton distribution of foodstuffs about the person has about it a chilling inevitability. Looking at the front of my T-shirt as I write, I can see traces of lunch, including an inch-long smear of what was a delicious gravy, and suddenly, some fifty-five years on, have some sort of fellow-feeling for my former joint headmaster.

As far as I can remember, Brooke's subject was Latin, but it also fell to him to administer beatings and to warn us about the, harrruuumphhh, changes that were about to occur in our bodies. For some of my friends these changes were already well underway, and one of them, Patterson, could already masturbate to issue. I, despite lonely hours dedicated to practising self-abuse, could achieve nothing other than a scarlet prepuce and consoled myself for my sexual inadequacy by taking up smoking. This had the positive effect of putting me off serious smoking for life, and when I left Woodlands for Shrewsbury I was pleased to give it up entirely. Well, I say 'entirely' but I did briefly smoke a pipe during the months in the mid-sixties in which I attempted to sell crop insurance in West Texas. I did this because I believed, mistakenly, that smoking a pipe would make me look pretty sophisticated and thus more attractive to the corn-fed country gals I encountered in the small towns I visited. I abandoned the practice when I dumped a bowl of hot ash into my lap whilst approaching Abilene and recognised that inexpertly smoking a pipe whilst driving was potentially lethal in the short term as well as the long.

Obtaining cigarettes at Woodlands was never easy and those of us sophisticates who smoked had generally to make do with fag-ends we found discarded in the school grounds – until, that is, someone recognised that we could smoke blotting paper instead. This also had the advantage of being something we could do indoors, it being more appropriate for the pupil to be carrying blotting paper than a third of an abandoned Craven A. Thus it was that three or four of us would gather around the fireplace in the school library and light up with relative impunity. Over a period of weeks we came to believe that the different colours of blotting paper gave different taste sensations and that, although all blotting papers were pretty good, some were better than others. 'Ravenscroft's got some red,' the word would spread as we headed for the library, bright-eyed at the thought of the thrills that lay ahead. Obviously all the blotting papers tasted the same – like, well, burning blotting paper really – but I identified similarly fraudulent connoisseurship years later in sixties London when smoking dope with other hippies. To be honest, I never cared much for smoking resin anyway as it almost invariably made me feel sick, but whenever anyone announced that we were smoking Peruvian Black or whatever else it was that was considered a superior brand, I thought back to Woodlands School and the old blotting-paper scam.

In the final week of each boy's sojourn at Woodlands, he would be called into the Revd Brooke's office for what might loosely be styled 'sex education'. There is little doubt that we really needed this. We had heard that the masturbation in which we indulged whenever possible would lead to poor eyesight, disfiguring spots, rounded shoulders and rapid mental deterioration, but apart from this knew little or nothing. From time to time rumours would spread around the leavers. 'Girls,' someone would announce excitedly, 'are not allowed to have long-handled hairbrushes at school,' and we'd exchange knowing glances without ever fully understanding what the significance of this information might be. Brooke, I'm afraid, did little to clarify the situation, possibly because he didn't really know much about sex himself.

'When you get to your next school,' he'd say, 'you'll find that, er, if you have a jug already filled with water and you add more water to it, it will overflow. Well, good luck (consults piece of paper) at Shrewsbury. Come back and see us sometime. Goodbye.' If it hadn't been for one or two happy accidents in the intervening years, I could easily have alarmed Sheila on our wedding night by smiling winsomely and cooing that I'd pop upstairs and prepare the jug of water.

Although several of my friends admitted to having sisters, none was prepared to discuss the differences that they might have noticed – how shall I put this? – in the subtle geography of their sub-navel regions, and I had absolutely no idea about the precise nature of these differences until one afternoon not far from Ludlow.

I was staying with my godmother, Ethleen, at her splendid home, Ashford Manor. The manor seemed to me to be about as splendid as a house could be and was later to serve in my imagination as Blandings Castle and all the other grand houses about which P. G. Wodehouse wrote. It had an implausible amount of grassland to the front and a lake with, I believe, a small island in the middle of it. In the yard stood a dilapidated old late-twenties Bentley, then seen as a rather quaint and mildly desirable used car rather than as a long-term investment opportunity. Sinking into the eternal mud alongside it were the remains of a chain-driven precursor of the Frazer Nash. Ethleen was married to Kit, who earned his living flower-arranging and had prodigious amounts of hair issuing from his ears. Despite the wonderful house, the family was always rumoured to be seriously short of money, to the extent that Kit would have, in wintertime, to shoot squirrels for the pot.

It's hard to imagine that any fifteen-year-old today would play hide-and-seek, but that is what we fell to doing that glorious summer afternoon. Specifically, we – Ethleen's children, their friends (all previously unknown to me) and I – played the hide-and-seek variant in which anyone finding the person who is It stays with them until everyone else has found them. I don't remember the details but I imagine the last to join the chortling throng is It for the next game. Anyway, when it fell to me to be It, I hid in the outside toilet and waited to be discovered. 'They'll never find me in here,' I expect I thought as I chuckled that sinister chuckle that so frightened little Maisie Chambers that November night so long ago. Five or ten minutes later, the door opened and a girl, name unknown, slipped into the darkened lavatory alongside me. Before the door closed fully, she announced that she was desperate to go and, pulling down her knickers, sat all unheeding on the toilet. Nothing in my fifteen years had prepared me for what I glimpsed as the door shut and the light fled. I had enough self-control, I'm proud to say, not to shriek out loud, and I'm grateful that I didn't slump to the ground in a fit of the vapours, but something, I knew, was wrong. Terribly, terribly wrong. What, in God's name, had happened to the poor child? Should I leave my hiding place and summon help? These and other, darker thoughts raced through my mind as we awaited the arrival of a third hide-and-seeker. It was to be six years before I had a second such experience, but by the time it came along, I was more than prepared for it – although I did have to be taken on a sort of guided tour of the area first. But I've often wondered who that girl was and whether she realised what an effect she had had on my young imagination. If she should be reading these lines, well, thank you, ma'am.

We'd driven the back roads so we wouldn't spend the whole day in traffic, but the strategy hadn't worked. Somewhere south of Stow-on-the-Wold we were caught in a line of cars that advanced a mile every half-hour, and never really understood why. Was Stow, we wondered, Sheila and I, where Madonna had an estate, and had she caused public roads to be closed in case a member of the public saw her in her shorts? I reminded Sheila that a public right of way runs so close to our house that persons enjoying their inalienable right to roam have a pretty good chance of seeing one or other of us on the lavatory and we further wondered what the chances would have been if we had attempted to get that footpath closed. Not good, we concluded.

By five thirty that evening we had reached our destination, the site at Eastnor Castle of the Big Chill Festival, where I was scheduled to play records an hour later. Having zigzagged across the site for an hour carrying the ludicrously heavy transparent record box I had considered, a few years earlier, would finally after all this time make me look pretty damn cool, we were not in the prettiest of tempers when we arrived outside the Finlandia Cocktail Bar. Well, I wasn't in the prettiest of moods anyway. As we stood outside, surveying the open-sided tent for the equivalent of an artists' entrance, someone in the crowd outside noticed us and started applauding. Within a few seconds, several hundred other festival-goers had joined in. This, I thought, only happens in Cliff Richard films. 'They probably think you're Bob Harris,' Sheila whispered. I harrumphed and we made our way into the tent.

I'm often mistaken for Bob Harris, despite the fact that we look very little alike. He is slimmer and redder than I am – and taller – yet hardly a week passes without someone saying to me, 'I remember you. I never used to miss the *Whistle Test*, you know.' 'I do believe you've got me confu—,' I start, but they're off again. 'Yes, never missed it. What about the time (insert name of tiresome seventies prog-rocker of your choice) was on then?' On at least one occasion, in a North London pub where a somewhat truculent Scot identified me as Bob and grew increasingly indignant as I insisted I was not, I have been forced to concede, with a world-weary but, I hope, not bitter chuckle and shrug of the shoulders, that I was indeed Bob Harris and that I was glad he had enjoyed the programme so much. I've asked Bob whether he ever encounters anyone who believes he is me. He assured me that he does not. I consoled myself later with the thought that Bob has probably not, at least not recently, been asked by anxious stage management whether he would mind playing a few dull records in order to quieten the over-excited dancers on the floor, as I was. I was also invited to kiss a large, florid and sweaty man, something I had not done since my teens. I accepted the invitation, to shrieks of approval. When had Bob Harris last kissed a man on stage, eh?

I left Woodlands at the end of the Easter term 1953, having still had no luck with the masturbating but having avoided – by days – the stigma of being the first boy to leave the school without having passed his swimming test. I blame my mother for my lack of distinction in the pool and on the beaches, as she felt the best way to teach a very young child to swim was to carry it out to sea and drop it into the waves. She had done this at Rhosneigr when I was four or five years old with frankly disastrous consequences. I had sunk from view in a trice and had been plucked from the sea a few seconds later determined never to allow my head below the surface of any water ever. Having failed my swimming test – one length of the school pool – on at least half a dozen occasions, the school authorities had finally wearied of pussyfooting about, and as the rest of the school was sitting down to lunch I was led to the poolside, lowered into the water and compelled to swim my length, with a lifesaver on either side of me instructed to push me back if I attempted to make my way to the side.

During that summer we stayed, as we usually did, at the Red House at the Lion Rocks end of Broad Beach, Rhosneigr. Years later, Francis and I spent two of the saddest weeks of our lives in a caravan parked on open land at the other end of the beach as Father tried to persuade us – and, I suppose, himself – that a semblance of normalcy could be maintained after he and Mother had gone their separate ways. I still feel pangs of guilt about the way we teased him over the lumps in his custard.

At the end of the summer I went to Shrewsbury School. As was the custom, I was taken down a day early in order to, in as far as it was possible, acclimatise. Father and Mother both turned out for this strange and terrible day, at the end of which I was left in what was styled a waiting house. This was across the road from the House for which I was intended, Riggs Hall, and was superintended by an A. J. Hagger. It has to be said that this Hagger and I never really got on. Although it would be handy for these present purposes to attempt, as so many other autobiographers have in the past, to pass myself off as a bit of a rebel, a man flouting convention, kicking against the pricks, the roots of the Hagger/Ravenscroft J. R. P. conflict lay squarely in my inability to pay attention for more than a few seconds at a time. Looking back on it, I rather suspect that I actually failed the Common Entrance exam I had taken at Woodlands to get into Shrewsbury, but was nodded through because my father, Uncle Bill, and both grandfathers had been at the school, serving their time there without anything that could be classed as distinction. I bucked this family tendency in that first term by coming bottom of the school.

I had been placed in the Third Form which, despite sounding as though, however poor that might be, it was at least better than being in the First or Second Forms, was not. There was no First or Second Form and the Third Form was, in fact, roughly the equivalent of what was called elsewhere a Remedial Form. To be fair to the brothers, few of us were authentically stupid. It was just that we had our minds on other things and I was secretly rather proud of being bottom of the school. It gave me, I attempted to convince my parents, a distinction that could only be surpassed by being top of the school, something which, I argued, they must concede was unlikely to happen. It also meant, I pointed out, warming to my task, that they could avoid Speech Day, when there was a centuries-old tradition that the entire school filed past the headmaster and 'capped' him. ('Capping' being a form of salute that involved touching the back of your head at the place where a skull-cap would have been if we hadn't stopped wearing them during the reign of William 'n' Mary. You were supposed to cap any member of staff you encountered regardless of where you encountered them. Failure to do so was rewarded, I expect, with a beating. Most things were. More on beatings shortly.) Parents were expected to gather before the school buildings to witness this excessively tedious parade and Mother and Father would, I assured them, look favourably on me for relieving them of their irksome duty in this matter. My parents were not, alas, convinced. Years later, I endeavoured to rid myself of some of the many ghosts accumulated during my years at Shrewsbury by agreeing to address morning assembly at Eton. The morning passed in a bit of a blur, to be honest, but I remember being told that pupils were offered some sort of alternative to assembly. I'm guessing here, but it was probably something character-forming like being keel-hauled by naval reservists in period costume, so my assembly attracted quite a throng. I'm certain I said nothing either interesting or amusing, but was afterwards taken on a quick tour of the college – that should probably be College – and was particularly struck by one building in which the very brightest students were herded together for their own protection. They were, it was explained to me, so busy translating the works of obscure Central European philosophers into Assyrian in their heads and things like that, that not only did they not know to come in out of the rain but they also walked into brick walls and fell down stairs pretty regularly. 'We were like that in the Third Form,' I thought to myself and felt almost proud as I turned my back on the build-ing – which was called something odd – as it would be – Moth, perhaps, or Gutters.

Hagger's response to just about everything I got wrong was to beat me. These were fairly informal beatings, during which both of us remained fully clothed throughout. I didn't much care for being beaten and never developed a taste for it later in life either, but I certainly was used to it. At home, Mother had beaten me regularly from a very early age. She hadn't wanted me to grow up to be a sissy, she explained years later. These beatings were informal in that there was no prescribed number of blows, but formal in that they came about as the result of a rather horrid ritual. If I was considered by Trader to have transgressed in some way, she would make her way to the bottom of the stairs and shout the words, 'Are you there?' If my mother heard her from where she lay on her bed reading romantic fiction, she flung herself out of the room, along the hall and down the stairs, grabbing 1) a belt and 2) me, as she flew. Then I was hauled into the dining-room, bent over the table and beaten until Mother grew weary of it. No questions were asked. It sufficed that Trader had shouted, 'Are you there?' If Mother failed to hear the question, I escaped un-punished. There seemed to me to be something attractively mediaeval about this form of justice.

Most of the beatings I received from Mr Hagger were for offences which would have been offences in no other place on

Earth – except, perhaps, for another public school. Our lives were hedged about with a system of rules and privileges without equal outside the military and, as is also the case in the Army, it was impossible to get through a day without breaking rules or overlooking privilege. Some of these were so arcane that to this day I don't know what they meant. For example, only members of the School First Eight were, I believed, allowed to have clocks on their socks. If you have any idea what this means, I'd prefer it if you kept the information to yourself. I like the picture I have had in my head for fifty years of clocks on socks and don't want mere reality to spoil it for me. There were paths and corridors on or in which you were not allowed to speak, have your hands in your pockets or, in some cases, walk, set against which fatuous restrictions were the twenty minutes between nine thirty and nine fifty at night officially set aside for 'milling'. This was not, perhaps disappointingly, an opportunity for what *Chambers Dictionary* describes as 'grinding by crushing between hard, rough surfaces or more or less similar operations', although, interestingly, that is a pretty neat summary of what went on. Milling consisted of rough games involving rolled-up socks, improvised goals, diving recklessly over and under iron beds and sometimes what might be considered an excess of physical contact. Riggs was the only House in which milling was allowed and we were much envied as a result.

We new boys had a great deal more to do, needless to say, than school work and developing in three elements free, to run, to ride, to swim – as the prayer had it. We also had to cope with douling, colour tests and, unless we were fortunate enough to be grossly deformed, with being loved.

Douling, my clever friends told me, derived from the Greek

word for a slave, and in your first two years at school you could be compelled to do almost any task by either a House prefect – they were called monitors – or your study monitor. These tasks could range from boiling an egg to giving someone a hand job. Monitors summoned douls by stepping into the corridor and yelling either 'Dddddddoooooooouuuuuulllllllll' or 'Doul doul doul doul doul doul.' For one you had to run to the monitor no matter what you were doing, for the other you ran only if you weren't already engaged in school work or on a task for some other slave-master. Looking back on it all, it seems amazing that anyone of spirit put up with it for a minute, and the amazement grows when you consider that the founding fathers of *Private Eye* were all at the school, albeit in different Houses, and presumably went along with the system both as douls and monitors.

When all the available douls were lined up, the monitor would select usually the last to arrive or, if they were so minded, the cutest, to clean shoes, press cadet corps uniforms, run somewhere with a message. These things were just tolerable.

Intolerable were the demands made by study monitors. A study might consist of three or four citizens, with the senior being the monitor and the junior the doul. A boy called Cox was my study monitor for a year and amongst the tasks he assigned me on a regular basis was that of boot-polishing his bicycle tyres. When he adjudged them clean and shiny enough, he would take his bike for a short spin in the mud before telling me to start again. Strong though the temptation might have been, telling him to go fuck himself would have resulted in serious punishment. However, I'm currently operating under no such constraints, so: Go fuck yourself, Cox.

Another study monitor obliged me to perform an even more unwelcome service during what was supposed to be a period for doing homework. This period, during which we were confined to our studies, was called 'top schools', but for my study monitor it was 'hand jobs'. If for some reason my tormentor didn't require a hand job, possibly because he had already compelled another small boy to give him one, he loaned me to one of his two friends and I was obliged to service them instead. This man – and although it is tempting to name him, I'm not going to – was, I think, the only genuinely amoral person I've ever met. Towards the end of our time together, he compelled me to agree to meet him in a public toilet in the cemetery on the outskirts of Shrewsbury, where he raped me. Oddly enough, much as I hated the experience, I think I had become so accustomed to systematic sexual abuse that I wasn't especially traumatised by the experience. However, it was many years before I could bring myself to tell anyone what had happened to me, and when I did tell Sheila, my wife, one afternoon in the eighties as we drove through Shrewsbury and past the cemetery toilet block, she found it, I think, more upsetting than I ever did. We have not spoken of it again.

Of course, life at Shrewsbury was not all about being beaten and buggered. From the Third Form I moved to the Lower Fourth, thence to the Upper Fourth and eventually to the Fifth. I served in each of these with comparable lack of distinction, although I did win first prize in an essay competition, which, I was assured, no-one else had entered. Sadly, my original thoughts on What The Individual Can Do To Promote International Goodwill, which won me a book of cartoons, many of which I didn't understand, are lost. So is the book of cartoons.

Over me throughout this time hung the threat of university.

I had, I now understand, a somewhat jaundiced view of university. University to us seemed to mean Oxford or Cambridge, and people who failed to get into one or the other would, having thus disgraced their families, do the decent thing and enlist in the Kenya Rifles for five years. I was pretty certain – and it is surprising that no-one at any stage attempted to disabuse me of these notions – that university would be a sort of ghastly fusion of Shrewsbury with *The Student Prince* and that on my first day as a fresher – whatever that was – I would be compelled to stand on a four-hundred-year-old oak refectory table and sing 'There Is A Tavern In The Town' in Latin. Believing this as I did, you'll understand why, when someone told me that if I didn't buck my ideas up and get on with some work I wouldn't go to university, I believed that I had been given the secret of eternal happiness. So I didn't buck my ideas up at all, nor did I get on with some work. Instead, I allowed my life to be transformed by hearing first, Lonnie Donegan, then, Elvis.

Chapter Four

By a strange irony, this morning's mail (August 16th 2004) brings not one but two envelopes from Sharon Donegan, Lonnie's widow. One advertises a forthcoming musical called *Lonnie D.*, featuring Peter and Anthony Donegan, a Live Skiffle Group and Full Supporting Cast. The musical is to debut at the Whitley Bay Playhouse. The second envelope brings me a programme from the Royal Albert Hall dated Monday 21st June. On that night a Host of Stars paid tribute to Lonnie Donegan and I should have been there. In fact, I had volunteered my services as compère but was delayed in northern France on my way back from the Sonar Festival in Barcelona by car trouble. That an appropriate tribute to Lonnie Donegan was long overdue was not in doubt, and, if nothing else, the Albert Hall concert boasted one of the strangest line-ups I've ever seen – or more accurately, I suppose, not seen. Chas and Dave were there, as were Rolf Harris, Gerry Marsden, Rick Wakeman, Billy Bragg, the Barron Knights, Roger Daltrey, Joe Cocker, Van Morrison and the traditional Many Others. This line-up illustrates perfectly, for me, the dilemma at the heart of Donegan. Interestingly, a similar dilemma lay at the heart of Elvis's music.

Lonnie's first hit, 'Rock Island Line', the only one of his records to have much of an impact in the US, reached the UK charts in the first week of 1956, four months before Presley's 'Heartbreak Hotel'. I imagine I heard it first, as many other people would have done, on one of the BBC's several family request programmes, either *Housewives' Choice* or *Family Favourites*.

Housewives' Choice was a daily, mid-morning programme with a guest presenter. Anyone visiting us incognito from the Planet Zbzzz at the time would have assumed, from listening to it, that housewives were some sort of sub-normal minority and that the wedding ceremony through which almost all house-wives would have gone in the fifties was part of the process by which a portion of their brains was removed. As to why this might have been done, well, our visiting alien might have had to get back to us on that one.

Family Favourites, on the other hand, had regular presenters, the married couple Jean Metcalfe and Cliff Michelmore. In the form in which I most frequently heard it, it had transmogrified slightly into *Two-Way Family Favourites* or even, although rarely, *Three-Way Family Favourites*. In the two-way form the programme brought together British troops serving in occupied Germany and their families. In the three-way form, troops stationed in Cyprus were also included in the fun.

Both programmes featured pretty conservative music –

although it must be remembered that there wasn't much popular music at the time that wasn't conservative, and that the forces have rarely been a hotbed of radicalism anyway. Glenn Miller and his Orchestra featured an awful lot, as did Doris Day, Guy Mitchell, Frankie Laine, Johnnie Ray and Winifred Atwell. Selections from *Oklahoma!*, *Carousel* and other popular musicals were also on pretty heavy rotation. (I was sufficiently affected by these to have carried to the present day a peculiar affection for that 'Everythin's up to date in Kansas City' song from *Oklahoma!*, particularly the faux-rusticity of its second line: 'They've gone about as fur as they can go!' That 'fur' gets me every time.) The request programmes also featured lots of light classical stuff – the name Rudolph Friml strikes a dull chord here – and it appeared to this impatient and sceptical teenager that no programme could be broadcast without the inclusion of 'The Nuns' Chorus' from whatever it is that 'The Nuns' Chorus' comes from.

The aforementioned Day, Mitchell, Laine, Ray and Atwell all recorded for Phillips Records, and you could pretty much gauge how well you would get on with people by discovering which of the five they cared for. For me, Guy Mitchell and Doris Day were unacceptable – too, you know, bright and wholesome – although I did, I have to confess, buy the latter's 'A Purple Cow'. There, I've said it. Of the others, Frankie Laine was my favourite. Mother had taken me to see him at the Liverpool Empire, and where I had been expecting a faintly ruffianly figure in appropriately ruffianly clothing, I got a slightly plump chap in a shot-silk suit who must have been nearing thirty. Frankie still sounded good though and I dutifully waited outside the stage door for his autograph, which I didn't get. I did the same for Johnnie Ray, thrilled by the press's lofty disapproval of his freakishly overemotional performances, with a similar lack of success on the autograph front. I did get to see, on the other hand, teenage girls morph into screamagers and was much moved by the sight and sound. I never got to see Winifred Atwell, alas. I had most of her records though and they are the only records by any one of the quintet that can still sound pretty exciting – with the exception of Frankie Laine's 'The Kid's Last Fight'. That can still stand up in any company – which was more than the Kid could do, of course.

But Lonnie's 'Rock Island Line' was something else. It had the narrative strength of 'The Kid's Last Fight' whilst allying this to a sense of space and freedom, a kind of take-it-or-leave-it spirit that made everything that had gone before sound overcooked and claustrophobic. However, even 'Rock Island Line', which had been recorded pretty much as an afterthought some two years earlier as part of a Chris Barber Band traditional jazz session, paled into something close to nothingness by comparison with Lonnie's first Pye Nixa 78, 'Lost John' coupled with 'Stewball'.

A few days before Lonnie died, I went with my Radio 1 colleagues Louise Kattenhorn and Hermeet Chadha to see the King of Skiffle in his Nottingham hotel room. Awash with painkillers, he had given his customary full-blooded ninety minutes the night before and looked seriously ill – as, indeed, he was. But he was nevertheless kind and funny and tolerated my telling him, not for the first time, how much his music meant to me. Somehow I found myself singing a verse from 'Lost John', the one that starts 'Lost John need a pair of shoes of his own,' and Donegan joined in on the final, 'You couldn't tell whichaway Lost John gwine.' 'I have sung with Lonnie

Donegan,' I thought as we left, with Lonnie telling me as I closed the hotel door that he would teach me to play guitar the next time we met. 'I have sung with Lonnie Donegan!' If someone had told the fifteen-year-old version of me that this would happen, it is difficult to imagine what the effect might have been.

Further astonishing records followed Pye Nixa N 15036. There was *Skiffle Session*, with its bleak, yellow-eyed 'New Burying Ground', the storming 'Bring A Little Water, Sylvie', and that rare thing, an LP that made the singles chart, *Lonnie Donegan Showcase*. On this, Lonnie hit what I still regard as his peak, with the skiffle group's searing version of the hackneyed old favourite 'Frankie And Johnny'. I have played this to dozens of people who, if they have known Donegan at all, know him only from the novelty 'Does Your Chewing-Gum Lose Its Flavour?' and 'My Old Man's A Dustman' hits and they have been amazed. Amongst the amazed have been Omaha's wonderful Black Keys and Detroit's White Stripes. Jack and Meg were so impressed by the intensity and sheer out-thereness of Lonnie's performance on 'Frankie And Johnny' that the only words Jack spoke when he picked up a Brit Award a few months later were, 'Remember, Lonnie Donegan started it for you.' And he did.

Since I was, oh, I don't know, about that high, I've always described the moment in which I first heard Elvis on the radio as being the defining moment in my life. It's certainly up there with the first time I saw Sheila and Alan Kennedy's goal against Real Madrid in the Parc des Princes anyway. I heard Elvis, as I had probably first heard Lonnie, on *Two-Way Family Favourites*. I'm sure that somewhere out there in the wilder reaches of the internet there is probably a site that would tell me exactly where and when 'Heartbreak Hotel' was played – and for whom – but, you know, life's too short. I've always characterised the record as being played for a L/Bdr Higgins in BFPO 15, but this, I'm afraid, is something that I have made up. Suffice to say that Elvis was described as 'the new American singing sensation' and that certainly hit the nail on the head. It may not sound like much today, but 'Heartbreak Hotel' had the effect on me of a naked extraterrestrial walking through the door and announcing that he/she was going to live with me for the rest of my life. As Elvis walked in, Frankie Laine and Johnnie Ray tiptoed out and nothing was ever the same again. There was something frightening, something lewd, something seriously out of control about 'Heartbreak Hotel', and alarmed though I was by Elvis, I knew I wanted more. And I got it. I could still sing you every note of every song on that classic first eponymous LP and maybe one day I will. Although other rock 'n' rollers, notably Gene Vincent, were, in time, to take precedence over Elvis, the only time I've ever bid in a serious auction was when an Elvis 45 on Sun was up for sale. Mind you, this wasn't just any old Sun 45. It was one signed by Elvis's band. Here was Scotty Moore (guitar), Bill Black (bass), DJ Fontana (drums), and Elvis had signed his corner of the sleeve, 'Elvis Presley (singer)'. That record, I reckoned, belonged in my house.

Unable to face the stress of the auction, and knowing that if I attended in person I would almost certainly end up getting carried away and bidding more than we could afford, I asked my friend and literary agent, Cat Ledger, to act on my behalf. I can hardly bring myself to type the words, but Cat was authorised to bid up to three thousand pounds. Fortunately for me, the bidding went way beyond this ridiculous figure and the record is now probably in a bank vault in Tokyo or Los Angeles. Wherever it is, it ain't here where it belongs.

There was depressingly little interest in either Lonnie or Elvis in Riggs Hall, The Schools, Shrewsbury. In fact, there was a good deal of low-level hostility to popular music or, indeed, twentieth-century classical music, in the House. In the study I was in when rock 'n' roll entered my life, the records of choice were a recording of Handel's Zadok the Priest from the Coronation of George VI and a recording of the same king's magnificent wartime speech in which he quoted from the poem 'A man stood at the gate of the year'.

At one point, desperate to discover someone else who cared for Lonnie, Elvis, Gene and the rest, I took some records along to a meeting of something called, with wilful inappropriateness, the High Society. This, I knew, was a jazz society presided over by a stuffy youth named Comyns who was Head of House. He was spectacularly stuffy about the record I had taken to the meeting. Anxious to impress the Society, I had taken along Earl Bostic's 'Sleep' and 'Flamingo' coupling, believing that in this I had found a record that would bridge the gap between us. Comyns didn't care for it at all, delivered himself of a few damning thoughts on Bostic's broadness of tone, then showed me the door. As I walked disconsolately back to the House, I wondered what Comyns would have made of Gene Vincent's raging 'Race With The Devil'. Not a lot, reason insisted.

Apart from the Devil's music, the principal consolation in the young Ravenscroft J. R. P.'s life came from football. Not so much the professional game, in which no-one seemed interested (I had supported Liverpool since the 1950 Cup Final, which they had lost 2–0 to Arsenal, in recognition of which I allowed no Arsenal supporters into our house except Robert Wyatt and Alfie until the mid-1990s. I'm still not convinced that I did the right thing in reversing this policy either), but in playing myself. I was an old-fashioned right winger – you know, take the ball to the line, cross it, that sort of thing – although I would rather have played on the left wing in emulation of my boyhood idol, Billy Liddell. A portrait of Billy hangs to the present day in our dining-room and his was the first autograph I ever collected. On my first ever solo trip to Anfield, I had seen Billy getting off the bus – in those days players travelled on public transport – and had grabbed a flier for the Socialist weekly, *Reynolds News*, and asked him to sign it. I have this in a special place in my dad's old desk and it is perhaps the most sacred object I own. I had it on me when Liverpool beat Real Madrid in the European Cup Final in Paris, as I had when they beat Bruges at Wembley. I went to the Paris game with John Gorman out of the Scaffold, having managed to get a flight to France on the plane that carried the players' wives. John and I both contrived to wear red trousers. I can't say that either of us looked very good in them.

After the game we found that we had become part of a group of about twenty or thirty scousers bent on celebrating. To this end we went into what turned out to be a bikers' bar not far from the Champs-Elysées. As something of a coward, I was nervous about this, but it turned out that Parisian bikers, despite looking magnificent, all cheekbones and immaculate leathers – but did they have bikes, I wondered? – were prepared to yield to jubilant Liverpool supporters. The other French people in the bar defied the stereotypes and were generous and friendly. They joined in, as best they could, with our singing and with the beer fight that erupted at about two in the morning. After this, and drenched from head to toe, the bar emptied on to the street, we sang the most beautiful 'You'll Never Walk Alone' I've ever heard, and adjourned to our various hotels, cars, vans and campsites. Gorman and I were staying, entirely fortuitously, at the same hotel as the Liverpool squad and in the morning came down to breakfast to find Bill Shankly at reception, paying his bill. As he prepared to leave for the coach outside, I darted forward and offered to carry his bags. Apparently, the great man didn't find this odd at all because he agreed at once. I regard this as being my greatest sporting achievement. A photograph of Bill is the only picture allowed to hang in our kitchen. It is before me – as they say – as I write and I have just walked across the room to check the caption. It reads, 'Liverpool manager Bill Shankly, supporting a campaign for more sports facilities in the city.' The only other people in the picture are ordinary Liverpudlians and I often wonder who they are, especially the bloke on the left laughing at whatever Bill is saying. As they have been in our kitchen for twenty years or more, I feel as though I know them anyway. Our daughter Florence, recently graduated from Liverpool University, is named in tribute to Shanks. Florence Victoria Shankly Ravenscroft – now there's a name to reckon with. Contemplating the grotesqueries of the modern game, I wonder whether Bill would be able to find a role in football in 2005? Would he even want to?

I had been to the Wembley game in 1978 on my own and had stood alone on the Kop. When Dalglish scored his winning goal, a huge lad standing in front of me turned and jumped into my arms as we all surged forward. Under his weight, I fell to the ground and for a moment feared for my safety. I trace my recurring back problems to this moment but I didn't care then and I don't really care now. I have seldom felt such joy. People say, 'But surely, John, the birth of your children . . . ?' Close, I concede, but Dalglish and Kennedy's goals top that particular chart. 'What about when you and Sheila got married then?' they persist, but I am deep in conversation with someone else, possibly about the Analects of Confucius but probably not.

My own football was, alas, woeful, although I was eventually awarded my House football colours at Shrewsbury. This, I know, was more for pluck and persistence than for making any serious contribution to the game. Over the years, I had developed the ability to kick a ball very hard and very accurately. I had honed these skills long before going to Shrewsbury on the Big Lawn at home. Francis and I had been joined at Haddon Corner on or after December 18th 1946 by Alan Watson Ravenscroft. Although Francis and I found the new recruit mildly interesting, we resented the fact that he was clearly Father's favourite. Looking back on it, this isn't altogether surprising as he was effectively the only one of us that Father really knew, and Alan can still, unwittingly, make me jealous by describing the occasions on which he and Father went walking together. Francis and I would get our own back by inviting Alan on to the Big Lawn to play football. To be honest, Francis had little interest in the grand old game and was more of a spectator than a participant as I would invite Alan to take up a goal-keeping position at the hedge. With the ruthlessness and, I like to think, skill of a practised executioner, I would turn and whack the ball straight at Alan. It usually hit him and carried him into the hedge, and when he had pulled himself out, he would run sobbing into the house to be comforted by Trader. Fifteen minutes later, twenty when he was a little older and a little wiser, the process could be repeated.

I brought these most particular skills to bear as a rough 'n' tumble right back for the Corinthians at Woodlands. (The other Houses were the Barbarians and the Free Foresters. Don't ask me why.) Again, I would have preferred to have been, as Billy Liddell was, left-footed, but whenever I tried to kick the ball with my left foot, I fell on my back. The only game at Woodlands I can remember, apart from a cricket match during which I deliberately hit a boy called Pearson with a cricket bat and was nearly expelled, was a House match against the Barbarians, during which I was moved to centre-forward and scored two match-winning goals. The second of these I can still remember, and still wonder at the manner in which moments seem to slip into slow motion. I can close my eyes and see the heavy, sodden leather ball arcing away from my heavy, sodden leather right boot and beyond what sports writers call 'the goalkeeper's despairing grasp' into where the net would have been if we had had nets. This, curse it, is the only experience I have had that could have given me any insight into how Alan Kennedy and Kenny Dalglish must have felt during the European Cup Finals discussed above.

At Shrewsbury I played football whenever I could, to the point, some of my friends believed, of obsession, but I was always crap at it. Slow and clumsy and frightened of being hurt in the tackle, I must have been a liability even in the House second team, and the colours I was eventually awarded can only have been the equivalent of an E for effort.

Chapter Five

It rained again last night. It is raining now. It will rain this afternoon and tonight and tomorrow. Fortunately, it didn't rain yesterday afternoon. Yesterday afternoon William and his Zahra, Alexandra and her Ashley, and Flossie, currently a solo act, met up with Thomas at V2004 in Chelmsford. 'The most corporate event I've ever been to,' said Alexandra, still seething with resentment at having her plastic bottle of vodka seized by security. The only drink available was, it seems, Virgin Cola. As they say, nice.

We're particularly interested in rain this week as on Sunday we are having a party to celebrate my becoming a pensioner and what is, according to experts in the field, our pearl anniversary. There will be a marquee in the field across the road and the other field across the road will be available for car-parking, and we don't want some Glastonbury-style mudfest, if only because the possibility exists that the *East Anglian* might get to hear of it and would print a brief paragraph under the caption: DJ IN A SPIN. They've done this several times before in stories about us and enough is enough, guys.

I'm at the kitchen table again, listening to Archie, now eleven months old, saying his first word. He says his first word a lot. It is a sort of sung 'Hello,' or at least something that follows the cadences of the standard 'Hello.' Archie has spotted that saying – or singing – 'Hello' goes down very well with his core audience, which, this morning, includes Caroline, who has been coming in twice a week to help with the cleaning ever since Sheila had her brain haemorrhage in 1996. Caroline is as fast a cleaner as exists on Earth and this morning she is going to have to address the small discolouration on the bathroom floor that marks the spot where Archie managed to deposit a small turd when our backs were turned yesterday. When our young people returned home, slightly drunk, from Chelmsford, there was a murmured suggestion that perhaps the turd had been left by me as an involuntary and poignant symbol of encroaching senility. I struck back by asking how they had managed to get drunk on Virgin Cola but it turns out that tiny bottles of Patagonia red wine from Argentina were available at three pounds each. Even the avaricious promoters of some of the most unspeakable festivals of the 1960s – I'm thinking in particular of those held in the hills above Buxton – would have raised their conjoined eyebrow at that.

At the second of these, in 1969, it rained mercilessly from slate-dark skies from start to finish. I was to appear as compère and spinner of the platters that mattered, but when I arrived on the site found that my work was likely to be somewhat restricted as no microphone had been made available for my use and there were no decks set up either. The stage manager, who had turned up for work, in a strictly non-ironic manner, in the evening wear he wore for his day – or night – job as manager of a club in Buxton itself, took me down to his house to pick up his home stereo in the hope that somehow we would be able to connect this luxury item, with its smoked-plastic cover and range of features, to the PA. I must have presented a deeply comic figure scurrying about the stage, begging roadies to help me to effect this. I don't remember that I ever managed to play a single record all day, although I did contrive to make a succession of stage announcements of the 'Will Snotter and Woot meet Dave in front of the stage as Dave's forgotten his insulin?' variety. These were staple fare at festivals of the period, and judging from the extraordinary number of them, either unprecedented numbers of diabetics were attracted to prog rock or 'insulin' was actually a shorthand for illegal exhilarants of one sort or another.

I don't actually know who played at that Buxton Festival – it is, I suppose, just possible that no-one did – but Chuck Berry certainly didn't. Rumours of Chuck's non-appearance were enough to enrage the large number of rockers who had arrived on the site, many, it was said, without paying. Chuck Berry was the only reason for their having made the journey to Buxton and they demonstrated their ire through redistribution of the mud that a bountiful providence had put at their disposal. What equipment there was on stage, including the stage manager, sundry roadies and the compère, was soon covered in mud, with every prospect of more on the way. In the meantime, the rockers, many of them by this time stark naked, were having what seemed from the stage to be a strangely homoerotic mud fight immediately below us. No band in their right mind would have considered taking to the stage under such circumstances, and in the total absence of any security I trudged off across the fields to a secure area far enough away that it might easily have been in a neighbouring county, to speak to the police. I found them warm, dry and enjoying cups of tea. When I explained that I feared things back on the site could well turn nasty, they expressed their regrets before explaining in their turn that they couldn't lift a finger until an offence had been committed.

Surely, I suggested, the prevention of crime was part of their remit, but it turned out that in this part of Derbyshire at least, it was not. I trudged back through the mud to take up my place on the stage again.

No sooner had I returned to my role imploring Pete and the other lads from Chapel-en-le-Frith to meet Boffo stage left, when a large mud-imp clambered from the swamp and asked me in what I thought a rather rough manner whether he could himself make an announcement. He was holding what in that yellow-grey light appeared to be a knife, but could, I have to admit, have been almost anything capable of a dull glitter. I looked out across the festival site at the struggling rockers, the drenched and dispirited music-lovers, and recognised that I could, within minutes, be on the road for Suffolk, and with luck could reach home in time for *Match of the Day*, and handed him the microphone. 'Not only can you make an announcement, my friend,' I told him, 'but from now on, you're the compère. Good luck.'

As I squelched away from the festival I was already formulating my thought-provoking theory, since taken up by sociologists worldwide, that the rock festival was the post-war generation's substitute for National Service. Turning to look back up the hill as I reached the exit, I saw three lads standing in the mud, their boots sunk in it, facing inwards, with an army groundsheet providing their only solace and shelter. As a depiction of utter misery it was hard to beat, and in the bitter light of that wretched afternoon, a light that rendered the scene almost monochrome, it seemed as though it could be an image from the Great War.

It's hard to believe it now, I admit, but when I was thirteen or fourteen, I was kinda cute and therefore craved by quite a few older boys. They were not, generally speaking, interested in penetration, but more, as we have seen, in what we have come to know as relief massage or even, in the absence of the below-stairs staff or hunting dogs they possibly slept with at home, warmth. Having experienced few physical expressions of affection at home – something that would have been true, I imagine, of almost every boy in the House – I was rather flattered by these attentions and was aware, too, that the only people to whom I could turn for help were, by and large, the very people who yearned to cuddle me. In the meantime, my own sexual experiences continued to be entirely solitary in nature.

Although the public-school system was supposed to be awash with what we now know to be paedophiles, I never, despite my tip-tilted nose and prettily turned ankles, attracted the attention of lascivious members of staff. In fact, I never heard of anyone who had, and the only example of which I was aware of what we might style 'inappropriate behaviour' occurred when a young, brilliant and odd master was caught in the park on the town side of the Severn with a small boy perched on his chest. I even survived unmolested the sharing of a tent on an ITC camp (ITC = Initial Training Corps) in Wales with a housemaster who was to go on to achieve notoriety at another public school for his near manic enthusiasm for what we know as TDSU beatings (TDSU = Trousers Down, Shirts Up). In fact, this housemaster was possibly the first adult to treat me as something approaching an equal, and in sharing with me some small part of his considerable knowledge and understanding, made me realise for the first time that there was pleasure to be derived merely from knowing stuff. I also, during this week in Wales, drove a car for the first time, despite being but fourteen years of age. The car belonged to an older boy who later described me as 'flirtatious' but was content, nevertheless, to allow me to drive his Austin 7 for miles along the single-track roads of the area – which I've never subsequently been able to identify – in which we were camping. He also reminded me, in a note accompanying a fifteen-second film he had found in an attic showing me climbing the school bank in a coquettish manner, that he had taken me to see the Crew-Cuts, hit recorders of 'Crazy 'Bout My Baby' and 'Sh-Boom', at the Liverpool Empire. I had also borrowed money from him that I have never repaid. What a tart!

My unspeakable loveliness was not, alas, enough to stop me from falling foul of the billions – OK, I exaggerate – of rules and regulations that hedged about our lives. Most of these referred to bizarre privileges granted to older boys – there were paths that could only be used by school prefects, known as praeposters, for example, and other paths on which you couldn't whistle, or talk, or have your hands in your pockets, or run until you had been at the school for two, or three, or four years – but we were also supposed to be able to identify, when ordered to do so by a boy in a position of authority, members of staff, their subjects, classrooms, wives, children, addresses and even, where appropriate, their pets. On Sunday evenings, cowering first-years were tested as to their knowledge and understanding of these arcane matters by the Head of House. These tests were known as Colour Tests, and if you failed them, you were beaten.

You were also beaten, of course, for whistling, talking, having your hands in your pockets or running where you were not privileged to do so, and Michael Palin's film about public school life, *Tomkinson's Schooldays*, in which miscreants were crucified on the school wall and compelled to take part in hopping races across uneven countryside, always seemed to me to be more documentary than fantasy. Michael came to Riggs a year after Francis, some three years after I arrived at Shrewsbury, but being a rather clever boy, started out in a higher form than the one it had taken me three years to achieve.

There were, needless to say, no hopping races as such and crucifixion was rare, but it was compulsory to take part in some identifiable sporting activity each day of the week. Failure to do so resulted in a beating. A game of football counted as a 'change', as these sanctioned activities were known, as did a game of cricket, an hour on the river, a game of fives or what was called a 'benjie'. I don't know why these runs along a defined course in the vicinity of the school were called benjies – possibly in honour of some boy who had died doing one – but you had to do a benjie every week. The course took you along a footpath across fields, through the cemetery in the Gents of which I was deflowered, and along the busy bypass and back to the House. I reckon the course was probably about a mile and a half long. Before starting your run, you had to persuade a senior boy to time you and failure to complete the course in less than thirteen minutes meant you had to do it again. (I've just re-examined that claim and can't believe I've got it right, but that's what I remember.) It was possible to make the task easier by ducking the portion of the run that took you through the cemetery, but if you were caught doing this, you were beaten. You also had to be careful not to post a suspiciously good time and thus get picked for some sort of competitive race in which your deceit would be uncovered.

The beatings you got for not completing a change or, indeed, for forgetting to register your change in the book provided for the purpose, were splendidly ritualised. The beatee was obliged to proceed at ten o'clock, immediately after milling, to the landing on which the Cadet Corps uniforms were kept in a long, low cupboard. The victim would then bend over the cupboard and the Head of House would administer four or six strokes, depending on the gravity of the offence, with a split bamboo to a pyjamaed backside. The split bamboo was chosen, it was said, because if the cane was turned in such a way that the split landed at ninety degrees to the pert bottom awaiting its arrival, it would hurt upon impact, then, having spread and pinched the skin, hurt again upon being withdrawn. After the beating, which you were expected to endure without crying out, you thanked the Head of House for his attentions, returned to your dormitory and the rest of the House could start breathing again, having temporarily ceased breathing lest by doing so they missed any whimpering you might have allowed yourself. Unfortunately, you could not discuss what had just passed with your friends because talking after lights out was forbidden. The punishment for talking after lights out was, you may have guessed, a beating.

Within the past year I have received several letters from a

former Head of House inviting me to contribute funds for a scholarship to be set up in the name of our Housemaster, R. H. J. Brooke. In his first letter he reminded me, lest I had forgotten, that he might have been compelled from time to time to beat me. He expressed what I took to be mild regret that this had been the case, and when I wrote back explaining that I didn't have the reserves of wealth that he assumed I did, I told him by way of consolation that I bore no grudges, understanding that he was only, after all, obeying orders.

Oh, no. Not 'self-deprecating' again. This time it's in the *Independent on Sunday* magazine, *ABC*. Sometimes being self-deprecating is perceived as good, as in 'John turned, and as he turned the evening sunlight fell across his even features, illuming his fine nose and the determined angle of his jaw. He smiled a self-deprecating smile. "No, you are too, too kind. I played virtually no part in the Restoration of the monarchy," he protested.' At other times, self-deprecating ain't so good, as in 'Whereupon the air turns self-deprecating' (*Independent on Sunday*, 29 August 2004). This time it's my oft-repeated remark to the effect that you can see what, for reference purposes, we'll call 'my career' as based on either a selfless dedication to the cause of public-service broadcasting or a shocking lack of ambition. I concede that I have said this in public and in private far too many times, often allowing the evening sunlight to fall across my face as I have done so, but the reason I have repeated it so often is that it is true. I am genuinely ridiculously proud to have worked for the BBC for as long as I have and am grateful that I have been paid not the spectacular sums imagined by some critics, but enough that we can afford to run four cars ('run' is a little inaccurate here as two of the cars are in sheds in the garden with every prospect of remaining there) and to have a bottle of wine with our meals. I'm also grateful that in all of the thirty-seven years I've worked for Radio 1, no-one in management has ever said to me that I should either be playing something that I'm not playing or not playing something that I am. I doubt that would have happened in the commercial radio sector. Admittedly, one junior-management dork and one DJ from the Aspirant Showbiz side of the DJ tracks did tell me in the early days of hip-hop, back when it was, as it is so often proclaimed, 'fresh' and, indeed, idealistic, that I shouldn't play it on the radio because it was, and I quote, 'the music of black criminals'. This, I felt, told me more about the individuals concerned than it did about hip-hop. Apart from that – and students, stand by, because here comes one of my guiding principles for Getting Along Just Fine With Management – Johnny Beerling, a much-criticised (often by John Walters and me) Controller of Radio 1, who has since turned out to be rather a good geezer, once asked me, following one of the occasional schedule changes that have made me old before my time, if I could make the first half-hour of the programme a little more consumer-friendly in order to ensure that it chimed seamlessly with the programme that preceded it. Whereas someone like Andy Kershaw, a great but combative broad-caster, would have put himself on an immediate war footing, issued an ultimatum and breathed fire in all directions, I smiled winningly, promised instant cooperation and continued to pro-gramme as before. Five or six weeks later, Johnny stopped me in the third-floor corridor of Egton House to thank me for act-ing so promptly upon his request and to assure me that the new policy had made all the difference. This will be the first notice Johnny has had that no such new policy had been introduced.

What had changed was his perception of what he heard issuing from his radio.

Johnny Beerling was the man behind three of my all-time favourite Radio 1 moments. The greatest of these – and one of the most extraordinary events I've had the pleasure of witnessing – was the Bay City Rollers at Mallory Park event. This is a story I've told so many times that there will be those who can virtually sing along with my account, but for those unfamiliar with it, I'll save it for a page or two. Johnny was also responsible, in conjunction with the World Service, for taking Sheila and me to Russia. We went to Moscow for the first time during the Yeltsin era and it was everything you would have wished it to be – bitterly cold, paranoid, snow-covered, resentful. We stayed in a huge and terrible hotel – 'All the rooms are bugged, so be careful what you say,' advised Johnny – and the food was disgusting, although doubtless better than that being consumed by Muscovites themselves. They, of course, were not allowed into the hotel unless, we quickly deduced, it was to give Westerners a quick blowjob. We were advised against making any contact whatsoever with the locals. 'They will almost certainly be secret policemen,' it was explained, although without any further explanation as to what these secret policemen might find useful in listening to the vapid conversations of airhead DJs. With this advice firmly lodged in our collective consciousness, Sheila and I were thrilled when we got a phone call one evening from a man who wouldn't give his name but insisted that it was imperative that he meet us as soon as possible. Pulses racing, with beads of sweat on both our foreheads, we arranged to meet the caller at a remote Metro station the following day. The wisdom of this seemed in doubt from the moment we left the safety of our hotel immediately after another revolting breakfast, one during which I had, in a fit of petulance, broken a plate upon being told that Sheila couldn't enter the breakfastation area wearing a coat – or without wearing a coat. I forget which. An ugly incident threatened, with the ever-present security personnel stiffening and taking steps towards me, although they fell back when they recognised that such behaviour was symptomatic of Western decadence. Perhaps, on the other hand, they were deterred by the glint of steel from the dirk tucked into my waistband. We'll probably never know.

The Moscow Metro system is, as with all such systems outside London, a matter of common sense, and we had little trouble finding the station where we had agreed to meet our mystery caller. We were, in fact, quite pleased to leave the train because, although we thought that after two or three days in the city we looked pretty Muscovite ourselves, we clearly didn't and all our fellow passengers watched us unswervingly throughout our journey with a mixture of curiosity and hatred.

We stepped from the train on to a poorly lit platform on which there appeared to be not a single living soul and it was at this point that our confidence started to evaporate. My imagination started generating newspaper headlines of the TOP DJ MISSING IN MOSCOW variety and I consoled myself by further imagining the disappointment of most British readers when they realised that it wasn't Noel Edmonds who had gone astray but some bugger they hardly knew.

We stood on that cold, ill-lit platform for what seemed – and there's no other way of putting this – like an eternity, until we detected movement in the intense gloom at the far end of the platform. Slowly, horribly, a figure shuffled towards us. As it drew near we recognised it as the figure of a man, a very big man, a man stooped and, we noticed when the inadequate light of a ten-watt bulb fell on his face, essentially toothless. (It is possible that there is no such thing as a ten-watt bulb, but I'm trying to build a little atmosphere here, so bear with me.)

The creature spoke.

'Hello, I'm Mischa,' it said.

And it was.

Mischa, it turned out, was one of those rare people who you feel upon first meeting that you have known all of your life. He had grown up in some military town so hedged about with security that it appeared, so he said, on no maps, and he was certain that however much life improved for former Soviet citizens, he would, on account of being born in this town – which even now I dare not name – never be allowed to leave Mother Russia. Our new friend appeared to have nothing that he could readily identify as a job, but lived, as so many did under the burgeoning freedoms being exploited by the more cunning former Communists, by his wits. These, we quickly realised, he had in quantity, despite his claim, flattering though it was, to have learned English the better to understand what I was saying about the music on the programmes I introduced on the BBC World Service. (Self-deprecation alert.) 'You must have been disappointed, Mischa, when you recognised that all I was saying was "That was . . . and this is . . .".' He laughed a great laugh and led us from the platform on which we stood to another and thence to a flat overlooking Red Square. Well, not exactly overlooking, to be honest, but from the snow-covered roof of the block in which the flat was located you could see the lights of Red Square. We know this because much later that night, we – Sheila and I, Dave Tate of the World Service, Mischa and the young couple who occupied the flat – climbed through the pigeon-filled roof space, half mad on the horrid sugar water they styled 'champagne', and out, covered with birdshit, on to the roof for a snowball fight. Few things in our lives have been more beautiful than that drunken brawl on the rooftops of old Moscow.

From then on Mischa was our unofficial guide to Moscow – and later to Leningrad/St Petersburg also. He was with us when we were taken by suspiciously well-heeled local business interests to a restaurant which had been in business so long that, we were assured, Tchaikovsky had dined there. Judging from the state of the Gents the management had, in tribute, no doubt, to the troubled genius, left them uncleaned since he himself had pointed Percy at the porcelain. The champagne-styled product flowed like champagne-styled product, a band played, amongst other things, 'Rock Around The Clock', and those of us representing the BBC in the crumbling grandeur of the place talked bollocks at the pitch of our lungs. At one stage I overheard Sheila explaining to Dave, a regular travelling companion, why it was that I never danced. She spoke briefly of the pain I had experienced at dancing lessons in Neston and Willaston village halls, pain that had stayed with me since, despite the award that Francis and I had won for our polka in Willaston, and explained to an incredulous Dave that despite my status as a veritable King of Rhythm, she and I had never danced together. When I heard this, I rose unsteadily to my feet, muttered something about there never being a better time or place to rectify this sad omission, and led Sheila on to the dance floor where I proceeded to give her a good kicking in some of the more complex figures of the Schottische. We have not danced since, there being, I think, a sort of poetry to our only having danced in the room where Tchaikovsky danced.

To return briefly and with a pretty show of reluctance to
Neston and Willaston village halls. When Francis and I were
driven for the first time to dancing lessons in the former we
showed wisdom beyond our years – approximately ten and
eight – by waving a farewell from the door before entering
and walking in a purposeful way through the hall, out through
the back door and into the toilets. Mother, we learned, had
done something similar as a young woman when delivered by
the chauffeur to the imposing entrance of Liverpool's Adelphi
Hotel to, I imagine it was hoped by my grandfather, ensnare a
young man with prospects through the medium of dance.
Mother, slightly plump and devoid of anything identifiable as
confidence, had similarly locked herself in the lavatory.

When our trick had been discovered, Francis and I were
compelled to dance, and as the shyest boys in the class had to
have as partners those young women considered by our gallant
peers to be the least comely in the room. I danced regularly,
therefore, with a strapping lass who regardless of the season
always had mud on her legs, whereas Francis honed his
waltzes, foxtrots, gavottes, military two-steps and the rest with
a preternaturally thin girl who was a good head taller than
him. The only dance I could get my feet around was the waltz
and I could only do that in straight lines. One afternoon, my
mud-covered partner and I had made our way diagonally
across the room, as was our wont – if she's reading this, I'm
sorry I was so crap – and had reached the corner in which we
would have to disengage, turn around, then re-engage, when
we became aware of a commotion in the opposite corner.
When we went over to investigate, we found Francis in tears,
standing over his partner. Somehow he had contrived to render
her unconscious during a spirited mazurka – or whatever – and

the image of the hapless girl on the unforgiving boards of Neston Village Hall, a trickle of blood oozing from the corner of her young mouth – no, I've made that last bit up – remains with me to the present day and may well be the reason I don't dance. Safety first, eh?

Mischa was on the platform when our party took the midnight train from Moscow to Leningrad/St Petersburg some days later. The temperatures were so low that if you stood for too long in one place, your Doc. Martens froze to the platform. The four-person sleeping compartments on the overnight train were clean but cramped and had frosted windows to prevent wolves, I suppose, from looking in on us as we trundled across the boundless snowfields of European Russia. Sadly, they also prevented travellers from peering out and, although there probably wasn't much to see anyway, Sheila and I felt that our poetic souls, such as they are, would harmonise perfectly with the thousands of square miles of pine, snow and wolves we were passing through. There was an area of glass about the size of a child's hand that remained unfrosted and we spent the night taking it in turns to gape through this. I don't think either of us saw a single damn thing but that somehow wasn't the point.

Mischa somehow reappeared within a few hours of our arriving in St Petersburg and told us that whatever else we did, we must visit the cemetery where Tchaikovsky – him again! – Rimsky-Korsakov, Rachmaninoff and the rest of the boys were buried. This we did, thereby missing the opportunity to spend an afternoon with the rest of the BBC team, who had opted to fraternise with someone like a Deputy Minister for Culture and Overseas Development in the Grand Hall of the Congress of the People. Or something.

Sheila and I seemed to be not just the only people entering the cemetery, but the only people on Earth when we found the way in. Inside the cemetery walls it appeared to be a strictly monochrome world, the massive black of the tombstones and the occasional patch of unfrozen footpath like a Factory Records sleeve against the snow. Tchaikovsky and the rest were interred in the furthermost corner of the cemetery – if they are no longer, word has not yet reached me – and we stood in respectful silence before them, attempting to look as though we had a serious interest in funerary architecture whilst thinking, as best we could, deep thoughts on the subject of Life and Death. As we stood, I felt a tug at my sleeve. I turned angrily, thinking that I wasn't really in the mood to be mugged, not here, not now. A small man – not, reason insisted, a member of the mugging classes – stood before me. With a sigh I made as world-weary as I could, I reached into my pocket for a rouble or two to pass on to him along with a patronising smile. 'It is you, isn't it?' he asked. 'Love your programme on the World Service.' And he scurried away. 'At least he didn't think I was Bob Harris,' I said to Sheila as we headed for the gate.

Johnny Beerling also led a Radio 1 expedition to Japan. I am not an enthusiastic aviator but know that I must seize any longhaul opportunity that comes my way. Sympathisers, aware of my unease, often suggest intoxication as the best means of eliminating fear, but a degree of research has shown that no matter how pissed you get, there's still an area, roughly located in the centre of your forehead, from which an unwelcome voice chides correctly, 'You may be pissed – but you're still scared.' I have found that a cocktail of rare and exotic herbal tranquillisers, harvested by small, brown slave-children from the impenetrable forests of wherever it is that they still have impenetrable forests under the direction of men wearing only penis gourds, do the trick marvellously provided they are taken in conjunction with an awful lot of chemical tranquillisers derived, recklessly, from other people's prescriptions. A friend it would be madness to identify recommends horse-tranquillisers, but I have not yet sunk this low.

Tokyo was, initially at least, rather disappointing. I had told people, with the infuriating certainty of someone who doesn't really know what he's talking about, that I imagined being in Japan to be as close as you get on this planet to travelling to another planet. Tokyo looked from the airport bus pretty familiar, the only light in our lives coming from the young woman who had been assigned by a bountiful Providence to look after our little group. She told us that her name was Florence – which it manifestly wasn't – and she pronounced this convenience name, naturally enough, as Frolence. There was much innocent pleasure to be derived from trying to coax Florence into saying Frolence. Our daughter Florence still has to endure being called Frolence on occasion by her adoring father. I'm sure she treasures these moments deep down. No, really.

It is difficult, looking back on it, to know quite why we were in Japan in the first place. Johnny had arranged for us to do programmes from the window of a Yamaha shop in Shibuyu-Ku, programmes presented by Janice Long but with me as our roving reporter. Johnny thought, I suspect, that the residents of Tokyo would be wildly excited at having this exoticism in their midst, but, of course, hardly anyone had ever heard of Radio 1, and although everyone was polite and pretended to be thrilled when it was pointed out to them, we felt faintly

fraudulent nevertheless. Inevitably, much of my roving report-
ing took me to record shops and in one of the biggest of these
there was an impressive display of Peel session releases on
Strange Fruit. I was looking at this when a woman assistant
asked me whether I was interested in the records and I had to
explain that I sort of was and sort of wasn't. She looked understandably nonplussed, so I explained further, revealing that I
was the Peel mentioned on the sleeves. 'You are John Peel?' she
gasped. I dimpled modestly and admitted it, whereupon she
burst into tears. Whether these were tears of joy or disappointment, I've never been able to make up my mind.

We were also in Tokyo to make a documentary for Radio 1
about the Yamaha Song Contest. This programme was to be
presented by me, but made by Mike Hawkes, my producer at
the time. Mike and I got on well enough. He certainly liked his
music and knew quite a bit about it, but I always felt there was
a Mike in there somewhere that I didn't really know. He could
be absurdly secretive and liked to give the impression that he
was a major-league raver and ladies' man. In Tokyo he would
arrive at breakfast as though straight from some exclusive club
or other at which he had been the centre of attention. There
would be oblique hints that lissom Japanese models had set
their caps at him and even more oblique hints that he had, in
some manner, gratified them. There was no doubt that Mike
was good at his job, his strangely insect-like fingers fluttering
and darting over the controls of the various recording instruments we had with us. The actual Yamaha Song Contest was,
at best, lame. Superficially, it resembled the Eurovision Song
Contest, except that it was, in theory, global and the Japanese
had, in their efficient manner, left nothing to chance. All the
contestants we interviewed claimed to know in advance who

the winner was, as only the American contestant had been flown to Tokyo club-class. Whether this was so or not scarcely matters. It was the US contestant who won and our programme, put together overnight in a room with a very graphic earthquake warning on the wall, subsequently won a Sony Award. I thought it was rather wonderful to win a Sony Award for a programme about the Yamaha Song Contest, although I think that Mike and I probably deserved it – if only because we had had to record links to cover almost every possible eventuality, as Mike had to fly to Blighty before the contest actually took place. Thus, on the night of Sheila's birthday, when we should have been out partying heartily, the three of us sat on a hotel bed together, as Tokyo's glamour models huddled in some chic niterie discussing the non-appearance of the new James Bond in their lives, and I intoned, 'The fourth-placed Norwegian entry . . . the fourth-placed Malaysian entry . . . the fourth-placed Maltese entry' and so on until we had brought ourselves to the very brink of madness.

In the shop, in the daytime, we noticed, as shoppers scurried about shopping and probably wondering what these pasty Euros were doing in the place anyway, that most of the middle managers were women, almost all of the foot soldiers men. In the evenings, when we were taken out to be entertained, this was reversed, with the middle-management women having to wait on their underlings. Sheila and Janice Long were only allowed to join us after being designated honorary men. We usually went out to eat something we didn't very much like the look of, and, unusually, I was more up for this than Sheila. During our stay in Russia, a young Russian author had invited us back to his flat for dinner and, not knowing that we were vegetarian, had served up, with no little pride, great gobbets of fatty meat. Sheila and I knew that we had little choice but to eat the stuff, although we were unable to ascertain from what creature – ox, bear, pensioner – the gobbets had been hewn. In Tokyo we faced similar problems, particularly on a night when we were joined by a Yamaha executive who throughout the meal demonstrated his fondness – which I share – for country and western music by singing us a dizzying selection of numbers about pick-up trucks, bars, waitresses and highways. It would have been discourteous for us to have cried with but a single voice, 'Hey, you. Put a sock in it!' Instead we had to sit with every appearance of enjoyment until he had finished. The situation wasn't helped by the fact that the middle managers were serving us from what looked like an overcrowded aquarium under which someone had briefly passed a Bunsen burner. Fish that with a moment's veterinary attention could have been returned to the wild to resume fulfilling lives found their way in preposterous numbers on to our plates, and at one stage I swear I was eating some sort of anal sphincter. I would have to admit, under questioning, that I have never seen an anal sphincter detached from its host and hope that I never do, but if the serrated rubbery ring on my plate wasn't such a sphincter then I'd like to know what it was. Sheila sat through this meal ashen-faced in the grand manner, clearly wishing that she wasn't an Honorary Bloke for the night.

After feasting – or not, in my wife's case – we were taken to a karaoke bar. This was before karaoke, in its horrid European form, became virtually compulsory, and we were all pretty keen to discover what went on. We ended up in a small and virtually empty bar presided over by a Korean woman. The fact that she was Korean is important, as she was not only much taller than the Japanese boys and girls who were with us but infinitely more extrovert. We had noticed on the streets the difference in the sizes of the generations of Japanese passing by. The grand-parents were tiny and, as I always say, rather unfairly, about Noel Edmonds, could have walked under a coffee table with an umbrella up. The parents would be about Sheila's size. She insists she is five foot two, although sceptics, myself included, dispute this. The children, raised on burgers and cola, were vast.

We sat along the wall of the karaoke bar, hoping against hope that no freak of fortune would result in our being bullied on to the tiny stage to sing. Luckily, the Korean woman was happy to do as much of the singing as was necessary, despite the fact that all the records were in English, a language of which she spoke not a word. Her tour-de-force was the American Live Aid song, sung in its original by a panoply of stars including Bruce Springsteen and Bob Dylan. The Korean woman did all of the voices, male and female, and did them amazingly well.

I'd love to be able to credit the Korean woman by name, because she was what we doctors call 'shit-hot'. Several years later, I was opening the mail at home and amongst the pack-ages was one from the Public Baths label of Iowa City, Iowa. I think Public Baths ceased trading shortly afterwards, but they were favourites of mine at the time because they gave a US release to quite a few Japanese records it would have been otherwise impossible to buy in the West. In order to emphasise the Japanese-ness of the singles they did release, Public Baths stuffed the sleeves with Japanese ephemera. Bus tickets, hand-bills, postcards, all of them beautifully designed and produced, would tumble out of the sleeves, and amongst the bits and pieces that morning was a card for the karaoke bar we had been in and a picture of the Korean woman we had all so admired. If I could remember which record it was, I could go out to the shed, find it and tell you her name. She was a star though – no doubt about it.

And so we say goodbye to international travel – for the time being at least – and head for Mallory Park motor-racing circuit in Leicester.

I have the programme before me. BBC Radio 1 Race Day, it reads. Sunday, 30 July 1978. On the inside, Johnny sets the scene. 'On our special Radio 1 stage we shall be having live performances by one of Britain's number-one bands, Darts; the famous Road Show will be in action for most of the day, with disco DJ Froggy presenting all the Radio 1 DJ stars, and at three o'clock Paul Burnett will be broadcasting live on Radio 1, helped by the Goodies.' Sets the pulses racing even now, doesn't it?

I was never heavily involved with the Road Show. In fact, the only time I ever saw a Radio 1 Road Show was when I travelled to Brighton to review one for the *Observer*. I was impressed by the size of the crowd that had turned out to witness Gary Davies doing, frankly, not very much, and was grateful that I was in a position to view proceedings from some distance away. Gary was very much the pin-up boy of Radio 1 at the time and his every winsome smile at the audience drew shrieks of appreciation from the fans. Whenever I was stopped by young women outside Radio 1's Egton House, they never wanted to discuss with me the contents of my sizzling pro-gramme the night before but were instead anxious that I tell them whether Gary Davies was in the building. If he wasn't already in the building, when would he be arriving? And if he was in the building, when would he be leaving? I seldom knew the answers to these oft-repeated questions and was rarely believed when I told the young women this. They seemed to think that we all lived together in some nightmarish commune and that my claim to be unable to reveal details of Gary's plans for the day was a lie. Odd though this belief was, it was as nothing when compared with that of a woman who was convinced that I lived in a flat on Baker Street with Lou Reed and Stevie Wonder.

I was so intrigued by this belief – and was keen, as you might imagine, to discover whence it had sprung – that, I'm afraid, I rather egged my correspondent on by writing back to her with details of the life Lou, Stevie and I shared. How we dreaded the weeks in which it was Stevie's turn to do the cooking, I remember telling her. I also exchanged letters with a Greek woman who was under the impression that I was her lover. So grateful was she for my entirely imaginary services that she would, from time to time, mail me small amounts of money. This I would return to her, pretending to be a BBC officer appointed to do that sort of thing. 'I very much regret that our contributors are not permitted to receive cash gifts from listeners and accordingly I am returning the five pounds you thought to mail to (fill in name of contributor),' I wrote. On at least one occasion, my benefactor, a burly lass of some fifty summers, stood alongside me at Broadcasting House Reception whilst seeking information about my whereabouts and she failed to recognise me. I can only assume that she was another of those who had me confused with Bob Harris.

More seriously unbalanced was the beautiful blonde who arrived at Broadcasting House Reception and, upon being told that I was nowhere to be found, removed all of her clothes. As she had the sort of physique admired by students of the *Sun*'s Page Three – and by me, I have to add – this unexpected tactic was much appreciated by BH security personnel, who arrived in unprecedented numbers to decide what to do next. For years afterwards I was asked, whenever I walked through Reception on my way to the studio, whether any of my 'friends' would be turning up that evening. I knew exactly what was meant by this enquiry. The only other time this woman appeared at work, she lay fully dressed in front of the Land Rover I drove at the time, and there is little doubt that if our friend Madge, styled The Simple Village Maiden and the daughter of the artist Lawrence Self, had not been with me and had seen a foot sticking out from under the car despite the dark – it was after midnight – I would have dropped the Land Rover into first, pulled away from the kerb and killed the beautiful blonde.

I can vouch, by the way, for the excellence of the blonde's figure because for years she sent me photographs of herself naked, along with letters filled with bizarrely jumbled religious, racist and medical hints and suggestions, and demands that I do something about the lack of recognition – and money – she had received for having written all the songs so wrongly attributed to Paul McCartney and Paul Simon. I'm pretty sure that I recognised this woman, whose name is known to me, when I was last in Birmingham. She was standing alone, dressed in rags, in the city centre, an object of distaste and ridicule to passers-by. I'm afraid that I too, in accord with biblical precedence, passed by on the other side, not through a lack of sympathy but through having absolutely no idea what to do to help her.

But back to Mallory Park. Sheila and I drove to the circuit in our Volkswagen Dormobile, and as we drew closer to it, were astonished at the number of girls trudging in the same direction dressed in Bay City Rollers chic. What they knew and we didn't was that the Rollers, at that time the most screamtastic band in the country, were scheduled to make an appearance of some sort during the racing – there was, in addition to all the Radio 1 fun, a full programme of motor sport, including, for example, the Dunlop Star of Tomorrow Formula Ford Championship Race and the Allied Polymer Formula Ford 200 (Odd Numbers) Race along with a Dave Lee Travis Dragster Demonstration and the BBC Disc Jockeys Popstacle Race. For some reason I was excused from participation in the last named, so reached trackside in good spirits and with a Dormobile filled with insanely overexcited Rollers fans we had picked up along the roadside. These were, it seemed to me, mainly sturdy fourteen-year-olds whose stockiness was cruelly overemphasised by the tartan outfits they all wore. Having bid them farewell, Sheila and I made our way to the elite area on the inside of the circuit.

For those unfamiliar with Mallory Park, there is, in the middle of the western end of the circuit, a large lake, which has on its northern shore a dog's-bone-shaped island, linked to the mainland by a narrow footbridge. On the eastern end of this island, on that unmatched July afternoon, a mock-mediaeval tent had been erected from which we could watch the racing without being pestered by young persons anxious to secure an introduction to the Bay City Roller of their preference. Before I was able to make my way to this sanctuary, I made my small contribution to the feast of soul and reason by ferrying small groups of Radio 1 fans around the circuit at the motoring equivalent of dictation speed. I wonder how many of my passengers, who with better luck could have been driven by

Paul Burnett or Simon Bates, remember this experience as being one of the highlights of their lives.

Whilst I was so engaged, Sheila had made her way to the mock-mediaeval tent to prepare, as it were, the way of her lord, and I joined her there shortly after two p.m., during, of course, a lull in the feast of speed that enabled us to cross the track.

I arrived outside the tent as a helicopter was flying a handful of Bay City Rollers on to the western end of the bone-shaped island. On this was – and possibly still is – an observation point, a sort of two-storey greenhouse in appearance, and it was from this that the Bay City Rollers could see and be seen. Already a considerable number of their fans had run across the track and were standing, shrieking, on the edge of the small strip of water that ran between the mainland and the island. More joined them every minute, a tartan-clad flood that seemed, like a burst water main, to be effectively unstoppable. Their objective was, naturally, to get on to the island so that they could touch, at the very least, the hems of the garments – also tartan, of course – of their perky heroes. The narrow foot-bridge mentioned above was not a realistic option, guarded, as it was, by its own burly Horatius. (I vaguely recall that the wonderfully named Lars Porsena of Clusium played a part in the Horatius-and-the-bridge business but I forget exactly what it was, so can't include Lars in this story, alas.)

I was standing outside the tent, next to the excellent Johnnie Walker, and he and I both noticed a significant pop moment there at Mallory Park, albeit one almost lost in the turmoil. Throughout the seventies, the band Slade had enjoyed a considerable run of success with a string of records, including 'Mama Weer All Crazee Now', 'Cum On Feel The Noize' and the wonderful 'Bangin' Man', the misspelling of whose titles predated the gangsta rap enthusiasm for phonetic spelling by close to three decades. Lead singer Noddy Holder was another guest on that Mallory Park island, and when he crossed the bridge, passed Horatius and strode unnoticed through the Rollers fans, he must have thought, 'Well, that's the end of that then.'

But Johnnie and I had little time to dwell on the ephemeral nature of pop acclaim as the bolder fans, driven half mad by the proximity of the Bay City Rollers, had started to wade across towards the island, through the mud and weeds and, I suppose, duck shit. The only organised force available to attempt to stem this tide was, barely credibly, the BBC Sub-Aqua Club, whose members were dressed in flippers and wetsuits. Johnnie and I and the other guests watched in astonishment as these frog-like figures collected hysterical girls from the weeds and, in the absence of any reasonable alternative, carried them back to the opposite bank. Here, of course, the girls turned and started the trudge back through the water again. In the meantime, helicopters were ferrying in more Bay City Rollers – perhaps, like the Royal Family, they were not able to fly together – and, although I may have imagined this, racing had resumed. Certainly the scene resembled something Dante might have conjured up when trying to impress friends at a party, and unable to drink in the wild detail of it all, I turned aside for a moment to see what was going on on the lake itself. What I saw caused me to seize Walker's arm in an approximation of a vice-like grip. Hurtling back and forth on the pellucid waters of the lake was a speedboat, and in the speedboat was Tony Blackburn, waving to the crowds. The speedboat was piloted by a Womble. 'Look on this and marvel,' I murmured to Johnnie Walker. 'You will never see anything like this again.'

Chapter Six

The other weekend we had the party in the field across the road to celebrate my becoming an old-age pensioner. I have been allowed something of a preview of the benefits to be derived from this condition in that I have been allowed the pensioners' one-pound deduction from Friday lunch in the Chestnut Horse for several months now. The party was, thanks to the preparatory work done by Sheila, her sister Gabrielle, our Alexandra and numerous friends, a huge success. From where I sit I can see some of the vast slabs of Cheddar and several whole Stiltons left over from the buffet, and there is enough red wine in the house to give the whole village alcohol poisoning in the unlikely event that I would be unselfish enough to share it with them. Music was provided to universal acclaim by Scotland's Camera Obscura and by Slightly Soiled, the band fronted by local farmer Peter Jordan. Peter was harvesting until four o'clock in the afternoon, but through circumstances beyond my understanding – something to do with specific gravity, I think he said – he had to leave the fields for the glamour of our party. I often tell people that Slightly Soiled are my favourite band after The Fall and they certainly played a blinder that night. The band restricts itself to proven country favourites – they learned 'Lonesome Fugitive' just so that I could moan along with it – and a handful of rock 'n' roll classics, some of the lyrics of which Peter has committed to memory. 'Lonesome Fugitive' is important to me, particularly in its version by Roy Buchanan, because this is the song I sang to our children on the rare occasions it fell to me to sing anything at all. For my 45th birthday, an important anniversary for the old-school DJ, along with 33⅓ and 78, Sheila arranged for the children to be recorded singing along with Roy Buchanan's band and had the results pressed up in a limited edition of six 7″ singles. Also on the record are each of the children and their mother separately singing 'Happy Birthday', William, then eight, saying, as he often did, 'It's not fair!', Alexandra (six) shouting, 'Shuddddupppp!', Thomas (four) bellowing his mantra, 'Will you wipe my bottom?' and Florence (two) gurgling while the rest of the family giggled at her. This, as you might imagine, is a record I can't listen to without bursting into torrents of tinkling, faerie tears.

The only sad thing about my sixty-fifth birthday is that there was no-one there, apart from members of my own family, that I knew before I was about twenty-eight. The only person with whom I'm still in touch from my days at Woodlands, Sparrow Harrison (qv), was, he told me, taking care of security at a flower show in Denbigh – those North Wales flower shows can get a bit rough apparently – and I'm not in touch with anyone who was at Shrewsbury with me, nor indeed with anyone from either my two years as a soldier of the Queen or the seven years I spent in the United States.

I brood on these things quite a bit these days, and I expect that now that I am a pensioner I shall brood on them even more. I think the truth is that I was not much liked at Shrewsbury – one former acquaintance whose opinion of me was sought by an enterprising television researcher said, rather memorably, that 'John wasn't the sort of boy you invited home for the weekend.' I'm not entirely certain what the implications of that phrase are, but they cannot, I think, be good.

I had some friends, of course. Names such as Edwards, Saltmarsh and Stephens come to mind, but they were, in the main, much cleverer than I, were never in the same form, and presumably went on to University, then took over family businesses before becoming Lords Lieutenant of counties. My principal consolation therefore from the years spent at Shrewsbury was the huge benefit I derived from being in a House – and, for a memorable year, a form – presided over by R. H. J. Brooke.

In fairness to the school, our children would say that it provided me with the sort of education that enables you to talk for about twenty seconds on almost any topic, although there is no one thing about which you know a great deal. I mention the children in this context because they take advantage of my imperfect education on an almost daily basis when completing the quick crossword in the *Guardian*. Florence, in particular, has benefited from this and I think it would be fair to say that she and I finally bonded, after a few difficult years during which my role as a mildly embarrassing parent threatened to destabilise our relationship, through the combination of the

Clockwise from top:
John's parents,
Harriet and Bob
Ravenscroft; John in
Rhosneigr; John and
his brothers, Alan
(middle) and
Francis; John and
his father

Alan, Francis and John

SHREWSBURY SCHOOL

House R.H.J.B. Form Uiva. Name J.R.P. Ravenscrof

Summer Term, 1955

Age at end of Term 15.11 Average age of Form 15.6 Number in Form 24

Form Place 23rd Fortnightly Orders :— (Form Subjects only.)

	1	2	3	4	5	First Half Term	Second Half Term	Whole Term
	22	22	23	14	14	23	20	22

FORM REPORT

Latin 18. His is a great disappointment. His improvement during
French 22. the last month was only achieved under the direst
History 13. Threats, and at the same time was done at no great
Divinity 3. inconvenience to himself. He has quite a flare for
expressing himself in English, + if only he would exert
+ develop this talent, he could become quite a promising writer

Maths. B3 17 In the middle of term he seemed transformed
but it was

SHREWSBURY SCHOOL

House R.H.J.B Form UPPER IV B Name J.R.P. RAVENSCROFT

Michaelmas Term, 1954

Age at end of Term 15.3 Average age of Form 15.2 Number in Form 26

Form Place — Fortnightly Orders :— (Form Subjects only.)

	1	2	3	4	5	First Half Term	Second Half Term	Whole Term
	20	5	5	6	3½	13	5	7

FORM REPORT

Divinity 3 Good.

English 6: Good. Occasionally brilliant, but a little slap-dash.

Latin 14: Impatience of detail lets him down too ofte.
He is almost entranced at his own progress and his pose of idleness annoys me but
aggravates often. He would do well to drop it and to accept himself for what he is — a gifted
boy with an idle past and a future which holds possibilities. M.W.Y

Chemistry: Set 2. 17/21. Pleasant in form, but far from hardworking. ——

History 7=/26. Probably the only member of the form with much trace of imagination or literary ability. If he could learn that
he isn't one of the kings of creation, he could do very well. He won't always be   A.L. le Q.

Physics Set 2 20/21 His work in the second half was better but there is still plenty
of room for improvement. D.N.M.

French 14/26 Rather better results since half term, but his carefully
cultivated attitude of contempt is hard to bear. ——

Maths. B3 14/25 Vari...

Art : His work shows some...

HOUSE MASTER I am very
gradually losing th...
and he is replaci...

HEADMASTER He is gradual...
— apparently de...
a pose.

This Report includes all work...

SHREWSBURY SCHOOL

House R.H.J.B. Form III. Name J.R.P. Ravenscr

Summer Term, 1953

Age at end of Term 13.11 Average age of Form 14.1 Number in Form 1

Form Place — Fortnightly Orders :— (to be left vacant for New Boys.) (Form Subjects only.)

	1	2	3	4	5	First Half Term	Second Half Term	Whole Term
	14	14	13	14	14	14	14	14

FORM REPORT

His work has improved slightly during the second half term, but
is no reason why he should be bottom of the entire school. In spite of h
lazy attitude there are occasional gleams of intelligence and his gro
in Latin (14th) is not too bad. He has got to learn the habit of work.

DIVINITY 14 He seldom even brings the right book. His ink is messy in the extreme M.W.Y

ENGLISH 12 No fool & he spells well. Has taken too little trouble
to do much good yet. C.S.F.

HISTORY 13= He took - or appeared to take - little interest and did not really
Geography 13= bother to learn his work. ——

SCIENCE 11/14. He must attend far better in school, and put his mind to his work (when
out of school.) ——

FRENCH 12/15 He seems very lacking in energy. His carelessness is his chief
Set D. for he has some grounding in the subject. On the whole, unsatisfac

SET SUBJECTS

MATHEMATICS He seems to have no idea yet of wha
SET C2 work means. He does not do anything
23

Left: John before leaving for the US
Above: Ty Croes Camp, Anglesey, where John was posted
Below: John at UEA after receiving his first honorary degree, with (L–R) Florence, Sheila, Alexandra, William and Thomas
Below right: An invitation to attend an Old Salopian weekend for former pupils of Shrewsbury

THE OLD SALOPIAN CLUB

15 ASHTON ROAD,
KINGSLAND, SHREWSBURY SY3 7AP
Telephone : Shrewsbury 51163

Hope very much that you will come and attend
the Old Salonian week-end in October - you
would add a bit of tone to the gathering,
and present boys are not wholly convinced that
you actually exist, being a cross between
myth and legend. (What is the difference ? only
Hon. MAs know).   No reply expected - and no
rude remarks on the air.....

best wishes, Michael Charlesworth.

Above: Two
early pictures
of 'Gene'
Ravenscroft
Above, centre:
The beginnings
of the record
collection

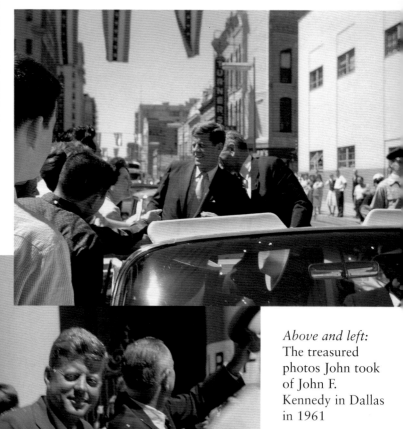

Above and left:
The treasured
photos John took
of John F.
Kennedy in Dallas
in 1961

DAVE JEFFREYS and NANCY SINATRA at recent Hollywood party where Nancy's new record "How Does That Grab You, Darlin'?" was released.

K/mentertainer

K/MEN's JOHN RAVENCROFT, 6 - 9 p.m., taking a few of the many requests that are called in every morning.

JOHN RAVENCROFT 6 AM to 9 AM	MARK DENIS 9 AM to 12 Noon	DAVE JEFFREYS Noon to 3 PM.

K/men 129 RADIO

CHUCK CHRISTENSEN 3 PM to 7 PM	BUDDY BUDNIK 7 PM to 12 Mid	JOHNNY DARIN 12 Mid to 6 AM

K/men 129 RADIO

DALLAS COUNTY CRICKET CLUB
1964-1965
John Ravenscroft
is a member in good standing
J A McDonald *C D Dransfield*
Sec./Treas. Chairman

Clockwise from top: Kmen newsletter; John Steele, a friend and co-worker at the cotton exchange; John experimenting with fashion; John with the Byrds, who refused to speak to him

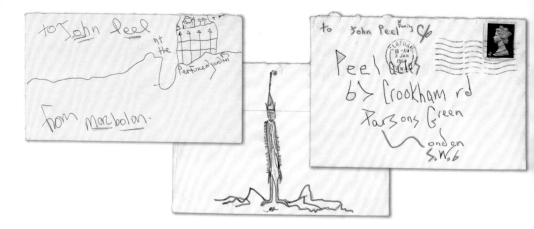

Above: Correspondence from Marc Bolan
Right: John, Pete Drummond and Clive
Selwood in Park Square Mews
Below: John on the deck of the *Galaxy*,
the Radio London ship

Left: John with
Captain Beefheart
and his Magic Band
Below: John in his
bunk on the *Galaxy*

Above: Broadcasting *The Perfumed Garden*
Below right: John signs autographs outside
Radio 1, watched suspiciously by his
childhood nanny, Trader
Below: John attends a memorial service for
Martin Luther King

Above left: John's mother celebrates her fiftieth birthday in style
Above right: John with his mother, dressed for a night out at Glyndebourne
Below: Francis, Alan and John with their father and Francis's son Sacha

quick crossword and the mobile phone. I still treasure the memory of the call I got one afternoon when shopping in Oxford Street. In its entirety, our conversation went like this:

Flossie: 'Writing desk, ten letters?'

Me: 'Escritoire.'

Flossie: 'Thanks.'

And only yesterday Thomas called home to ask about a clue in the *Observer* speedy crossword. 'Unacceptable, Dad,' he said, '6-3-4.' 'Beyond the pale,' I suggested. I wouldn't have been able to do these things without a public-school education, I'm sure of it.

After the programmes I usually cycled to Mother's house in Jameson Street. In the past I had travelled to John and Helen Walters' home in Croydon, then our friends the Knappetts, then the Proudfoots, or to the Lycetts on the Kilburn/West Hampstead border, but as London's traffic worsened and parking became more expensive and I grew fatter, it seemed a better idea to cycle the few miles to Notting Hill instead. The ride itself was usually fairly uneventful, although there were nights when there seemed to the slightly over-imaginative cyclist to be an undefinable air of menace as I pedalled, whereas if the air was warm and there were more people on the streets, London could seem almost romantic.

The night on which I was struck by a hit-and-run driver was, as I remember it, a pretty neutral sort of night. I was making my way towards Bayswater Road through Hyde Park Square when a car – colour, make, occupancy factor unknown – came out of a side road, clipped my back wheel and, possibly even unaware that it had hit me, disappeared into the night. I had fallen on to a small rectangle of recently laid Tarmac that seemed to me in my dazed state to be soft, even slightly warm, and not a bad place to spend a few minutes, possibly even the night, so I made no attempt to get to my feet. Despite the proximity of the Bayswater Road, there were no pedestrians or other traffic about in the square, so no-one in a position to rush to my aid, no-one to check my vital signs or dress my wounds. Hold on, I thought, what's this talk of wounds? Do I have wounds? I raised myself on one elbow to check, and in so doing became aware that there was a trickle of something warm and sticky from my nose. Alarmed by this, I wiped it away with my hand and, clambering to my feet, walked to a streetlamp to check whether it was blood. When I saw that it wasn't, I picked up my bicycle, and finding it, too, relatively undamaged, continued on my way to Notting Hill.

The following night I was recounting this fairly unremarkable tale to Kid Jensen, my Radio 1 Rhythm Pal, on air and our conversation was overheard by a doctor who phoned the BBC to let me know that this fluid that had issued from my nose could have been cerebro-spinal fluid, that this was – and, medics, I may have got this wrong – the stuff in which your brain floated and that the spilling of it usually indicated a fractured skull. I should, the doctor explained to the Duty Officer who took the call, report to hospital with a minimum of delay.

I spent the night under observation in the nearby Middlesex Hospital and was discharged at the crack of dawn with the welcome news that I had no fractured skull. However, one of the tabloids had picked up on my conversation with Kid as well, and ran a story to the effect that I had been rushed to hospital, where I had been diagnosed as having a fractured skull but had discharged myself in order to introduce that night's *Top of the Pops*. I rather preferred this story, with its overtones of reckless heroism in a fatuous cause, to the truth, and phoned home to discuss it with Sheila, who, it turned out, had been contacted by a rival paper anxious for a quotable quote and her reflections on my bravery and fortitude. She, knowing the original story to be almost entirely the product of journalistic imagination, pointed out that quoting, however memorably, on a fiction, was not something she cared to do. The second tabloid, thwarted, waited for an hour before phoning again to tell my wife that they had just heard that I had passed out and had been rushed back to hospital, and to ask did she have anything to say now? Fortunately, Sheila, recognising that if this second story had been true, she would have been the first to hear, neither panicked nor provided a quote.

Intriguingly, both tabloids had missed out on the only genuinely interesting aspect of the whole affair, something they could have headlined, DARK LORD SAVES TOP DJ. (I apologise for the apparent conceit of that imaginary headline, but as any student of the popular press will know, any DJ featuring in such a story is, by definition, a Top DJ, in much the same way that any woman who has ever had her photograph taken is a Model and if that photograph was taken by someone living in Paris or New York, a Top Model.)

The Story That They Had Missed was derived from the fact that my mother, Hat, had for some years shared half of her life with the actor Sebastian Shaw. They met, I believe, when she was staying outside Ludlow with my Aunt Ethleen, although not, as far as I know, in the outside toilet that had played such an important, if brief, role in my life. They met in the altogether more elevated surroundings of Ludlow Castle, where Sebastian was appearing in a production. I was never really comfortable with their relationship, although I never said anything – it was, after all, none of my business – but it seemed to me that Hat, always a pretty single-minded woman, had turned her back on most of her friends and on any possibility of a more stable relationship by devoting herself to Sebastian. Throughout their relationship, Sebastian had maintained a parallel relationship with another woman, one who was the very antithesis of Hat. Whereas my mother had never worked, was overweight, drank excessively and was content to live in what to the impartial observer might well be classed as squalor, the other woman had a highly responsible career in the twilight world of opera, was trim, rarely drank and lived in some elegance. Nevertheless, it must be said that the days she spent with Sebastian – the rota worked on a strict four-days-on, four-days-off basis – were, for her, happy days. If they hadn't travelled to Stratford-on-Avon – Hat's beloved 'Stratty' – they were in London, and my arrival at Jameson Street in the small hours wasn't always treated with the unrestrained glee for which I might have hoped. Conversely, when Hat was on her own she was often morose and hostile and, as I was likely to have been the only person she'd seen all day, tended to take out her frustrations on me. Despite this, we muddled along, and I kept her supplied with the US tour-jackets that record company promotions departments showered on John Walters and myself. She would report to me, with no little pride, that she had gone to the off-licence in either her Bob Seger Band or Boston jacket and been intercepted by an American tourist anxious either to discuss the band's latest record or, better still, to buy the jacket.

The night of the hit-and-run had been one of Sebastian's nights and occurred around the time of the Star Wars film, *Return of the Jedi*, in which he played Darth Vader. In the earlier films, the Dark Lord of the Sith had been portrayed by the actor David Prowse, who had been the Green Cross Code Man in a lengthy series of television road-safety films, but in the third film of the Star Wars trilogy, in which Vader was revealed as Luke Skywalker's father and was required to remove the helmet he had hitherto worn, the producers required an older man than Prowse and one who did not have the strong West Country accent of the Green Cross Code Man. The result of this casting decision was that I could brag that following my being wounded by a hit-and-run driver, I had my head bathed by Darth Vader. Not many people, I like to think, can make that claim.

Sebastian/Darth did occasionally come with Hat to stay with Sheila and me and word would spread amongst William's friends that the Dark Lord was in the house. The normally quiet lane that runs past our house before coming to a halt over the top of the hill, would fill with puzzled parents indulging normally epically indolent children who had, against all expectations, expressed enthusiasm for a walk, one that would take them past the Ravenscrofts' house. I expect these children, mainly boys, secretly hoped that as they dawdled past the house, Sebastian would leap through the front door brandishing his light sabre and challenge them. Instead, an amiable old gent would invite them in, if the mood took him, and would perform simple conjuring tricks for them – including the knocking-a-coin-through-a-table trick. Nowadays such neighbourliness would be interpreted as 'grooming' and hordes of vigilantes would crowd into our narrow lane to burn crosses and grunt threats. For myself, I still don't know how Sebastian did that coin-through-the-table business.

On one of the rare nights upon which I arrived at Jameson

Street with Sheila, Hat excused herself and with much huffing and puffing disappeared upstairs, to reappear ten minutes later with a bedraggled panda and a brown envelope. The panda, which I had last seen thirty or forty years previously, had been my constant companion as a child, and I had not known that it had survived the war. Most former panda or bear owners under circumstances such as these are obliged to reveal that their panda or bear was called Mr Smuggums or Boogie Bear or something equally cringe-making, so it is a source of some pride to me to be able to tell you that my panda had no name. It was female rather than male, but only because we had another panda, a pyjama case to adults but a living, breathing friend to Francis and me, which was more obviously male. (I don't mean it had a penis, just that it had bigger ears and seemed, somehow, male.) I was moved to tears by the sight of my childhood friend after all these years. She sits, as of even date, on the chest at my side of our bed, still keeping an eye on the young master.

In the brown envelope were my school reports.

Frankly, I could fill this book with details from these reports, along with orgies of self-justification, but to do so would risk maddening the reader anxious to hear stories about the stars. However, it would be useful, perhaps, to give you an idea of how other people regarded the infant John Ravenscroft.

The earliest report is dated December 1945, and comes from Miss Jones's kindergarten which, I had forgotten until now, was more formally known as Westbourne School, Wood Lane, Neston. As I said before, at Miss Jones's there was none of your Second Year Remedial action-painting nonsense. We did Arithmetic, History, Geography, Scripture, French and Elocution, amongst other things. My elocution was 'quite good for a first term', and I was allegedly 'very interested' in Scripture. My conduct was, disappointingly, 'good' and E. Aubrey Jones, Principal, came to the famous conclusion that 'Robin has made a very good beginning at school.' I have always told people, including you, that what she said was, 'Robin has failed to make much impression at school' – a better story, if, alas, untrue. Bugger!

The following term, my conduct had deteriorated to 'Fair. Not always obedient,' which is slightly more rock 'n' roll, and I was adjudged to 'be quite ready to try to sing alone'. I was still disobedient in the summer of 1946 and my Drill was 'fair'. By the spring of 1947, I was 'very interested indeed' in Scripture, and later that year had transferred to Woodlands, where S. P. L. Lloyd deemed me 'very good' at something called Repetition. My critics, including members of my own family, would insist that this is still the case. The headmaster found me 'an exceedingly nice boy'. When Woodlands was taken over by Messrs Brooke and Sinker in the Christmas term, 1948, things started to go wrong for the 'exceedingly nice boy'. 'We hope he will take more interest in all sides of school life next term,' the duo whined. Sportswise, I had 'not much idea of swimming' and apparently showed little interest in football.

As the new decade dawned, the decade that started with Liverpool's defeat by Arsenal in the FA Cup Final but was later to bring us Elvis, I was expressing myself well in English and 'developing interesting ideas'. I was 'excellent in pattern making'. Thank you, Miss Baker. I was four foot nine and weighed just over six stone.

By the following winter I was playing regularly for the 2nd XI as an old-fashioned full back and had 'proved to be an invaluable member of the side'. I tackled well and was always keen. Should any other former member of that 2nd XI be reading this, I wonder if they'll remember the unpleasant smell that pervaded the bus in which we travelled to a match with Heronwater. We spent the whole drive trying to locate the source of the reek and I can now reveal, for the first time, that it was me. As the bus left Deganwy, I attempted a discreet fart and it all went terribly wrong. I won't go into further detail, but I left my soiled underpants in the changing room at Heronwater and would like to apologise to whosoever it was who found them.

A further Christmas term (1952) and a further revelation. I had, according to the headmaster duo, been 'called on to be a prefect in an emergency' and fully justified their choice. I don't remember this at all, am deeply embarrassed that it was so and would much prefer to be able to tell you that I approached my teen years as a troubled and turbulent youth with a handful of gimme and a mouthful of much obliged. Whatever that means. When I left for Shrewsbury, I was five foot tall and weighed seven stone.

The first Shrewsbury report was appalling. There were fourteen of us in the Third Form and the fortnightly breakdown reads that I was 14th, 14th, 13th, 14th and 14th. I can't help but wonder who that poor moron was who came 14th in that third fortnight. I seldom brought in the right books (Divinity), was 'lacking in energy' and 'unsatisfactory' (French), had 'no idea of what work means' (Mathematics), and the headmaster recognised that I was 'idle' and 'evasive'. Even R. H. J. Brooke, housemaster and sympathiser, believed that 'we had better forget this term and start anew next term'.

However, halfway through that next term, when I had risen to Lower IV G, my form-master was able to write, 'he has behaved more like a reasonably intelligent boy of four rather than fourteen' and felt that, at the end of term, I 'remained as beastly as ever'. This, I'm afraid, given the time and the place, would be roughly the equivalent of the contemporary 'He's an obnoxious little prick.' Excitingly, I came eleventh out of seventeen and perhaps it was this that encouraged Brooke to write, 'Obviously there is something there, but it's going to be a long, patient and wearing struggle to get it out. I like the boy and think we shall succeed.'

By the summer of 1954, as Elvis was laying down his demos for Sam Phillips in Memphis, it was written that 'his (mine, not Elvis's) appearance and attitude in form are rather deplorable', but A. L. le Quesne, who taught me History, felt able to write, 'Probably the only member of the form with much trace of imagination or literary ability. If he could learn that he isn't one of the kings of creation, he could do very well,' and my house-master celebrated the fact that I was 'gradually losing the reputation of being the House's problem child'.

By the Michaelmas term of 1955, I was in Brooke's form, V C, as well as his House, but was suffering from a wrist broken in a tackle – interestingly, the very wrist that John Birt was to break in a disgraceful challenge many years later during a five-a-side game in a Holborn gym – and before this mis-adventure I had been top of the class for the first time in my life. This I can only attribute to the extraordinary forbearance and understanding of my housemaster, a man I – along, I think, with almost everyone in the House and many other boys in the school – absolutely adored. I think that on some level he recog-nised that there is a sort of curious success to be derived from what appears to be failure, that if you end up doing something that brings you great happiness, as I have, you have achieved this as much as the result of your perceived 'failures' as of your perceived 'successes'. A boy at a private school in the 1950s had extraordinarily little control over his life. Everything appeared preordained, predestined, and it dawned on me, as I battled through school and on into the Army, that the only available control mechanism lay in failure – failure to pass the exams necessary to take me on to University, failure to pass the exams necessary to take me on to officer training.

The following term, with O-levels looming, I dropped to third in Brooke's form. According to my reports I had missed much of the term through illness – this must have been when I was in the school sanatorium with a severe bout of measles. I had measles so badly that I was kept for a couple of weeks in complete darkness and thereby missed out on the opportunity to spend time with any of my fellow sufferers. Amongst these, at different times, were Richard Ingrams, Christopher Booker, Paul Foot, Willie Rushton and Michael Palin. The first four of these were very senior boys and probably wouldn't have spoken to me much anyway, but it would have been interesting to have been able to watch and listen to them. They were working at the time on a parody of the school magazine, the *Salopian*, called the *Wallopian*. This, you could argue, was effectively the first *Private Eye* and I wish I had a copy of it now. I even submitted what I thought was a hilariously funny piece, written very much in clumsy imitation of J. B. Morton, 'Beachcomber' of the *Express*.

Beachcomber's work is seldom discussed now but seemed to me then – as now – to be central to a tradition of what might be styled 'surreal' comic writing and performance that we Britons believe to be uniquely British but is almost certainly universal. Ingrams's anthology of the best of Beachcomber lies at my panda's feet by our bedside. Happily, my attempt at writing Beachcomber was rejected by the *Wallopian* editorial team.

Despite this rebuff, I have read *Private Eye* since I returned from California in 1967 and read it still, regarding it, despite its occasional error of judgement, as being as close to a newspaper of record as we have. The villains vilified, you feel, really merit vilification, and *Private Eye* has an impressive record of being correct in the long term even if sometimes incorrect in the detail. I was once invited to one of *Private Eye*'s lunches, famed, as they are, in folksong and legend, and sat next to Paul Foot. He was enchanting, clever, funny and kind, and I wished I had somehow come under his influence during my time at Shrewsbury. Ingrams I found cold, even hostile, and when I once discovered him looking for a studio in the basement of Broadcasting House and led him to it, felt that he still regarded me, then in my fifties, with the lordly disdain that he would certainly have shown in that sanatorium had I been in a position to speak to him.

Brooke, perhaps growing desperate for something positive to write about me, suggested in my report for that term that 'Journalism would seem a good career for him, for he has a sort of specious literary gift of the gab which might well stand him in good stead.' At the time, I thought nobody had ever said anything nicer about me – and suspect that Brooke would have known that as he wrote my report. A term later he wrote, affectionately, I was sure, that what was required was 'less Donnie Lonegan and more of the constructive effort'.

I was further heartened by my final Shrewsbury report, written when I was in the Remove and was at least a year above the average age of the form. Of my form-mates, I remember only Hall and Balfour, both about the same age as me and both, as I was, thoroughly enjoying their last months at Shrewsbury. Whoever taught us Latin that term – the signature is illegible – summed up my overall performance pretty accurately. 'Cheerfully incompetent,' he wrote.

Outside, the nightmare worlds of work and military service beckoned.

Chapter Seven

Family life had changed pretty radically during the four years I was at Shrewsbury. Francis still had two years to serve when I left and ten-year-old Alan was boarding at Tre-Arddur House outside Holyhead. Father was settled in Heswall with a second wife and Mother was unsettled in London's Rosary Gardens in a flat next to the Soviet TASS news agency. (She used to report that she was often disturbed at night by the cries of recusants and revanchists being tortured next door.)

I suppose that if Francis and I had not been away at boarding school for thirty-six weeks in the year, we might have spotted that a divorce was looming. We had heard our parents arguing, of course, usually about money and Mother's reluctance to stop spending it quite as quickly as she did. She made it quite clear that, as far as she was concerned, there was no possibility of compromise, and spent on. Much of the money went on clothes, either bought from Browns of Chester or from the boutique run by her friend Rene Williams on the front in Parkgate, and some of the outfits Mother wore when visiting Francis and I at Shrewsbury were the source of acute embarrassment to us. Before major events in the school calendar such as Speech Day, other boys would ask us whether our mother would be putting in an appearance as they were anxious, so they said, to see what she would be wearing this time. More extrovert lads than Francis and I might have welcomed this interest; we certainly didn't. Mother was particularly keen on hats that Father routinely suggested – with some justification – would, if turned upside down and fitted with a handle, have served wonderfully well beneath the bed as a pot. Not that Father was much of an authority on fashion, dressing, as he did, in suits of deeply conventional cut that were made to last for decades, possibly even lifetimes. Happily, Mother was willing to connive with me in the purchase of suits that pushed the school's clothing-list definitions to the max. There was a double-breasted, dark-blue number that I wore during my final year in Riggs Hall that made me feel as though I was wearing something from a particularly louche theatrical costumier. To the untrained eye, it must have looked exactly the same as the suits worn every Sunday by every boy in the school, but I knew – and celebrated the fact every time I wore it – that the suit was a shade lighter than everyone else's suits. You have to bear in mind that this deviant behaviour came at a time when virtually everyone, from the Royal Family to the humblest road-mender, wore a suit, shirt and tie to work, and if you had wanted, say, a red shirt, you would have had to travel to Ravenna or Nice or somewhere else in Mediterranean Europe to obtain it.

Neither of my parents knew that I had hidden in the bottom of a wardrobe at Haddon Corner a pair of very poorly made and extremely uncomfortable drainpipe trousers, of the type worn by Teddy-Boys in Liverpool and Birkenhead and beyond. These, together with the lime-green socks I'd bought along with the trousers in Scotland Road, were symbols of a wild-eyed rebellion I was anxious to keep from the rest of the family. I had had to summon up considerable reserves of courage to venture down Scotland Road, which was, at that time, one of the most notorious thoroughfares in the Empire. Bear in mind that I would have walked there in cavalry-twill trousers, a sports jacket, knitted tie and suede shoes, and you'll probably feel that you would have liked to give me a kicking yourself. However, it was in this uniform that I regularly visited the Shrewsbury House club in Everton to play five-a-side football, and although I was usually jeered at by residents, I was never attacked. Father found these visits incomprehensible and assumed I was taking a less than wholesome interest in young boys. In vain I would explain to him that I liked playing football and liked the fact that the lads in Everton were prepared to take me at face value, unlike the boys at Shrewsbury. To be fair to Father, some of the parents of the boys I befriended were similarly mystified and on at least one occasion wrote to him to ask what the hell was going on. It was upon receipt of this letter that he said to me, rather wonderfully I thought, even at the time, that he would give me a five-pound note if I came home and told him I had got a barmaid pregnant. I didn't like to tell him that, desirable though this might be, I wasn't 100 per cent certain of the processes involved in bringing it about.

I don't think either Francis or myself had any idea of what was to happen when we got a note from Father to warn us that he was coming to Shrewsbury in a few days' time, and wanted us to meet in the reception area of the Raven Hotel so that he could tell us something rather important. However, we both knew that whatever the important thing was, it was unlikely to be good.

When we arrived at the hotel Father was already there, and I have often wondered since what thoughts must have been tumbling through his head as he waited for us. He sat us down on an overstuffed sofa and, sitting on a chair opposite us, told us that he and Mother hadn't been getting on for some time, virtually since he returned from North Africa at the end of the war, and would be seeking a divorce. When the divorce was absolute, he continued, he would be remarrying – and this, he said, with the air of a man producing a rabbit from a hat, was the woman he would be marrying. With that, a small, rather unremarkable-looking woman who had been sitting nearby got up and came and sat with us. By this time, poor Francis was sobbing quietly in his corner of the sofa, whereas I, in my dual role as The Boy That Never Cried and older brother – let's make that Older Brother – turned, I suspect, a deathly white as I thought the 1950s, posh-boarding-school equivalent of 'What the fuck do I do now?'

I remember nothing of the rest of the day, beyond the walk back across the Kingsland Bridge with Frank. More than anything else, we were concerned over how the impending divorce would affect the attitude of other boys to us. Hard to imagine now, but it was viewed as something of a disgrace to have divorced parents and we only knew of one other boy of the 630 or so in the school who was similarly cursed.

Being back at home for the holidays following this bomb-shell – forgive the cliché, but for Francis and I it was nothing less and I imagine it was even harder to grasp for Alan, alone at Tre-Arddur Bay – was strange indeed. For reasons I never fathomed, I was sent to live in Heswall with my grandmother, whereas Francis and Alan stayed at Haddon Corner.

Granny, a redoubtable Glaswegian, lived in some splendour in a house in the Lower Village, Heswall, which was later coveted, apparently, by Ringo Starr. She lived alone, save for two maids, one of whom, a fabulously kind woman named Bessie whose generosity of spirit would have won her a place in any Enid Blyton story, shared our surname. We were always puzzled by this, but a recent letter from a listener to whom Bessie was Aunt Bessie assures me that it was merely co-incidence. Granny had left Glasgow in 1908 or thereabouts to marry our grandfather. Rumours persist within the family that she travelled south with a fabulous dowry, one amounting to many millions in today's terms, but all trace of this has vanished, alas. There's nothing like a bit of unfairly inherited wealth to boost the spirits, I always say. Francis, the family archivist, recently unearthed a photo of Granny taken at around this time and she certainly was a powerfully attractive woman. I'm not sure what the Old Testament has to say about fancying your grandmother, but I can't help but believe that it would have been unenthusiastic. To us, of course, she was infinitely ancient, infinitely wrinkled, with a quiet, patrician, slightly mystified and mystifying air. The teas she laid on were sensational, with enough cakes and jellies for each of us to have consumed our own body weight several times over. Although she liked a drink – dry sherry, in the main – and would start drinking early in the day, she would touch not a drop once the grandfather clock in the hall had struck noon. Then she would sit down to watch the horse racing on television and to place bets with Mr Pyke the Butcher, in Neston. These transactions were, at the time, quite illegal, but Granny enjoyed it all so much that even when off-course bookmaking became legal, she continued to place her bets with Mr Pyke.

I wasn't too happy about being billeted with Granny, despite her and Bessie's apparently limitless patience and kindness. The house was vast, dark and not a little spooky, in addition to being filled with what I took to be extremely valuable objets d'art. However, Granny was magnificent, being prepared even to take an interest in the records I carried home from Liverpool. I can remember playing her 'Ma, He's Making Eyes At Me' by the Johnny Otis Show featuring Marie Adams and the Three Tons of Joy – it reached Number Two in the Charts in November 1957 and is one of the most raucous records ever released – and Granny gave me the impression that, against all the odds, she really rather cared for it. Mind you, she also gave the thumbs up to the Isley Brothers' 'Shout', another splendidly boisterous record, so, on some level, plainly knew her stuff. As with so many other members of my immediate family, I wish I had known her better. I was already determined that whatever might happen to me later in life and assuming that I mastered something other than solitary sex, any children I might father would never be sent away to school.

It was said within the family that Father had had some sort of nervous breakdown, but this may have been a device to hide from us the bizarre rituals that had to be observed by anyone hoping to obtain a divorce. To get a decree, it was necessary for one partner, almost invariably the male as it would have been entirely destructive of a woman's reputation for her to have accepted the role, to affect to commit or be taken in adultery. I don't doubt that many a husband or wife actually seized the opportunity to really be adulterous, to feel the hot breath of a third party on their necks, to thrill as an unfamiliar hand probed . . . well, you get the picture. Less libidinous would-be divorcees would feign adultery, checking noisily into some tawdry hotel or pub with a woman (or man, presumably) hired for the job, signing the register in their own names and generally making it obvious to all and sundry that, by God, they were up to no good. Father, by all accounts, was not terrifically keen on sex, referring to the commission of the reproductive act as 'that farmyard activity', so probably took the second course.

In the meantime and despairing that I would ever find work, he had the good sense to invite one of his competitors in the Liverpool cotton industry to take me on as an office boy without portfolio, probably reasoning that my incompetence would bring his rival to his knees. This rival was an immensely likeable man called Tony Hinde, in reality one of my dad's best pals and a character you could easily have encountered in one of P. G. Wodehouse's stories. The company he fronted was called Baumann-Hinde and Co., and had offices at the back of the Liverpool Cotton Exchange (now demolished), from which you could see the Liverpool Stadium, famous as a wrestling venue and the venue in which I had seen, in 1954, the Obernkirchen Children's Choir.

The Obernkirchen Children's Choir had provided me, then a fabulously naive fourteen-year-old, with a range of thrills, most – although not all – entirely proper. At the time of their global smash 'The Happy Wanderer', the charts had been record- rather than sheet-music based for less than two years. Until the change in 1952 that saw Al Martino's 'Here In My Heart' achieve eternal pub-quiz question status as the first record to top the Hit Parade, everything was based on the sales of sheet music. It was perfectly possible, as in the case of a huge tune such as 'Love Is A Many-Splendoured Thing' or 'Three Coins In The Fountain' for the pop-picker to be able to make their choice from twenty-five, even thirty recorded versions of the number. But what was exciting to me was that it looked as though the Obernkirchen Children's Choir's record was going to be the first in history to spend an entire year in the Top Twenty. To my bitter disappointment, it dropped out on the fifty-second week, only to pop back in again the following week. This made the pain – a pain which I still feel to the present day – somehow even worse.

Mother took me to see the Choir – I can't face typing 'Obernkirchen' again – at the stadium on their first and possibly only British tour. In addition to being a musical treat, the event was also significant culturally and, for me, sexually. Let's deal with the culture first.

This was, you'll hardly need reminding, less than seven years after the end of the war, a war in which Merseyside had taken a pounding from the Luftwaffe from which, you could argue, it never really recovered. Liverpool and Birkenhead were scarred with vast areas of rubble – the 'debras and ollers' (debris and hollows) on which my friends in Everton played football when Shrewsbury House was closed – and to bring seventy or eighty German schoolchildren and, one supposes, a fair few chaperones, into Liverpool to perform German songs in German was quite a bold initiative. At almost the same time, it is worth observing, Hermann Goering's massively armour-plated Mercedes was drawing crowds, including me, to a showroom in Birkenhead.

Now to the sex. From the very first number the Choir

performed, I had my eye on a chorister about three rows back on the left. Father would have approved of the fact that this chorister was a girl. From our position in the middle of the stadium audience, it was not really possible to discern her features too clearly, but I loved the way she moved and became obsessed with her in the way that you can when you are fourteen and pretty stupid. After the concert I made some effort to attempt to identify the distant object of desire but was clearly doomed to failure. In fact, I don't think I ever learned the name of any member of the Obernkirchen Children's Choir, but I can still see 'my' chorister in my mind's eye and would wish her to know that she was loved. I wouldn't want to pretend that I still get an erection at the thought of her – the diabetes has taken care of that – but I certainly did for several years afterwards.

I had no similar yearnings at other concerts that I went to with Hat. This was probably just as well, as the concerts featured, amongst others, the Four Aces, Duane Eddy, Bobby Darin, Clyde McPhatter, Liverpool's own Billy Fury, Johnny and the Hurricanes, Eddie Cochran and Gene Vincent.

Chapter Eight

In my final terms at Shrewsbury there had been a lot of loose chat about my future career path. The consensus seemed to be that there was virtually nothing for which I could sensibly be described as having an aptitude, the family business was on its last legs and was stupifyingly boring anyway and there seemed to be few opportunities available in our part of the country for aspirant Lords Lieutenant of Counties. There were even fewer for aspirant Margraves. I've been told that we don't have Margraves in this country and that they are restricted to Central Europe, but I still have a hankering to be one nevertheless. Perhaps in the expanded Europe I could become Margrave of the Marshes, the title for which I yearn.

Brooke had suggested that it was possible that I might be able to forge some sort of nightmarish career from my enthusiasm for boisterous records and for writing overlong and facetious essays. Further to this, the only prize I won at Shrewsbury was for the writing of just such an essay. This answered at wearisome length the set question, 'What Can The Individual Do To Promote International Goodwill?' As far as I know, there was only one other contestant and his contribution must have been very poor indeed. I wish I could recall what it was that I suggested that the individual could do in the promotion of international goodwill, but can remember not a word. My prize was a five-pound book token. It should be remembered that at this time, the mid-1950s, you could buy a stonecutter's cottage in Snowdonia for not much more than five pounds. Having no need for a stonecutter's cottage, I spent my winnings on a book of cartoons collected from all over the known world and the change on a pint of beer. I had had little experience of drink and although I would love to be able to detail a story of teenage drunkenness, vomiting in the Prince Rupert, clumsy interference with the clothing of a barmaid leading to premature ejaculation and more, I cannot. Not yet anyway. From time to time I used to sneak into town with a boy named Roditi to watch Shrewsbury Town play and Roditi, who was a year older than me and rather swarthy, had no problems getting served in one of the pubs near Shrewsbury's riverside ground. Mind you, neither did I – and I looked like a twelve-year-old girl.

Whenever our son, William, full name William Robert (after my Dad) Anfield Ravenscroft, complained about the Anfield part of this splendid name, I would silence him by pointing out that had I supported Shrewsbury rather than Liverpool, he would be William Robert Gay Meadow Ravenscroft. That usually stopped his whingeing and, indeed, that of his sister, Alexandra Mary Anfield Ravenscroft.

Prior to these pints in Shrewsbury, the only alcohol that had passed my lips was the cider that we were fed in the way that today young persons are fed cola drinks, and I didn't experience drunkenness until I was a soldier of the Queen and found that the unceasing battle we waged to keep our island home free from the Red hordes massing, as it were, at the gates, meant that a man needed something more than cider. It was during one of the several discussions I'd had with Dad – at his instigation, always at his instigation – about work, that I was reminded of something I had read, to the effect that in Victorian times the eldest son took over the family business, the middle son went into the Army and lost limbs and/or eyes overseas before coming home to marry the doe-eyed daughter of the local aristo, and the youngest son – usually, it seemed, an imbecile – went into the Church. I was, I revealed to Father, prepared to forgo my rights as the eldest son and take on the mantle of imbecility instead. As he was rather prone to introducing me to people as 'the family idiot', he couldn't marshal many arguments against this.

I have to admit that I didn't really believe in God, but imagined this no bar to progress in the Church of England. I secretly believed – and still do, I suppose – that no-one actually believes in God any more than they believe in the Tooth Fairy or Inspector Morse, but have never been awfully good at defending this position in debate. But, I mean, come on . . . !

My failure to believe in anything much other than the primacy of Liverpool Football Club – a belief that has itself taken a bit of a hiding in recent years – was not affected in a positive way by my confirmation during my second year at Shrewsbury. I had, I'm afraid, so far misinterpreted holy writ as to come to believe that the simple laying on of hands would, in some extraordinarily mystical way, enable me to see through girls' clothing. Looking back on it now, I cannot imagine how I came to believe this – but believe it I did. Thus it was that when I walked solemnly back down the aisle of the school chapel following my blessing by the Bishop of Lichfield, I cast a glance in the direction of the back rows of the congregation where the daughters of members of staff worshipped. Imagine the bitterness of my disappointment, nay, disillusion, when I couldn't even see through the outer garments they needed to keep themselves from freezing to death in that place. I had read in some unsuitable book that the daughters of working people were obliged to wear what were styled 'breast clothes', yet despite my new status as a fully fledged member of the Church, not a breast cloth could I see. I can tell you, friend, I was a bitter boy.

Yet despite this, and despite my confusion over the fact that you could be beaten for persistently being late for Chapel, something that seemed to me to run directly counter to the Christian spirit of forgiveness that we were constantly hearing about, I was still prepared to offer myself up as a servant of the Lord. This was more to do with the pleasure I took in the language and the singing of psalms – there was a Te Deum by, I think, Stanford, which was sung in canon, that I loved – and, once again, the influence of Brooke. My housemaster preached but rarely, perhaps once a year, but when he did you'd have believed whatever he invited you to believe. His texts were rarely drawn from the Scriptures, but whatever he said and however amusingly he said it – and he was a genuinely funny man – I felt that he had some unnerving, although not un-welcome, window into the blackness of my soul.

Dad was, by all accounts, pretty keen on the Old Testament

– the King James version, of course. I don't think he'd have cared for the ridiculous new Bibles that flood out of the US and seem to have been written with the sole purpose of providing justification for Washington's foreign policies, any more than I do.

Happily, Radio 4's *Home Truths* programme provides me on an almost weekly basis with opportunities to reacquaint myself with the Old Testament. Why, this very week a Chris Robbins wrote to the programme on the subject of his father's initials. As a schoolboy, Chris had not known them – but then, what schoolboy does know his father's initials or, come to that, what his father does for a living? Upon enquiry, our correspondent had discovered that his father's initials were, in fact, E. H. The H. stood for Hezekiah, the E. for Er.

Now, I have to admit that until this week I had not heard of Er, and it turns out that his story was grim but interesting. Interesting in that it sheds a different light on one of the Old Testament's most regularly traduced characters, Onan. These things, let me remind you, took place back in the days of heavy-duty smiting and begetting and all that trouble over the mandrakes. It seems that Judah went in unto Shuah and she bore a son and called his name Er. Then Judah went in unto Shuah again and she bore him another son and called this one's name Onan.

A few years later, to cut a long story short, the Lord was displeased with Er, by now a married man, and smote him. And not content with this, He told Onan to go in unto Er's wife and lie with her. Onan, being a decent sort of chap by all accounts, thought this was a bit tough on the widow and, not to put too fine a point on it, spilled his seed upon the ground rather than in his brother's wife. For this refinement of feeling, he too was smitten. So Onan, whatever you may have believed hitherto, was, in fact, a thoroughly moral man and not the wanker everyone thinks he was.

Perhaps you can tell from my sensitive treatment of this frankly beastly business that I could have played a convincing minor role in the Church of England, but it was not to be. Instead, after a few months spent as a telephonist/office-boy in the Liverpool Cotton Exchange, I applied for early call-up and became a soldier instead.

I was born, as I have remarked before, just a few days before the outbreak of war, on 30 August 1939, and when the Government decided, in 1960, to do away with National Service, they decreed that no-one born during the war or, of course, after it would have to serve. If I had allowed events to take their officially specified course, I would have had to enter the Army, Navy or Airforce at the age of nineteen and a half or thereabouts, but recognising that, whatever happened, I was fated to serve my Queen and Country, I applied for early call-up and shortly afterwards was ordered to report for a medical and for intelligence tests.

All the Scousers with whom I took the tests were somewhat wiser in the ways of the world than I was, and when I bragged to some of them afterwards that I'd done really rather well, they pointed out that, given that the medical tests couldn't really be faked and that the Forces would take you anyway if your body gave off warmth or the doctors could detect the flickering of a pulse, the only chance you had to dodge the column lay in failing the intelligence tests. I suppose you could argue that by passing the intelligence tests with such high marks I had merely demonstrated how lacking in intelligence I truly was.

Some months later, having applied to join the Royal Artillery, in the maintenance of a family tradition going back almost twenty years, I got what I suppose really were my marching orders and was instructed to enlist for basic training in Oswestry. This basic training I remember with mixed feelings. Having had some training in the Combined Cadet Force at school, a body of boys attached to the KSLI or King's Shropshire Light Infantry ('King's Silly Little Idiots,' our Drill Sergeant volunteered when I told him this), I was reasonably competent at drill and, to be honest, rather enjoyed it. Also the discipline, although tough enough, was no rougher or more pointless than many of the things I'd encountered at Shrewsbury. On the minus side, my recently acquired stepsister, Carol, was going out with the 2nd Lieutenant responsible for our training programme. Carol, a likeable girl for whom the description 'fresh-faced' might have been coined, was the older daughter of my stepmother, Alta.

Father had been engaged to Alta prior to meeting and falling in love with my mother on a skiing holiday in Wengen. My grandfather had already expressed disapproval of Father's relationship with Alta anyway, as he found it shocking that she was determined to study medicine – at Edinburgh – and to become a doctor. She was never good at disguising the fact that she didn't like me, or Francis, in the very slightest. Alan, Father's favourite, she liked least of all, possibly because Alan was roughly the same age as her younger daughter, Sue, and showed signs of a boyish interest in Sue's sub-navel delights, as he styled them.

But Carol, who was undergoing training to become an orthopaedic nurse in Oswestry, was never anything but helpful and generous to me during what was an uncomfortable three months. Her tit of a boyfriend, whose name, alas, is lost in the mists of pre-history, was a different matter. He never seemed to bother to memorise the names of any of the other recruits in our troop, relying solely, when attempting to demonstrate to NCOs that he knew what he was doing and could be a stern disciplinarian when necessary, upon shouting out my name and giving me a dressing-down. On the mercifully few occasions upon which I met him at home or with Carol, he insisted that I call him 'Sir'. You have to be a rather special sort of twerp to do that, I think.

Upon completion of our training, it was clear that, excellent as I might be at drill – except for changing step on the march, I'm afraid – I was likely to become that rare creature, the ex-public-schoolboy who failed to get a commission. Once again, I was exercising the only option open to me. Getting a commission would, reason roared, mean spending most of my time with men like Carol's ex and that was definitely not what I wanted from Army life.

After basic training, 23558538 Gunner Ravenscroft J. was posted to Larkhill Camp on Salisbury Plain. He didn't much care for it.

Larkhill was much, much harder than anything I had ever hitherto experienced in life. I had never, for example, en-countered men who were prepared to fight for what appeared to be nothing at all, although I had punched the boy Bardsley for bullying Francis at Woodlands and a rather sensitive, bespectacled lad called Smith who had been put up by several of my friends to pouring a bottle of Quink ink over me at Shrewsbury. Smith had sat down rather abruptly when I hit him and burst into tears. Although this might seem to some a satisfactory conclusion, I felt terrible, and if Smith, who I have been told went to live on a remote island and think beautiful thoughts upon leaving University, is reading this: I'm sorry.

But some – a lot – of the lads at Larkhill seemed to be in the grip of some sort of psychosis and life for a wan youth with a posh accent could be very unpleasant. I managed, through policies at the heart of which craven cowardice lay, to avoid getting beaten up, but it was often a close-run thing. The only pleasure I got at Larkhill – and fate has kindly blotted out almost all memories of my few months there bar this – was of doing overnight guard duty in the vehicle sheds. If sufficiently emboldened, you could climb into the cab of a Matador and have a better sleep there than you would have done amongst your testosterone-maddened fellow soldiers in the bearpit that was the billet. Even better than this was the fact that, as day dawned, the nearest non-military building to the vehicle sheds was Stonehenge, and to see Stonehenge emerging from the gloom and mist and (occasionally) into the early-morning sunlight was intensely moving, even giving me, in the unpleasant circumstances under which I found myself living, something that analysts might have identified as hope. Further hope was given to me by the couple running the camp's Salvation Army canteen. I don't think I ever knew their names but I owe them a lot. They were extraordinarily kind and patient with a soldier – and there must have been others – who couldn't cope with the macho culture of Larkhill and their generosity spawned in me a lifelong affection for the Salvation Army. I know it is customary for people with jobs like mine to imply that they give enormous sums of money to charity and that they cry themselves to sleep each night thinking of disadvantaged kiddies. I'm not hypocritical enough to attempt to give you that impression, but the largest part of the miserly sums I do dole out goes to the Sally Army.

Perhaps realising that I was possibly heading for some sort of crisis, the Salvation Army couple helped me to prepare an application for a compassionate posting out of Larkhill. Frankly, I would have gone anywhere else on Earth, but, at their suggestion, I based my application on the fact that my parents had but recently divorced and that my ten-year-old brother Alan, on whom I was genuinely a considerable influence at the time, needed to have me somewhere close to where he was boarding at Tre-Arddur Bay, Anglesey. I expected the War Office, or whoever it was to whom I mailed this application, to reply with a terse 'Horseshit!' so was amazed and delighted when I received word from HQ that I was to be posted to Trials Establishment Royal Artillery, Ty Croes Camp, Anglesey. The camp, shortly to become Trials Establishment (Guided Weapons) Royal Artillery, was a few hundred yards from Cable Bay, where we had spent many a day fooling about in the sand and on the rocks when I was a child, about five miles from Rhosneigr, where Grandpa Ravenscroft had lived for years and where we had spent almost every summer of my young life, and about fifteen miles from Alan's school. As a bonus, Ty Croes was unlike most other military establishments in that there was an officer for every two or three men and, as a consequence, the place was relatively relaxed. Only relatively, mind.

I was billeted for the next eighteen months on the edge of the camp's parade ground and had an otherwise uninterrupted view out over the grass and rocks to sea. I've had holidays that were worse.

On that first night at Ty Croes, I came across the first Geordie I had ever met. His name was Geordie Coleman and he looked like a footballer. Perhaps he was. When I first heard him speak, I assumed that he must be part of the influx of Hungarian refugees that had recently fled their country for ours. It was to be several weeks before I could understand a single word he said. Geordie Coleman was by no means the only surprise I was to encounter at the camp.

My first job at Ty Croes was a range watch detail. Implausibly glamorous though this may sound, it seemed to consist mainly of painting radar sets and the generators that powered them. These were daubed in the ubiquitous olive drab and much of the day could be wasted in travelling to stores for more olive drab and to the fuel point for more diesel for the generators. I quickly learned the necessary skills of petty theft and evasion, along with a grudging respect for the Lance Bombardiers, Bombardiers and Sergeants who controlled almost every aspect of our dull lives. Parallel to this grew a grievous lack of respect for the officers who believed they controlled almost every aspect of our dull lives. The worst of these by far were the junior officers, the Second Lieutenants and Lieutenants who were, in the main, the same age as me and every bit as stupid. These had gone through the processes associated with the War Office Selection Board, processes in which there was still a slight prospect that I might find myself involved if I didn't watch out. I like to think I put paid to any such prospects I might have had when I inadvertently marched a troop of men through one of the neat, if rather sentimental, flowerbeds outside the guardhouse.

As an indication of how stupid these junior officers could be, we treasured the experiences of members of our troop, F Troop, at the hands of one supercilious little shit, the son of a senior officer, who remains nameless only because I can't, alas, remember his name. One bitterly cold night, this ninny appeared in our drill shed with instructions that a generator was required and should be started before, rather than the infinitely more sensible after, being towed to the location at which it was required. These generators were rarely easy to start at the best of times, and starting them grew harder as temperatures dropped. I took the precaution of never learning how to start a generator, but they had, as I recall, three alternative systems available. The first was, of course, a self-starter; the second, a handle; the third, something whereby a special cartridge was inserted into the starter motor and fired, thereby, it was hoped, starting the generator. The generators themselves were mounted on gun-carriages in order to make rapid deployment easier. There was, needless to say, no mechanical or electrical connection between the free-running wheels of the gun-carriage and the generator. Nevertheless, our Second Lieutenant, frustrated when the generator could not be started by any of the methods conventionally considered feasible, ordered a truck to be brought down to drag the gun-carriage around the square, presumably in the hope that this would somehow jump-start the generator. Obviously anyone observing that this was a complete waste of time and resources would have been nailed for insubordination, so the truck arrived and a half-hour or so was spent dragging the generator fruitlessly around the parade ground. Oh, how we laughed.

The days passed in painting radars for the greater good of the free world, playing football in the drill shed with cotton waste or whatever we could find that was kickable, and making our way as slowly as possible from one point to another. After a few months, I was assigned to one of the several theoretically secret projects that TE(GW)RA was working on. This was code-named Yellow Fever and was to take up the next year of my life.

The best thing, from a military perspective, about Yellow Fever was that it would speed up and simplify the means by which anti-aircraft guns and their operators deduced the point at which a shell and its target would, hopefully, meet. As it stood, pre-Yellow Fever, this involved a long-distance radar set about the size of a large truck that located the target at distance, passed the information to a smaller radar and thence to the guns. These were then trained on the target – aimed, if you like – manually by the several gunners assigned to them who upon receiving the order, 'Fire!', fired. Once again, what you may interpret as sensitivity to the nation's defence needs and the understanding that, even now, it is best to remember that walls have ears, is less to do with discretion and more to do with my never having had to work on these big guns and therefore having little real idea what went on. Yellow Fever, which was about the size of the cab of a large truck, was unusual in that, unlike the conventional sets which had a rotating aerial on top, the entire thing spun round. This meant that when something went wrong – it was described to me as being the equivalent of a fuse blowing – the entire set would spin around out of control, the two operators clinging to specially provided handles to avoid being flung out. If it had worked properly it would, I expect, as these things are always tipped to do, have brought about the end of warfare as we understood it and made life safer and better for all of us. Which brings me to . . .

The best thing, from a non-military perspective, about Yellow Fever was that it rarely worked. The equipment was located some distance from the main camp and outside the security area, and we were lucky to be working on it over the summer of 1959, one of those summers that people will tell you that we don't have any more. The sun shone, warm breezes blew, seagulls – possibly including cormorants and kittiwakes – wheeled and swooped in the swooning air and we sat and painted olive drab anything that seemed paintable, played football, or, in my case alone, I think, clambered on to the rocks, from which I could see the Bungalow, Grandpa's house – no longer occupied, alas, by Grandpa – to sit by the water, to watch the waves breaking and to muse on Life, the Big Picture. Boffins, in the meantime, would be peering into the entrails of Yellow Fever and wondering what the hell had gone wrong this time. As potential cannon-fodder, a humble Gunner who had every prospect of remaining a Gunner, I played no part in the technical life of Yellow Fever, despite having passed the exams to become a BII Radar Operator. I had done this, as a man essentially unfamiliar with passing exams, through learning the drill book parrot fashion. This entirely satisfied the Army's examiners, who presumably felt that an understanding of the contents of the drill book was surplus to requirements.

I wouldn't want taxpayers to think that their money was being completely wasted on us though. From time to time, Yellow Fever worked, and when this happened planes were summoned from RAF Valley and flew over us at high speed and low altitude, effectively hidden from our view – and, alas, that of Yellow Fever – against the sun-dappled backdrop of distant Snowdonia. This was undeniably exciting, and as we knocked off work to start the twenty-minute walk to the camp for our half-hour NAAFI break, we were proud to be able to talk of the contribution we were making to the defence of the free world. Actually, that's not true at all, but leads neatly into an account of a demonstration of the potential of Yellow Fever before high-ranking NATO personnel that took us to Manorbier in South Wales.

Most of the lads with whom I shared a billet at this time came from Clydebank, and I have regretted as much as I have regretted anything in my life that I lost contact with them upon demob. They were all, needless to say, called Jock. I remember Jock Hamilton and Jock Steel in particular and suspect that they may have been of the party that took the languorous train journey down to Manorbier. At one stage we were travelling through wooded country in cattle trucks, mercifully cattle trucks that had evidently been free of cattle for some time, trundling along in the soft sunshine for hour after hour after hour. Upon arrival at Manorbier, we had a couple of days of rehearsal, during which Yellow Fever behaved impeccably, before the day on which the NATO chiefs were due to be impressed.

That morning dawned wet and blustery and the demonstration didn't go well. Not at all well. My only contribution was, at a certain point in the introductory remarks, to come smartly to attention, double forward and switch something on. I accomplished this without a hitch, but on the return journey tripped over a cable and fell flat on my face. The NATO chiefs didn't laugh, but then I suppose NATO chiefs seldom do. Things went rapidly downhill from there and by the end of the day thousands of shells had been fired at a series of drogues that were being towed through the heavens above us without a single hit being scored. This, I'm pretty certain, effectively marked the end of Yellow Fever. It certainly marked the end of my involvement with it, as I had volunteered to take on the recently vacated job of Battery Runner.

My suitability for this job, I explained to Capt. Jones, the only officer in our Battery for whom it was possible to have any respect, was based on the happy combination of my having four O-levels (English Language, History, Geography and Mathematics) and a James 150 motorcycle which I was prepared to put at Her Majesty's disposal in order to speed communication between officers and men – a winning combination, I'm sure you'll agree. Capt. Jones certainly did.

Chapter Nine

It was said that the first rule for the National Serviceman new to military service was never to admit to having special skills and to volunteer for nothing. Perhaps, on a technicality, that's two rules. By and large, this – or these – remained a sound First Principle – or sound First Principles. Everyone claimed to have been caught out by an NCO's question about their ability to ride a bike, viz:

'Any of you 'orrible little men know how to ride a bike?'

'Oh rather, Bombardier. I can ride a bike.'

'Well then, run over to the Sergeants' Mess with this comically heavy package, then double over to the cookhouse and report for potato-peeling duties.'

That sort of thing.

My own 'bike-riding' moment came during a lecture from a small arms expert about the Bren Gun. I had disassembled and reassembled Bren Guns on numberless occasions in the school cadet corps, although I'd never actually fired one. Obviously, instructing bored National Servicemen in the use of weapons, even automatic weapons, can't have been a lot of fun and our expert, a sergeant, had built his talk in such a way that he had left the only mildly amusing aspect of the gun to serve as a sort of punch line. Unfortunately, I was just a little too much of a smart-arse to hold back, so when he looked up, pointed at the Bren and asked whether any of us knew what this part of the weapon was called, I stole his thunder by declaring that it was the Barrel Locking Nut Retainer Plunger. The instructor was, reasonably enough, livid. 'Right then,' he growled. 'If you're so fucking clever, you can reassemble these two Brens and double around the square with them until I tell you to stop.'

Which I did.

From then on, I kept my mouth shut. At least, until the massed Jocks in the billet invited me to join them on Christmas Rear Party. This, let me explain, isn't nearly as much fun as it may sound to some of you. Christmas Rear Party simply involved staying on camp over the holidays, maintaining, if you like, a sort of skeleton staff. Amongst the duties involved was clearing up the Sergeants' Mess in the wake of their Christmas party, and it was because of this that the boys from Clydebank and myself volunteered for duty.

We had already discovered the unexpected advantages of volunteering to assist in the removal of officers' families from one location in Rhosneigr or Aberffraw to another. Firstly, the officers' wives usually felt bad about this and plied us with tea and cakes. I'd like to be able to tell you that they occasionally offered us sexual favours as well, but that would be completely untrue. It was widely believed that something was added to the

tea to eliminate any sexual urges we might have and it must
1) have been true and 2) have worked. I don't remember anyone in our billet claiming to have had any sexual experiences at
all during the eighteen months I was there, even with officers'
wives.

After tea and biscuits, we would pack domestic equipment
into tea-chests, taking care to put objects we liked the look of
near or on the top. Then we would carry the tea-chests out to
the truck and, when the truck was full, would set off for the
family's new home. As we slowed for sharp corners or hump-
back bridges, we would throw the pre-selected items out by the
roadside – we never took valuables or indeed anything that
might be missed, concentrating instead on things that would
improve the quality of our lives in the billet. Then, after work,
I'd ride the same route on the James and collect the stuff we'd
thrown out of the truck.

Similar principles – or lack of them – applied to the
Sergeants' Christmas Party. All we were required to do was
turn up the following morning and tidy up the considerable
mess. Upon arrival in the somewhat unprepossessing building,
my companions and I were not surprised to find that there
were still sergeants present. Fortunately for us they were all
unconscious and, apart from alarming us by emitting the
occasional low groan, did nothing to hinder us in the execution
of our duties. We had been told by those who had volunteered
for rear party the previous year that although a record of the
drink and cigarettes sold was kept pretty scrupulously at
the start of the evening, this book-keeping fell into disarray
before being abandoned entirely in the small hours. Thus no-
one had the slightest notion of what stock had been sold and
what remained and it fell to us to remove as much as possible

of what was left before anyone regained consciousness. This was easy to do fairly inconspicuously when you were wearing, as we were, baggy denims tucked firmly at the ankles into gaiters. My Scottish mates must have been the toasts of their respective communities when they came home for Hogmanay a few days later, groaning under the weight of Army-surplus Scotch and Navy Cut. We did even better than this on the night of the big fire.

The alarm first sounded at about two in the morning at almost the same moment as a bevy of NCOs arrived in the hut to bully us from our beds. 'It's just a sodding drill,' we grumbled to each other as we dressed. Now, Queen's Regulations stated at the time something to the effect that troops called out on a fire drill were to wear tin hats and boots. What was worn in between was not specified, so we trudged out into the cold and dark in our tin hats, boots and pyjamas. We then fell in and were marched on the double to a marshalling point in front of the Camp cinema. As we ran, we noticed that the Quartermaster's Stores were ablaze.

It was – and may still be – a tradition in the Forces that whenever thefts from stores reached a point at which the most skilled book-keeper could no longer mask the deficits, the Quartermaster would set the place on fire. I'm afraid that in our cynical way, this is what we assumed had happened. As we fell in again outside the cinema, a few hundred yards from the blaze, I took care to take my place at the back, reasoning that if anyone was required to risk their lives to save mountains of old greatcoats and stuff, those at the front would be chosen. To my horror, the squad was turned about so that I was now at the front as we doubled towards the fire.

Upon arrival outside the stores, I had an axe thrust into

my hands and was pushed into the blazing building with instructions to throw out whatever I could find. At the time I thought it was all a bit of a laff, but if the building, which was eventually all but destroyed, had collapsed on me, I'd have stopped laughing in double-quick time. It wasn't long before the faces of the Clydebank posse, who had quickly assessed the business potential of this conflagration and had been ordered to recover whatever I and my fellow involuntary firemen threw out, started appearing at the windows with specific requests. 'Can you no find any toasters, John?' I remember being asked as I went about my heroic work, roof beams crackling above me, asbestos panels exploding all about me in the heat. This was undoubtedly the greatest danger I faced during my National Service – except, possibly, during the unhappy few months during which I was goalkeeper for the Camp hockey team. This, I'm afraid, is something else for which I had volunteered.

I have mentioned that we didn't have a very high opinion of our officers, with the exception of Capt. Jones, but Army life provided us with absolutely no opportunities to attack them physically without ending up in Shepton Mallet, the military prison. However, we were sauntering down from Yellow Fever one day and passed the Camp's hockey team defence playing a practice game against the attack. As we watched we saw a Capt. Hogg take a particularly violent blow from the wayward stick of an opposing player and fall, moaning softly, to the ground. 'There's more to this hockey than meets the eye,' someone muttered. So it was that, more out of bravado than anything else, I offered my services as a goalkeeper, promising that I would do my utmost to injure any officer who came up against me.

Unfortunately, this too rather backfired. Being the goal-keeper in Army hockey was, I quickly found, Not A Good Thing. Not A Good Thing at all. I was much more likely to be injured than to be in a position to inflict injuries and, worse than this, as the only man from the ranks of the common soldiery in the team, I had to travel to away games on my own in the back of a truck. As the officers sped away from Ty Croes in their MGs and Triumphs, I was clambering over the tailgate, forbidden by Queen's Regulations even to travel up front with the driver. I once travelled this way all the way from Ty Croes to Aldershot. Before and after the games none of my team-mates spoke to me and they spoke rarely during the game other than to chide me for allowing the opposition to score. I was a crap goalkeeper, they were crap human beings.

Dreesen got our address from Georg at a-Musik in Köln and hopes I will like his record. Becky from Darlington wants to thank me for playing a track by her band, We Start Fires, on Radio 1 the other night and wonders whether I could mention the band's tour dates. Data Error Records in Mahlow have sent a white label of an LP by Hakan Lidbo, currently our favourite Swede, and Jeff from Orrell Park, Liverpool, who used to be in the key gore metal band, Carcass, wants to record covers of country and western favourites and has enclosed a demo of his version of 'Sunday Morning Coming Down'. Hindzy D from East London sends, without an accompanying note, his 'Baked Beatz' EP on the Sting label. (This has nothing to do with the tiresome crooner of the same name.) Hindzy's record will be what is currently called grime or eski or sub-lo or 2.2 or 4.4 or underground garage. It is not a good idea to use any of these names on the radio, as listeners will e-mail or text to tell you that no-one, but no-one, calls it that any more. This morning's charity appeals come from the Salvation Army and from the Children's Food Fund.

Unusually, I'm looking forward to hearing all of the records that have arrived in the morning mail and may have to incorporate some of them into this week's programmes, thereby messing up the running-orders I have spent the weekend – and a lot of Tipp-Ex – preparing. Title, artist, duration, composer(s), publisher, label, catalogue number, LP or EP title (where appropriate) and track or side and band number must be listed. There are those who find it really strange that I type my own running-orders (on a typewriter that I bought in Barcelona earlier this year that doesn't have a + or a & but has a range of mildly amusing Spanish characters instead), but I counter their sophistries by pointing out that this is the only way I can be reasonably sure that the information I have before me as I drone away on the radio is accurate. I may play the wrong tracks sometimes in the heat of battle, or play the right tracks at the wrong speed, but the information, at least, is sound. (Someone produced a rather good badge last year, on which, beneath a picture of me, was printed 'Right Time, Right Place, Wrong Speed.' I really liked that. It somehow caught what I perceive as the spirit of the programme. Sometimes critics suggest that I play records at the wrong speed deliberately to appear cute, but I argue that there would be something deeply unwholesome about someone my age trying to be cute.)

Last night Liverpool played Manchester United on television. You're not going to catch me slagging off United when I know there may be United fans reading this book. For them: if you've ever wondered where Manchester is, it's about halfway up England on the left. Liverpool lost, but I wasn't watching. I was trying to sort out some of the boxes of demo (demonstration) CDs that clutter every room in the house, making myself busy, knowing that if I watched the match I'd get more wound up than was good for me.

Disposing of the demos is just about the most depressing aspect of what we'll laughingly call 'my work'. They come, in the main, to the BBC address and from all over the world. There was one from Peru in yesterday's mail here at home. A few weeks ago, in the spirit of research, I counted how many demos had come in that day. There were 158. Now, assuming a five-day week that makes 790 a week, although, to be honest, I doubt we get quite that many. Let's settle for 400 a week. Now, assuming each one to be 15 minutes long, that's 100 hours of listening out of a week containing 168 hours. Deducting from that the number of hours spent sleeping or trying to get to sleep (56), that leaves 12 hours a week for eating, drinking, going to the lavvy, watching TV, listening to records, typing running-orders, looking in wonder at Archie, our grandson, and dancing naked in the copse next to our house. Common sense would tell you this means that not every demo gets heard. Last night, as Liverpool slipped to defeat at Old Trafford, I was moodily carrying boxes of CDs – most heard, some unheard, all at least a year old – to the skip in the driveway. Amongst these are letters from and photographs of the bands. It's when you look at these that the enormity of what you're doing hits you. These letters, friendly, sometimes slightly cheeky, written perhaps to demonstrate that the writers are independent, carefree, a little out of control, and the photographs of brooding youths looking, if not like our own children, at least like some of their friends, make you want to listen to their music again, hoping against hope that you'd missed something the first time, that you'd be able to phone right away and ask them whether the band was still together and whether they'd mind if you played a track on the radio. Sometimes I get to do this, but not often. So, I'm sorry, Mip, Autolump, Amber Views, What's That?, 84 Days, Bitten By A Monkey, Wake-Up Call, Pocket Gods and thousands of others. I hope – I really do hope – that one of these days you'll be able to visit me in the Stowmarket Home for the Bewildered and shout, 'Listen, you old twat. You were wrong about us.'

Finally, as a service to aspiring musicians, Louise Kattenhorn, currently my Radio 1 producer, and I are working on a list of things not to write in any press release you might be planning to include with your demos. There'll be a detailed list later, but for now, consider these: avoid the word 'jazz', don't claim a lifelong admiration for the New York Dolls, the MC5 or the Stooges (this will mean you are almost certainly either Swedish or German, wear leathers and are in your late thirties) and, if possible, don't have a saxophone player in the band. That should be enough to get you thinking, I imagine.

Back in our hut at Ty Croes, we had little time for music. Amazingly, if we all gathered around the furnace to listen to anything, it was *The Goon Show*. Despite our Monarch-in-Waiting's enthusiasm for the Goons, they have not, I think, stood the test of time. In the twenty-first century Sellers, Secombe and Milligan sound, well, childish. I never met Harry Secombe or Peter Sellers, although I did, in the late 1960s, sleep with a Yugoslavian woman who claimed that she also slept fairly regularly with Sellers. She danced almost nightly at a club in a mews off Bond Street called Revolution and would get ready for her nights there in the flat I shared in Park Square Mews with the photographer Peter Saunders, known to all my chums as Beautiful Peter as he was, undeniably, beautiful. My Yugoslavian friend would change every night into what I can only describe as a gold-effect chain-mail bikini, before setting off in search of the popular, if apparently deeply unhappy, Goon. If she failed to find him, she would return to Park Square Mews and sleep with me.

Spike Milligan I did once meet, when I stood in for a guest who had failed to appear for a programme on the British Forces Broadcasting Service (BFBS). I didn't like him at all. For a start, Milligan seemed to have no interest in anyone other than himself and seemed to regard me as some sort of threat, which I most certainly was not. I had been rather excited at the unexpected opportunity of meeting him and was disconcerted when he chose to attempt to obliterate any of the drab answers I was giving to the drab questions I, as a stand-in, was being asked, by making hilarious Goon-type noises until the presenter turned back to him.

Those of my fellow gunners who gathered around the radio listening to *The Goon Show* – the massed Jocks, Peter Edgson, Stan Williamson, Neil Bell, the ex-miner from the Midlands, Bill Stott from Bolton (we were a shifting population, of course, so I don't remember all the names) – would have been as saddened as I was to have encountered Spike Milligan in the kind of temper he was in on that lunchtime programme on BFBS.

Musically, my only real ally was a man with whom I attempted to start a skiffle group. He played guitar and I sang. Now, only in Bedlam would my voice have been considered tuneful, but this didn't deter us from attempting to take the stage during one of the infrequent dances held in the Camp cinema. Fortunately, we had barely left the wings before we were ushered forcefully from the stage. Drink had, I'm afraid, been taken. I don't remember what song we planned to sing, although my feeling is that it could have been 'John Henry'. He was, you'll recall, a steel drivin' man. Unusually, I do remember the name of my guitarist, but also remember that many years ago, when I mentioned it on the radio in connection with the same skiffle-based incident, I received a letter from him in which he threatened to take legal action if I ever mentioned him in public again. So I won't.

By this time and inspired, as always, by Lonnie Donegan, I was beginning to take an interest in the blues. I started, as so many had before me, with Sonny Terry and Brownie McGhee. Sonny and Brownie toured Europe frequently, allegedly loathed each other, and their music, except for when Sonny takes off on one of his deeply rural harmonica solos, now sounds rather anodyne. From them I moved on to Houston, Texas's Sam Lightnin' Hopkins, mainly as a result of an LP released by Doug Dobell's record shop at 77, Charing Cross Road. This LP, *A Rooster Crowed In England*, was later to help in securing me my first radio spot on WRR in Dallas, and I remember playing it to Mother – whose interest in listening to what I probably represented to her as the outcry of an oppressed person was, I fear, minimal – and being disappointed at her failure to be moved. But I loved Lightnin' – still do – and have more records by him than by anyone else other than The Fall. (I'm guessing at that. You'd quite reasonably question the sanity of anyone who knew that sort of thing off the top of his or her head.) Mother was much more impressed when I brought home, a few months later and mere weeks before I set sail for the USA, an LP by Muddy Waters. It's difficult to imagine now, but in the later 1950s those of us who took our music seriously were deeply troubled by the thought of electric guitars. Da blooz, as we saw it, involved the acoustic guitar and the acoustic guitar only, and we never thought, for example, how much Robert Johnson or Son House would have loved electric guitars and what astonishing music they might have made if they had had access to them. (Students. See my paper on Caravaggio and the spray-paint revolution.) But Muddy's guitar playing on that LP was a revelation.

(I've just been to my card file to look for the LP and am slightly crestfallen to find that I no longer have that copy I played to my mum, although I have all the tracks on more recent releases. In passing, under what would you file Muddy Waters, M or W? His name was plainly neither Muddy nor Waters, it was McKinley Morganfield, so his professional name was as much a construct as, say, Howlin' Wolf. Nevertheless, Muddy is filed under W, whereas Howlin' Wolf is filed under H. I can't imagine that any sane person would file Howlin' Wolf under W. If you do, don't get in touch. And then there's Bo Diddley. Some other time, eh?)

I mentioned Peter Edgson earlier. Edgy was the only man in our billet who had actually seen action, in Cyprus. Although we never discussed it with him, we had been told semi-officially that he was the only survivor of a truckload of men blown up by EOKA. Although he was that rare thing in our hut, a southerner, he was going out with a girl who lived in Kirkby, outside Liverpool, and as I rode the James up to Liverpool for the football almost every weekend, he frequently took his place on my pillion. The James was not a powerful bike and the ride along the coast road, through Bangor and Conwy and Queensferry, was not necessarily an easy one, but I could usually get to Anfield in time for the kick-off. On a Sunday night, I would chug back out to Kirkby to collect Peter and we would ride back overnight. In the winter this was a total bastard of a ride and most weekends we would have to stop in Penmaenmawr or Llanfairfechan to run about and attempt to discover whether we still enjoyed the manifold blessings of blood circulation.

A few weeks before I was demobbed, at a time when the honorary title of scouser had been passed on to me, following the demob of Alan, our Bombardier and a former Golden Gloves boxing champion, six or seven of us headed for Liverpool and the Empire Theatre to see Gene Vincent, Eddie Cochran and Billy Fury.

By the time I get to the end of this book, I may well have compiled a list of the Ten Best Gigs Of All Time, and there is no doubt that Eddie Cochran and Gene Vincent at the Liverpool Empire will be in any such list. The concert confirmed me in my lifelong love for Gene Vincent in particular, although Eddie Cochran was nearly as good. But Gene looked as I dreamed of looking, completely out of control. He almost completely ignored the audience, staring wild-eyed into the wings as though demons lurked behind the Empire's plush curtains. From time to time, he would fling his damaged leg – held together, we were told, in defiance of medical reason, with pins – over the microphone, and that unearthly high, almost feminine voice that I sang along with in my bedroom echoed like something abandoned and fearful in the Liverpool night. Gene was perfect, exactly how I had hoped he would be, and all I have to do to recapture that night is listen to 'Race With

The Devil' or 'Who Slapped John' or any other of dozens of classic tracks. Perhaps the fact that Gene never really made it commercially in the way that he surely should, helped to endear him to me. Years later he made an album for Dandelion Records, the label that Clive and Shurley Selwood ran with me as a sort of artistic director, and although it wasn't a great record, it was still a Gene Vincent record. As Gene himself sang, 'B-I bickey bi, bo bo boo,' and it would be a churlish man or woman who didn't agree.

We travelled to the concert on the James and in a dilapidated car owned by a regular soldier named Ginger Foord. Ginger was one of but a handful of regulars prepared to spend time with National Servicemen and was a man who, to paraphrase the words of Lonnie Donegan, had many a first-class tale to tell. I can still close my eyes and see Ginger at the wheel of his car as he and I raced side by side along a long straight stretch of road near Hawarden.

My final report, as issued to every soldier upon demob and rarely anything other than generous – many of the lads had to use them as references to help them find work out in civvy street – read 'This man has failed to show any sign of adjusting to the military way of life.' I was rather proud of that, having done it without ever getting into serious trouble. My sins were, I suppose, more of omission than commission and although Dad once again took a rather dim view of what I regarded as quite an achievement, I imagined that Brooke would have smiled a wry smile if he had ever read the report. Although I was grateful to leave the Army, I had greatly enjoyed the year or so I had spent at Ty Croes. The camp remained pretty much intact long after National Service ended and years later, when a television company was making a film about National

Servicemen who'd subsequently become involved with the media, I returned to TE(GW)RA, then in mothballs. A researcher had told me that all of the camps at which those chosen to appear on the programme had served had been demolished and the land returned to civilian use. 'In fact,' she said, 'there's only one such camp left anywhere in the country.' 'Oh, yeah?' I replied, only marginally interested. 'Where's that, then?' 'It's called Ty Croes. It's in Anglesey,' she replied.

Thus, by default, I became the star of the programme, staying at the Maelog Lake Hotel, where my dad had drunk when we stayed in Rhosneigr as kids, sitting on the little footbridge over the river running from the lake into the sea – a river that my grandfather had devoted his declining years to keeping clear of weed, walking along the banks angrily swiping at the water with a cane – and waiting for Sheila to drive up from Suffolk with William, Alexandra and Thomas, then aged seven, five and three respectively. Sitting on the bridge and reflecting that I had known this place as child, soldier and now husband, and could associate it with my father and grandfather, both of whom were dead, it all got too much and I sat in the sunshine in floods of tears, my feet dangling over the water.

Sadly, the footage completed over that weekend was never used. No-one ever got to see me standing outside the cinema telling stories about the great fire and the skiffle group, or talking to the ancient locals looking after the Camp, all of whom pretended to remember me but couldn't possibly have done. The film people told me that every inch of the footage had been overexposed, but I knew differently. When I put the phone down after hearing the bad news, I told Sheila that it seemed I had been as crap an ex-soldier as I had been a soldier and we laughed.

In the weeks leading up to the point at which I ceased to be 23558538 Gnr Ravenscroft J. and became, once again, John Ravenscroft, Gentleman, I'd had several conversations with Dad about the future role I was going to play in society.

'What are you going to do with your life?' Dad had wanted to know, and I had replied along the lines of, 'Well, you know, just hang about and watch the world go by, I suppose.' To this, Dad played his best card. 'I'll send you to work in the USA, if you like.' Startled, all I could do was mutter, 'Yeah, OK. See if I care.'

With this studied indifference, I thought I had called his bluff. Six or seven months later, when I boarded the SS *Eugene Lykes* in Liverpool, bound for Houston, I recognised that he had called mine and it was too late to cry, 'Come on, Dad. I was only kidding.'

To give him his due, my father had been nothing if not thorough, having arranged with his friend Arnold Ogden of the Townhead Mill, Rochdale, that I should work for him until such time as I left for Texas. This, I imagine, was probably at the insistence of Alta, our stepmother, who would not have wanted any one of us Ravenscroft boys hanging around the house in Farr Hall Drive, Heswall, to which they had moved. In the event, I rather enjoyed my time at the Mill. I stayed, during the week, in a bed and breakfast, keeping myself very much to myself, riding my stepsister Carol's old Lambretta back to Heswall at the weekends. The work itself was hard and dirty and very noisy, it being my responsibility to help two other men break open the bales of cotton that had been winched up the side of the building, before chucking it into machines that broke it up further before sending it down into the body of the mill. The idea was that I should move every week to another part of the mill to learn more, but I found the raucous mill-hands, almost all women, considerably more than I could cope with. They, probably with good cause, found me a pretty ludicrous figure, and within hours of being assigned to a different part of the mill I had usually found my way back to the breaking room where I had started. Eventually, someone recognised there was little point in attempting to teach me milling and left me there.

Over the six months I worked in Rochdale, I grew fitter and stronger than I had ever been in my life and I loved my nightly walk down from the mill, across a small park and up the other side of the valley to my lodgings. My social life was non-existent and my evenings were spent in my room, reading Beachcomber, Nathaniel Gubbins, Robert Benchley, James Thurber and P. G. Wodehouse. Beachcomber's 'Sideways Through Borneo' I virtually knew off by heart. I would, if any-one had thought to canvass my opinions on the situation in which I found myself in Rochdale, have expressed myself entirely happy. I might well have gone on to claim that I would be content to carry on working at the Townhead mill for the rest of my life.

Unfortunately, Dad was still concerned over my inability to make any impact on the social life of Heswall, a failure that contrasted dramatically with Carol's membership of, so it seemed to me, every golf, tennis and sailing club in the area. I was enormously envious of Carol's social skills and have always thought of her as being older than I am, although she insists that she is not. On the other hand, I found the bulk of her friends seriously obnoxious, over-confident and in the front room having a drink with Carol's mother and my father – and calling him 'Bob' in what I regarded as an insolent manner –

while I cowered in the back room listening to Lonnie Donegan.

My only concession to Dad's wishes was to join a football club called the Liverpool Ramblers. The Ramblers were almost exclusively public-school types who were crap at football and met in a bar called the Crooked Billet. Upon entering the Crooked Billet, you found yourself at the top of a flight of steps leading down into the body of the bar and it seemed to me that, in the manner of figures in an H. M. Bateman cartoon, every-one spun around to check out new arrivals at the top of the steps. On the third occasion I put myself through this ordeal, there was as I entered, I felt, a certain amount of tittering from my team-mates gathered on the floor. I froze in the doorway. Eventually, some languid oaf detached himself from the crowd at the bar and sauntered over. 'Excuse me, old chap,' he said. 'Are you playing for the Ramblers this afternoon?' When I nervously confirmed that I was, he raised his voice slightly to say, 'Perhaps, then, you'll be a good fellow and do your flies up.' This was greeted with guffaws from, it seemed to me, the entire company. I never went back.

Chapter Ten

I left for Houston, Texas, in the spring of 1960. Dad came to see me off. He was, I was told years later, incredibly sad to see me go, but at the time I never recognised this, being too obsessed with my own feelings, all of which could have been grouped under the general heading of Terror. Apart from my Uncle Michael, Mother's half-brother, I knew no-one who had been to the US and had absolutely no idea what to expect. Nowadays, with people owning holiday homes in Florida or popping over to New York for the shopping, this may seem barely credible, but my understanding of American life was cobbled together from reading the *National Geographic*, cheap adventure magazines, *Jazz Journal* and *Jazz Monthly*, and from listening to Lonnie Donegan's cover versions of Leadbelly and Woody Guthrie songs. There would therefore be loads of burly men in checked shirts standing beneath redwood trees, possibly the very men I had read about in such yarns as *The Yank Adventurer Who Discovered the Valley of Chained Blondes*, ruddy-faced pioneers in dungarees, and etiolated black men almost permanently engaged in running like turkeys through the corn, catching that southbound train and attending rural funerals. The reality was very – and in some ways disappointingly – different.

The *Eugene Lykes* had an uneventful crossing and the five other passengers and I were bored stiff most of the time. In mid-Atlantic we were heartened by a succession of the most astonishing sunsets I've ever seen – so much so that I would lie on the only deck to which we had access and stare into the skies until it grew dark – and when we entered the Gulf of Mexico, with its dolphins and flying fish and temperatures twenty degrees above anything I had experienced previously, I did feel as though I was en route to another planet rather than another continent.

As we drew close to the mouth of the channel that takes vessels from Galveston up to Houston – the only waterway on Earth, the captain told me, ever to have caught fire – you could smell the oil long before you could see the hundreds and thousands of pumps on the shore. The heat and the smell of oil was intoxicating and it was easy to believe that amongst the figures I could just make out on the shore were Ol' Riley, Lost John, Betty and Dupree, Frankie and Johnny and Tom Dooley. And could that train be the Old 97, or the Wabash Cannonball, or an engine on some spur of the Rock Island Line? And was that woman with the shapeless bundle making her way from one cluster of wooden shacks, little better than garden sheds really, to another, possibly Sylvie bringing a little water? I was entering Lonnieland.

That first night in Texas was spent in a hotel in downtown Houston. There had been no-one on the quayside to meet me when we docked, no-one to say, 'Hello, you must be John,' but I wasn't bothered. As soon as I'd checked in, I went for a walk. Even at night the heat was overwhelming and I was amazed at the number of people still wandering about downtown in mid- to late evening. Most of these were black, and although I had seen black men and women – mainly, Dad had told me, Somalis – in Liverpool, I had never imagined being in a place where half the population was black. Here a man was having a heated argument with a news-vendor, there was surely what must be a high yeller gal leaning into a car, talking to its two male occupants. From time to time as I walked a door would swing open, there'd be a blast of beery air, a babble of voices, the smell of sweat and the sound of a record I was pretty sure I knew. It would perhaps be embarrassing to go in, although not as embarrassing as the Crooked Billet. Maybe I'd try the next one I came to.

In the event, I ended up back in my hotel room, unable to sleep with the heat and the excitement. In the morning I caught the train to Dallas.

My dad had arranged that I should learn yet more about the cotton industry from a company based in Dallas's Cotton Exchange with whom he did business. I was met at the station by a man who had, as I discovered within seconds, not only heard of Gene Vincent but had, he claimed, played in his band at some stage. Being still high as a kite on heat, dust and the first twenty-four hours of my American experience, I had no difficulty in believing him.

I was taken first to the YMCA, where I was to live for two months, and thence to the office and sample room in which I was to work. Here I met Joe Black and John Steel, the first black men to whom I had ever spoken. John, a clever, proud and resentful man, endeared himself by asking me, when we were first introduced, 'John, how you is?' He repeated this question each and every morning I worked alongside him in the Cotton Exchange. I thought then and think now that John Steel was one hell of a guy. I often wonder what became of him.

The boss of the company – I can't for the life of me remember his name or that of the company – didn't seem as interested in me as I had hoped and expected. He didn't seem to know much about my dad or Strauss and Co., the family business, either. And this was not the full extent of his ignorance.

'Hey, John. Where you from?' he asked when I was shown into his office.

'England,' I replied, modestly but accurately.

'England,' he repeated. 'Is that in France?'

I met a lot of this sort of thing in Texas. Folks, even those who appeared educated, even sophisticated, had very little idea what went on outside Texas, even across the border in Louisiana. (A Dallas-based attorney was to tell me a few years later that a degree from some Texas universities – he mentioned Texas Tech in Lubbock in particular in this context – was roughly the equivalent of one of our O-levels.) From time to time, I would meet men who had served with the US Army in Europe, and they too seemed to have noticed little about us as they spent time in our midst. Many seemed to be under the impression that there were only a few hundred people in the country, and that if we weren't all related to one another, we would at least know each other pretty well. 'I met this guy, Bill, in your Leicestershire (pronounced Lye-sester-shire) during the war,' a fairly typical conversation would run. 'Do ya know

Bill in Lye-sester-shire?' When I replied, carefully, that I didn't
believe that I did, they would seem hurt, even slightly resentful,
as though I was in some way making fun of them. I was
eventually to capitalise on this naivety when the Beatles hit the
US. I never, to be fair to myself, claimed to know them – but
then, I never told whosoever it was with whom I was discussing
the lovable mop-tops that I didn't know them, either. Again,
more a sin of omission than commission, I like to think.

It became clear to me pretty early on in my time in the
Cotton Exchange that no-one was going to bother to teach me
much about the cotton trade, but that I was to be treated as
cheap, foreign labour. I was reasonably content with this. It
meant that I spent most of the day with Joe and John and that
sometimes we'd work on in the sample room after the white
folks had gone home. Then cans of Country Club Malt Liquor
would appear as if by magic and I would go down to the
barbecue joint on an otherwise vacant lot next to the Exchange
to get our suppers. John and Joe, being what my white co-
workers called, in a strangely affectionate way, niggras, were
not allowed in the barbecue so would have gone hungry without my taking advantage of the privilege of being a slightly
liverish pink.

On a couple of occasions, John and Joe took me with them
when they went out to a club after work. I would be aware that
I was the only white person in there but never felt ill at ease
over this – at least, not until other (white) people expressed
incredulity at what I had done. It saddened me when I recognised that there was a kind of colour-coding within the club
anyway, with Joe, who was much darker-skinned than John,
usually leaving us early to sit with similarly coloured men and
women in a different part of the venue.

My time at the YMCA, which was only a couple of blocks from the office and was astonishingly cheap, came to an abrupt end when a fellow resident attempted a sort of rather half-hearted rape. I was having a shower in a cubicle in the communal shower room when a stranger rushed in with a frankly enviable erection. When he made it plain where he hoped that this erection would finish up, I punched him in the face. He sat down and started crying, saying, 'You didn't have to do that.' He was right too. It's yet another thing about which I've felt bad ever since.

Nevertheless, I started looking for alternative accommodation and quickly found, on Gaston Avenue, an inexpensive boarding house. This was presided over by a magnificent old gal named Miss (pronounced Mizz) Smith, and most of the seven or eight other residents were members of a surveying crew. One of these, a guitar-playing son-of-a-gun named Edgar Wortham, from Waco, Texas, was about my own age, and he undertook to show this somewhat withdrawn, even slightly neurotic loner, from somewhere he'd never heard of, how life in Dallas should and could be lived. The late Viv Stanshall, on his day as amusing a man as I've ever met – and as clever – once said that the British issue invitations in the certainty that you won't have the bad manners to accept them, and there is more than a kernel of truth to this. In Texas, on the other hand, when folks said, 'John, you must come and see us real soon, d'ya hear?' they meant, 'John, you must come and see us real soon.' This generosity of spirit took a bit of getting used to, and the first few times Edgar invited me to join him and his co-worker and best mate, Vallee (after Rudy Vallee), in the bar next to the drugstore a block nearer to town than the house we shared, I made my excuses and didn't go. Eventually, after yet another lonely night spent listening to the r 'n' b records on which I was spending too much of the puny wages I was getting from the Cotton Exchange, I went along with Edgar and Vallee and several other of the drifters staying temporarily under our roof. One of these was a Canadian, Tom Chouinard, and I have since read that there is a Canadian author of that name. Same man? I have no idea.

Once in the bar, we were joined in our booth by an extraordinary young woman named Myrna. Myrna, who claimed kinship with the actress Myrna Loy, must have been about twenty-five, and promised everything but gave, as far as we knew, nothing. She was the sort of woman who would wait until some stranger had put money in the jukebox selector at his table, then get up, go and sit on his knee and select as many tracks as he had paid for. Edgar and I yearned for Myrna, as did almost everyone else in the room, but neither of us would have dared to lay a hand on her. As far as we could tell, the only men Myrna cared for were dangerous men, either big, brawling, bruised men or those slight, wiry men with expressionless pale eyes – a local speciality, it seemed – who you could easily believe would kill you as soon as look at you. When one of these came into the bar, I always deemed it wiser to get up and leave without finishing my beer.

However, I did enjoy success, of a strictly limited sort, with one of Myrna's friends. I had been in Texas for the six months my permit allowed me when I realised that if I applied for an extension, the next six months would take me past my twenty-first birthday. I was keen to do this, realising that if I went home it would be to some overblown event involving people – possibly including some Liverpool Ramblers – I didn't care for or really know, at which I would be the unwilling centre of attention. So I applied for an extension to my visa, it was granted, and I spent my twenty-first birthday watching Peter Sellers in *Two-Way Stretch* on my own in a cinema attached to Southern Methodist University (SMU). Result, I thought.

Shortly after this, I was in the bar, as usual, with Edgar, Vallee and others, watching Myrna working the room, when we were joined by a small, slightly ill-kempt woman of indeterminate age who introduced herself as Myrna's friend from the frankly squalid apartment block across the road. A few hours later, I found myself in this apartment block trying to explain to Myrna's friend that I had no working knowledge of the exact geography of the area I was eager to explore and asking whether she could, as it were, act as my guide. With a sigh, she obliged, and the sigh had hardly died on her lips before I was rolling on to my back, saying 'That was amazing,' and asking when I could see her again. She said, 'Never.' I thought she must have been joking but it turned out that she wasn't. Nevertheless, thanks to her, I was now a MAN.

A few weeks later I was in another apartment with another woman, this time aware that I should attempt to prolong the oafish thrusting for a little longer – even, oh, I don't know, up to a minute. The lucky woman was lying on her sofa as I tussled with her, and after thirty seconds or so I opened my eyes to enjoy the look of ecstasy I expected to see on her face. She had her head tipped sideways and with her left hand was leafing through a magazine on the adjoining coffee table. She didn't want to see me again either.

1961 was a presidential election year in the USA and I was still working in the Cotton Exchange when, on consecutive days, the candidates paraded through downtown Dallas. The Nixon/Lodge parade came through first, all open cars, smiling local Republicans, marching cadets from A&M University in College Station and the drum majorettes of SMU in inspiringly short skirts. I tiptoed away from work to watch and, as the parade passed, noticed that spectators were running from the pavements to shake the candidates' hands, so ran forward myself as the parade inched past me and shook hands with Richard Nixon. Difficult to imagine such a thing happening in this century. I've always told people since that Nixon had a cold, clammy hand, but I'm not sure that he did. Mind you, no-one has ever disbelieved me.

The following day, the Kennedy/Johnson parade followed the same route, with the same cadets and the same majorettes. There seemed to be more people on the pavements and it seemed they were in sombre mood. Although Lyndon Johnson was obviously one of them, Kennedy definitely was not. He was a Yankee, a Catholic and, it was universally agreed, a smartarse, and folks had, to a degree, turned out to hate him. At one stage, low on the hill that ran up Main Street from the area where Kennedy was, a couple of years later, to die, the motorcade came to a standstill opposite me. Seizing the moment, I ran forward to shake JFK's hand. 'Good luck, Mr Kennedy,' I said. 'Hey, you're from England,' he replied. When I told him that this was so, he asked me where from exactly, why I was in Texas, whether I liked it and whether I planned to stay. I was amazed, as we talked, that a man running for President of the USA could be interested in what I had to tell him. Hell, I couldn't even vote for him. Then he noticed the camera in my hand. 'Are you going to take a photo?' the future President asked, and when I said I'd like to, he suggested I should go back a few steps then, when I was ready, shout and he'd grin at me. So I stepped back three or four feet, raised the camera and yelled, 'Hey, Mr Kennedy.' He smiled and I pressed the button before going back to the side of the still stationary car to thank him. 'What are you going to do if that doesn't come out?' he asked. 'Why don't you take another one over the windscreen of the car? Then you can get Mr Johnson in as well.' So I moved to the front of the car, leaned on the bonnet and took another photograph. When I ran back to speak to John Kennedy again, someone else was talking to him, but he still found time to nod and suggest that I went to the other side of the car to meet LBJ. This I did before hurrying back to work.

This is a story I've told, I'm afraid, hundreds of times, and each time have watched as my audiences have grown more incredulous. I have often imagined them wanting to ask whether there were Martians present at the events I described or whether I heard choirs of angels singing 'Hosanna!' as we spoke, and have wished that I could finish by saying, reaching into my back pocket as I do, 'and here are the photographs.' Alas, all I have been able to do is to say, pathetically, 'Unfortunately, my first wife burned all my diaries and photographs in a fit of pique one night, so I can't prove the truth of my story.' Eyes are raised, someone points out that it's my round and a few more people are convinced that I'm full of bullshit.

No-one believed me in the bar that night either.

Eventually my employers in the Cotton Exchange grew as keen to be rid of me as I was to start earning a decent wage and Dad, growing fed up with sending me large cheques on a fairly regular basis, got in touch with a friend of his, Lex Cairns, who was in the insurance industry and lived in some style in the Highland Park area of Dallas. Lex made a few phone calls and secured me a position as office boy with the K. T. Martin

Insurance Company. K. T. Martin dealt exclusively in crop-hail insurance and I imagine that my benefactor had persuaded him that my comprehensive knowledge of the cotton business would prove invaluable to him. I was put in charge of the company Studebaker Hawk and started a new life making several trips every working day to the main post-office downtown. This, I recognised, offered me the same opportunities for skiving that the job of battery runner had done at TE(GW)RA.

Before I left the Cotton Exchange, located as it was in the heart of downtown Big D, I had discovered, on Elm Street, on the black side of the Central Expressway (where it was known as Deep Elm, pronounced 'Ellum', as hymned in more than one record) a secondhand record shop. The records, almost all 7″ singles, were stacked on broom handles set on to a narrow table running around the walls, and looking back on it now, I wished I had had the money to back a truck up to the door and take the whole damn lot. As it was, I must have bought several hundred – at about twenty cents a time – over a year, although the only one I still own is Larry Bright's 'Mojo Workout' on Tide. The rest disappeared, along with several thousand other obscure/now collectable singles from various radio station chuck-out boxes, when I left the USA for the UK years later.

Over a period of time, other of my records started arriving from home, notably Sam Lightnin' Hopkins's 'The Rooster Crowed In England', a UK-only release on 77 Records that included a track called 'Blues For Queen Elizabeth' that I bet Our Sovereign has still never heard. (There's another track that asks the question 'Have You Ever Seen A One-Eyed Woman Cry?' and, d'ya know what?, I never have.) This record I took with me, along with a bunch of French 10″ LP releases by artists such as Big Maceo, Washboard Sam and Jazz Gillum, when I went along to visit radio station WRR at its HQ in the Texas State Fairground.

During daylight hours, WRR was, even for the time, a curiously old-fashioned station, broadcasting middle-of-the-road music that was really middle-of-the-road. I cannot be more specific, although the words 'Les Brown and His Band of Renown' leap unbidden into my mind because I never listened to WRR other than between the hours of ten p.m. and midnight. This was when a magical programme called *Kat's Karavan*, introduced either by Jim Lowe or Bill 'Hoss' Carroll, was on the air. During the day I listened to the pop stations KLIF and KBOX, as did, it seemed, almost everyone in the Dallas/Fort Worth area. Apart from the occasional terrible novelty hit (Paul Evans and the Curls' 1959 smash 'Seven Little Girls Sitting In The Back Seat', anyone?) KLIF and KBOX played wonderful music, with KBOX seeming perhaps a little more juvenile, a little more downmarket. As a guide to how good the music was, Lightnin' Hopkins had a number-one chart hit on KLIF with 'Mojo Hand'. If that means nothing to you, it's time to make some serious adjustments to your life.

But *Kat's Karavan* was something else. The DJs were wry, well informed – although not so well informed that you couldn't occasionally pick them up on some small detail in the life of, say, John Lee Hooker – and the effect of hearing Hopkins, Hooker, Howlin' Wolf, Bo Diddley, interspersed with comedy tracks from Jonathan Winters, Shelley Berman, Bob Newhart or Brother Dave Gardner (a big local favourite), booming out of the car radio as you cruised with your mates to Garland or Mesquite or Richardson to try your luck with the girls at a different drive-in, was galvanising. But the big man on *Kat's Karavan* was Jimmy Reed, and it remains one of my deepest regrets that I never saw him live. I may have claimed in the past that I did see him once, but if I did, I was lying. Mind you, Jimmy came to Dallas often enough, as did most of the great electric bluesmen – I suppose Muddy Waters and even Elmore James would have passed our way at the time, but if they did, I missed the posters. Anyway, they would probably have been playing at some club or ballroom on Hall Street in the black part of town, and by this time I'd have been too scared to go down there. Nevertheless, I did see Lightnin' Hopkins at Lu-Ann's, and dozens of chart acts such as the Coasters, the Drifters, Etta James and Jimmy McCracklin at huge shows at the Sportatorium. I even saw teen goddesses (realistically at this time probably post-teen goddesses) the Shangri-Las, at a bowling alley across the river in Oakcliff. This was one of those shows when current chart acts – dozens of them – would arrive in coaches from the previous night's gig, come on and do their hit and go back on to the coach until it was full enough to set off for the next venue. The only other artist I can remember from the Shangri-Las night was Troy Shondell ('This Time'). It is hard to imagine a more perfect teen name than Troy Shondell. What is frustrating is that there must have been dozens of other one-hit wonders I could brag about seeing on these Nights Of A Thousand Stars, if only I could remember who appeared.

After I had been working for K. T. Martin for a while, I started making the occasional trip to New Orleans – I have one of the finest collections of slides of Spanish moss on Earth as a result – with a couple of other English boys I'd met. Our main interest in New Orleans, I have to admit, was not centred on the music, the architecture of the French Quarter or the seafood, but a young woman billed as Chris Colt, the Girl With

The 45s. This, let me remind you, was long before implants and Chris Colt was 100 per cent the real thing – so much so that my friends and I used to follow her from seedy strip joint to seedy strip joint, paying inflated cover charges as we went, cover charges that included a 'free' drink that was ＊ that much bourbon and ＊＊＊＊＊＊＊＊＊ that much water. Not that we cared. I can't help wondering, as I muse, in a wholly healthy way, on Chris Colt, her 45s and her subsequent career, what she is doing now. Back in 1961–2 in the Vieux Carre, shaking her tailfeather in a bored sort of way to a scratchy record by Bill Black's Combo, she was a goddess.

The possibility has just crossed my mind that there may have been more than one Chris Colt, the Girl With The 45s. It is such an obvious name for a pneumatic stripper, after all, and I remember being told by the booker at Lu-Ann's that he knew for certain that there were at least six Sonny Boys Williamson working the Southern States at any one time, and no fewer than twelve Memphis Slims. I suggested to him that it would make for one hell of a night at the club if he booked all of the Memphis Slims simultaneously. I'd turn out for the Massed Memphis Slims, I enthused, but he'd stopped listening.

One weekend, my companions had elected at short notice to stay the night in New Orleans, leaving me to drive back to Dallas alone. For this I have been grateful ever since, although at the time I wasn't best pleased, for the drive gave me one of the greatest musical moments of my life. I had been driving for some time and it must have been two or three a.m. as I started through the richly forested area of East Texas known as the Piney Woods. There was little traffic on the roads and, as the road rose and fell through the trees and past tiny towns that were often barely more than a handful of bedraggled shacks, the moon, which shone brilliantly directly in front of me, turned the concrete to silver. I was listening, I imagine, to Wolfman Jack from XERB, over the border in Mexico, and as I came over the top of a hill to see another tiny town below me, he played Elmore James's 'Stranger Blues', 'I'm a stranger here, just drove in your town,' Elmore sang, and I knew that I would never forget the perfect conjunction of place, mood and music. Nor have I.

The work at K. T. Martin was pretty dull, but the office was brightened by some of my co-workers. There was a woman named Bobbie Umholtz who with her friend, Georgia, would often invite the foreigner in their midst to join them for the weekend at one or other of their homes in one of the feature-less tracts of inexpensive housing that surrounded Dallas, or to spend a drunken evening around a barbecue at the lake. Bobbie and Georgia were both married, although I remember little of their husbands beyond the fact that Georgia's was named Forrest. Bobbie was the first woman I ever heard say 'Fuck.' This aside, I was further awestruck by the generosity of my new friends, generosity made more remarkable by the fact that both couples had very little money to spare. They and their friends also introduced me to the wonders of drag-racing when they took me to Caddo Mills Raceway, Fort Worth. There wasn't much money to spare at Caddo Mills either and all the runners there were enthusiasts who had worked on their Chevrolet, Ford, Dodge Plymouth or Pontiac-engined cars in their own garages at home. Bobbie and Georgia also helped me when I had girlfriend trouble – which I did fairly frequently.

I had moved from Miss Smith's establishment to a more modern – and more expensive – purpose-built apartment across the road, accommodation I shared with a backwoods relative of Miss Smith's, Obie. Obie was, I suspect, gay, but gay at a time when even the existence of homosexuality would have been disputed by much of the population of Texas. Perhaps it still is. He was certainly a remarkably effeminate man and dressed in a manner that a decade or so later would have persuaded passers-by that he was a member of Duran Duran. He also found my enthusiasm for shagging rather distasteful although I have to admit that, having come to sex relatively late in life, I had developed a perhaps excessive enthusiasm for it. Thus the flat I shared with Obie was filled with a succession of rather scruffy, even poorly washed, but morally relaxed youngish women who were prepared to share my bed. I remember the names of none of these, and they probably don't remember mine either, but I'm grateful to whichever of them it was that gave me a copy of Rosie and the Originals' 'Angel Baby' and recommended the B side, 'Give Me Love'. What a gal.

Eventually Obie and I fell out over the women and I moved on to the posher end of Gaston Avenue, down towards White Rock Lake, to an apartment block filled with airline stewardesses and people with careers. Here I shared a flat with Miles and Charlie and a Mexican named Manuel Avila. Given the racial attitudes of almost every white person I met in Dallas, I imagine the only reasons the latter was allowed to share a flat with Miles and Charlie were that he didn't look Mexican, insisted that he was, in fact, Spanish anyway and came from a wealthy family. God only knows why they accepted me into their hateful little community. Miles, to be fair, was OK, quite bright and enough of an Anglophile to drive an XK 120 Jaguar, but Charlie Mann was one of the most disagreeable men I've ever met. In fact, I seem to remember that there was a Charles Mann who was a member of the Manson family and I've often wondered whether it could be the same shit. It is certainly easy to believe that it could have been. He was swarthy and short but good-looking in a swinish, dangerous sort of way, characteristics that found considerable favour amongst the airline stewardesses. He made it clear that he despised me, as much for my poverty as for my not being American, and he bullied me in pretty much the same way I'd been bullied at school. His bullying was never physical, although he was not averse to violence, and the threat of violence seemed to hang in the air whenever Charlie was in the room. I imagine that Miles was probably afraid of him too. The two of them spent their evenings in the club attached to the apartment, a club I couldn't afford to join and, indeed, never set foot in during the eighteen months I lived above it, and would return late at night with an airline stewardess or two they had picked up there. This entirely suited me, as I was going steady with a seventeen-year-old from Garland, another Georgia, who loved rhythm 'n' blues as much as I did. Georgia, a tough high-school dropout from the wrong side of the tracks – it is probable that all of Garland could be classified as the wrong side of the tracks, consisting, as it seemed to, of rows of used-car dealerships and cheap bungalows – was as fearful of Charlie as I was and she believed, from the way he looked at her, that he was perfectly capable of assaulting her. She was probably right.

I didn't make the right decision, or anything close to it, when I stopped seeing Georgia and started going out with a red-headed gal named Judy. Sounds like something from *Oklahoma!* or *Carousel*, but it wasn't that much fun. Judy was, ironically, an airline stewardess, with Braniff Airlines. Despite the veneer of respectability that this gave her, she was as hard as nails. About once a week, Judy would compel me to take her to a club called the Hi-Ho Ballroom – those of you who have seen the film *The Blues Brothers* would recognise the Hi-Ho Ballroom. The level of violence there, which occasionally involved guns, was astonishing, to the point at which going for a piss was actively dangerous. Many was the time I toyed with taking the easy option and just wetting myself rather than risk the Gents, but I'm proud to tell you that I never did. As often as not I would come back to find Judy, one leg thrown revealingly over the back of her chair, talking to some murderous-looking cowpoke who would drawl insolently something along the lines of, 'Hey, feller. Ya don't mind if I take the little lady for a dance, now do you?' I did, of course, but I'd seen what a bullet can do to a man. Don't like to talk about it, you understand. As a result, I would often make my way back across the blood-soaked car-park alone at the end of the night, leaving Judy in the scarred arms of a rural primitive.

To this day, I don't know why I put up with this. Judy wasn't even prepared to have sex with me, go to the drive-in movies or the drag-strip, or drive out to the Dairy Queen in Mesquite for an outstanding product called a Dr Pepper Icy. She didn't even kiss me much, but I was so besotted with Judy that towards the end of our relationship ('Call that a relationship?' E. V. Railton, Whitchurch) I used to drive her in my '63 Chevy Impala all the way to Kansas City – some six hundred miles away – to spend her weekends with Another, before driving back alone and sobbing. What a twat!, you might well be thinking, and you would be right to be thinking it. I even went so far as to propose to Judy – her surname was Garrison, by the way – and offer her a ring that I explained had belonged to my dear, white-haired old granny but which I had bought that afternoon downtown. She was having none of it, and I'd had about enough of her and moved on, looking for someone more downhome and who was not averse to feeling my hot breath on her neck as I cupped her glistening . . . well, you get the picture. I'd never even discovered whether Judy had orbs.

The '63 Impala casually mentioned above had replaced the first car I'd ever owned, a secondhand '58 Chevrolet Biscayne, a bottom-of-the-range item in what would now be seen as Norwich City colours. I picked this up one lunchtime from Friendly Chevrolet in Dallas and set off in such a hurry back to K. T. Martin's to impress my friends that I drove down the ramp on to the freeway and straight into the side of a truck. The kindly folks from Friendly Chevrolet jus' came right along and picked it up and fixed it for me and I drove it for two years before trading it in. I wish I had it still, although I suspect that Sheila would insist on a paint-job in Ipswich's blue and white.

'What I'm sort of hoping for is that after I'm gone, one or other of our children will claim that on a cold, still, dark night they could have sworn they heard the rattle of my stick on the road outside,' I explained to Alan. He smiled. It is not, of course, in the general nature of sticks that they rattle, but this one once served as a mop handle and still has in place the metal plates that secured mop head to handle. 'He doesn't need a stick at all,' I heard Sheila explaining to Rosemary, Alan's wife. 'He just likes to carry one about.' Actually the mop handle isn't really my favourite stick. That honour is held by a broom handle that disappeared shortly after I had used it in a doomed attempt to unblock the drains. There is a third stick, a handsome silver-topped cane that was a sixty-fifth birthday present from the women working on *Home Truths* – the Cows of *Home Truths*, as they rather ungenerously styled themselves – but this is for use on ceremonial occasions only and would not have been deemed appropriate for the post-prandial walk to the top of the hill the four of us were enjoying.

I normally undertake this hill-climb each evening when I take the dogs for a walk before they – and we – retire for the night. As dog-owners will understand, walking is not the principal purpose of this exercise, neither is exercise, but you can't talk about taking the dogs for a shit and expect people to be impressed. I'm always purposely vague about the precise nature of the hill, in the hope that whoever is listening to me will be unfamiliar with Suffolk and will assume it to be at least Pennine, if not actually Alpine. The truth is that the hill would barely count as a hill in most parts of the country, being more of a gentle slope that, measured from the green bucket in the hedgerow near the bottom to the end of the fence at the top, is 128 footsteps high. I check this every night, having decided that if it takes me 130 steps or more, disaster will befall the House of Ravenscroft. There are nights, possibly when the moon is high, when I attempt to better my record for the number of steps it can take, currently standing at eighty-five. An observer – and let us pray that there will never be such a person – would witness the strange spectacle of a portly gentleman dressed in the High Informal manner, often in pyjama trousers, stretching his fat little legs as far as he can as he proceeds jerkily up the hill behind the dogs, Nellie and Bernard.

I do a lot of this counting of steps even when I'm walking about in the West End of London. If I don't get to the top of the twenty-one steps that lead down to the BBC car-park in less than four hundred paces, I'll be involved in an accident on my way home. Makes perfect sense to me, stranger.

I had intended to show Alan a rough draft of the early chapters of this book, to give him the chance to scan them for inaccuracies, but never got around to it. At some stage, I'll have to give Francis the same opportunity, knowing that he'll scan the pages to the accompaniment of snorts of disapproval and cries of 'It never happened.' I'd also planned to ask Alan whether my compassionate posting to Ty Croes, to be close to him when he was at school in Tre-Arddur Bay, had had any measurable beneficial effect on him whatsoever, but forgot to do that as well. I don't suppose it made much difference, as all I ever did was occasionally save money from the twenty-five shillings I was paid each week for protecting our island nation from her enemies and take him and his friend Anthony Holden, now classical records critic with the *Observer*, for tea at the Bay Hotel. Both boys have grown to be quite bulky chaps, but then they were whippet thin and on one celebrated occasion ate their way through the Bay Hotel's tea menu twice. Afterwards we would clamber on the rocks and I would feel grown-up and responsible, a most uncommon series of sensations, before taking them back to the school.

I still drove the Impala when I started going steady with Nancy. Nancy Bowling was sixteen – seven years younger than me – and a student at Bryan Adams High School in Dallas. By contemporary standards ours might well be judged an 'inappropriate relationship', involving, as it did, a lot of sex, much of it al fresco, but for a non-graduate male without much money, high-school girls provided the only available dating pool. College girls only dated college boys, and in a culture where marriage at fifteen or sixteen was common, there were few unattached women over twenty – apart, perhaps, from airline stewardesses.

Nancy was petite and pretty, with a ball of bleached-blonde hair like candy-floss, as was the high-school fashion of the time. Anyone reckless enough to attempt to suit action to the romantic cliché about running their fingers through a girl's hair would have run into trouble immediately and would probably have had to be cut free by paramedics. When I first met Nancy she was dating my friend Johnny in a casual sort of way, but we both remained friends with Johnny when she transferred her affections to me. Nancy and I went out most nights, spending the evening driving around listening to Russ Knight, the Weird Beard, on KLIF or going to a drive-in movie. Whatever we did, we would make love before I took her home. At the drive-in movies this was easy enough. All you did was hook the speaker on the driver's window, get yourselves a supply of burgers and Dr Pepper, climb into the back seat, get partially undressed and go to it, secure in the knowledge that in almost every other car in the open-air theatre something along similar lines would be going on. We never used condoms and would have been astonished if anyone had suggested that we should. The monthly wait for Nancy's period seemed exciting rather than worrying and I think we'd both have been quite happy to have married if she had fallen pregnant. We also knew nothing of sexual techniques but enjoyed devising our own, tailored, as they were, to the back of that Impala.

If we didn't go to the drive-in, we went to the small cinema adjacent to Southern Methodist University to see the latest black-and-white British comedy, usually starring either Peter Sellers or Ian Carmichael. *Two-Way Stretch* was our favourite and we must have seen it a dozen times – this was, of course, before the age of the video. In return for my introducing Nancy to the wonders of British cinema, she introduced me to Bob Dylan. Nancy was the first Dylan fan I ever met and she could hear things in Bob's lyrics that I never could. Nevertheless, I persevered for Nancy's sake, and know that when, in 1965, after we had stopped going out together, Dylan went electric, Nancy would have welcomed the development.

After we'd seen *Two-Way Stretch* – or whatever – we'd adjourn to the shores of White Rock Lake and the back of the car. I don't remember that we ever slept in a bed together, Nancy and I. Ours was a car-bound romance in a car-bound culture. Sex at White Rock Lake had its own perils, its own excitements. There was a Park Patrol that cruised the windy, narrow road around the lake with the sole purpose of ensuring that no-one could experience penetrative sex on their patch. The rule was that everything was OK provided two heads were visible above the door-line when a torch was shone at them. This made oral sex problematic but not impossible, given the generous internal dimensions of the American cars of the 1960s and a certain degree of athleticism. (Illustrations available to genuine art-students only.) At the weekend, Nancy and I would drive out to towns, again sometimes little more than a collection of tumbledown sheds, with amusing names. Bug Tussle was a favourite and I've on several occasions suggested it as a fine name for a band, although, as far as I know, no band named Bug Tussle has yet surfaced. Jot 'Em Down was another favoured destination.

In many ways Nancy was the dream girlfriend. She was bright, funny, liberal – so many Texans of her age had serious problems with what they called 'niggras' – and she loved the same music as me. I've never really understood why we drifted apart, but we did, slowly and somehow painlessly. Looking back on things now, she was, after Sheila, the girl I have loved most. I often wonder what became of Nancy and hope that she has had – and continues to have – the happy life she deserves.

Another of Nancy Bowling's assets, when I reflect on it, was that she was not religious. Although vast numbers of Americans have since swallowed the notion that 'Blessed are they that have, for unto them more shall be given' and a ferociously aggressive religiosity to go with it, there was a more generous, although primitive, religious fervour in the state when I arrived there that was faintly attractive. I first became aware of this when I said to colleagues in the office during some discussion or other something along the lines of, 'Oh, come on. You'll be telling me next that you believe in Adam and Eve!' The looks of not unfriendly incomprehension focused on me persuaded me that in future I should add religion, as well as politics and race, to my list of topics deemed not suitable for even casual discussion.

In the meantime, exciting developments were afoot at K. T. Martin and Co. The company, although small, was a leader in the specialised field of crop-hail insurance. This, as the name insinuates, involved insuring farmers' crops against hail damage. Hail, in this context, isn't the girly-man hail we're accustomed to in Europe, but brash, exterminator hail, the individual stones often described as being the size of baseballs and which can destroy cars and cattle as well as crops. It was part of my job to ensure that we didn't accept an excess of risk in any territory, particularly in those states considered part of Tornado Alley.

This crop-hail insurance business had been running success-fully and efficiently for some years, but the boss, K. T. Martin himself, had a dream and that was to be able to offer farmers insurance against either an excess or a shortage of rain. After many years of research, K. T. believed, in 1964, that he had hit on the formula. The notion was that in the event of a farmer believing he – or she, I suppose – had a claim, rainfall measurements would be taken from the three nearest US weather stations, an average calculated and the claim processed according to this average figure. Now, I thought I could see something of a two-way flaw in this system: either the crops might be destroyed by rain at a time when very little or no rainfall had been recorded at the three relevant weather stations, or vast quantities of rain might have fallen at the weather stations but none on the insured crops. This would mean that farmers could legally claim and would have to be paid, even though their crops were undamaged, or that they could lose their crops and their claims would be turned down. Win–win or lose–lose either way.

Nevertheless, despite my reservations and armed with brochures, leaflets, information packs and more, I was sent out into West Texas with our man in the area, Harry Fuqua, to sell the idea of this rain insurance to small-town insurance brokers, feeling like a salesman charged with interesting the gullible in a perpetual-motion machine.

As Texans delighted in reminding me, their state is three times the size of the UK, and anyone driving around from town to town out there is going to cover a lot of miles. This Harry and I did. I remember one stretch, from somewhere like Midland to Nuevo Laredo, where you can drive over two hundred miles in a dead straight line on a road that barely rises or falls over the whole of its length. Nothing grows there that is higher than sagebrush and nothing is there that is manmade other than signs reading: DO NOT LEAVE YOUR CAR. SNAKE-INFESTED AREA. Nevertheless, Harry and I enjoyed our time crying in the wilderness, despite hardly anyone falling for our snake-oil pitch, even though the hilarity caused by my accent often resulted in the agents to whom we were talking summoning their pals and asking me to go through the whole damn thing again. But at night we would hit the bars, barbecue joints and bowling alleys of what seemed to me to be pretty much still the Wild West, and Harry and I had a good time out there. In one bowling alley, I accidentally discovered a technique for winning countless free games on a baseball/pinball machine and, just like in a film, as I won more and more free games, a crowd of excited jeanagers crowded around. Eventually, I walked away with over fifty free games on the machine, telling the young persons they could enjoy the rest of the night's play for free on me. I like to think that even now old folks in the community still talk of the night some English guy came to town and showed them how to whup ass on the baseball machine, yessir.

When we got to Nuevo Laredo, we crossed the border into Mexico and Harry led me through the mud streets to his favourite brothel.

Part Two

Shortly after returning to England in 1967, John began a regular correspondence with Tom Robinson, then seventeen years old, who had written to him after hearing his Radio London show The Perfumed Garden. *In 1968, he sent Tom the following letter:*

Dear Tom – a voice from the past.

It was really good to hear from you – I'd often wondered how and where you were. My address is 2, PARK SQUARE MEWS, UPPER HARLEY ST, N1. If you're ever in London call WEL 5847 and come and see me. I'm very Happy. I've found a lady called Pig, with whom I'm very much in love and that's nice after 30 years. You must come and meet her. I'm much calmer and more together now. My record company makes nice records that no-one buys much, vegetation sounds good the way you describe it. The tale of 'Ego Iuvenis Sum' sounds quite entertaining – I'd certainly like to hear it. Now I have five hamsters (4 Chinese, 1 of which is wandering around the flat having left her cage two weeks ago), the amazing Biscuit and a slightly eccentric gerbil called Uproar, they all, plus the Pig and I, send love to you and those you love,

John.

To refer to the circumstances in which I first met John as 'auspicious' or even 'mildly promising' would be misleading to say the least.

It was November 1968, and I was at college in South London, studying to be a chemistry teacher. One of my friends occasionally acquired, through her lecturer, tickets for recordings of television shows. I hadn't been to one before, but I had recently split up with a boyfriend, and found myself at a loose end one Friday night, so I trundled off with her to the Riverside Studios in Hammersmith to watch the recording of a show called *How It Is*.

One advantage of attending these shows was that you got paid. Nothing grand – no repeat fees or anything like that – but the meagre stipend of ten shillings was doled out once you had signed a contract promising not to leave before the programme was finished, and it paid for a few beers after the show. Of course, the downside was that you had to stay put no matter how soul-crushingly tedious the show became. The guests on the night I went included, bizarrely, the romantic author Barbara Cartland and the Liverpool group the Spinners, so staying in my seat may have represented the hardest ten shillings I ever earned.

To add to the general all-round fun and hilarity, there was a section in the programme when John, Ronald Fletcher and Richard Neville of *OZ* magazine would sit on high stools discussing current events and delivering what press releases like to call 'a satirical look' at the past week.

I was familiar with John's radio show, *Top Gear*, which I used to listen to on Sunday afternoons, though I wasn't the full-on, card-carrying hippy that he evidently was – I just liked some of the music. John was, don't forget, the man who was immortalised in the 'Pseuds' Corner' section of *Private Eye* magazine for writing that the music of Pink Floyd evoked the sound of dying galaxies. (He always said he was proud of that, though he was sure he'd pinched the line from someone else.) He didn't go in much for velvet, though he owned a kaftan, bought for an outrageous price from a shop off Carnaby Street. His suspicion that it had been a bedspread in a previous existence was one of the reasons why he could never wear it with the necessary conviction. Consequently it didn't last long in his repertoire, for which Swinging London should be eternally grateful.

But wherever there was the smell of burning incense or a gathering of hairy types in roomy velvet pantaloons (and that was just the girls), you'd find John. He was there, for instance, at the 24-Hour Technicolour Dream at London's Alexandra Palace in the summer of 1967, explaining to suggestible young women that he was the far-out DJ who did that *Perfumed Garden* programme on Radio London, and that if they played their cards right, they could accompany him to the next Exploding Peppermint Slipper 'happening'. However, the women in question inevitably turned out to be less suggestible than they had first appeared, and the line notched up an impressive 100 per cent failure rate.

The fact that John prepared for *How It Is* by walking past the queue outside with Richard Neville, inspecting the incoming audience for comely young females who might possibly be more suggestible than those sceptics at Alexandra Palace, indicates that the sophistication of his pick-up techniques had not increased noticeably in the year since the 24-Hour Technicolour Dream.

John had a gig to do straight after *How It Is*, so he scurried off before the recording was finished, though I can't say that I even noticed. But as my friends and I were getting up to leave and collect our ten shillings, Ronald Fletcher approached me in a very gentlemanly manner and handed me a note. It said, 'Would you call WEL 5847 on Saturday morning – about 11.30.' Below that was the word 'Peace.' There was no name, so at first I thought it was all very mysterious. Then, when the penny dropped, I thought, Well, what do I do now?

I went back to my digs in Putney and talked it over with my flatmate Terry, who encouraged me to call. At this point, I had no intention of doing any such thing. I must have been a little excited, though, because that night I phoned home and spoke to my sisters, whose sage and considered advice was, 'Do it! Do it!' Throwing reason, good sense and an innate suspicion of hippies to the wind, I ended up calling John the next morning. He asked me if I'd like to go to the cinema that evening to see *2001: A Space Odyssey*, which had just opened.

But at that point the conventional notion of a date started to fade. First, he said he would pick me up at five o'clock, once he'd heard the football results. I didn't mind about the football part, because I was a football fan as well, but I did think that it was a strange time of day to go on a date. Who goes out at five?

It wasn't what you'd call rock 'n' roll, but then John was full of little surprises. Despite being a hippy, he turned his nose up at dope. He had smoked it occasionally in his peace-and-love days, as he enjoyed reminding the children whenever the subject of drugs came up at home. But he became more partial to marijuana in his sixties than he had been in the 1960s, occasionally partaking of the odd monster joint at special occasions like festivals.

Mostly he had smoked grass when he lived in California. A couple of friends made regular drug runs into Mexico and stored their contraband in the wooden shed he called home. It was this supply that he sampled, though he said he never experienced the extreme effects predicted by both the drug's proponents – 'You'll see God' – or its opponents – 'You'll imagine you can fly and will jump off a tall building downtown and, in no uncertain terms, die.' What put him off the drug was returning to Britain and finding that the home-rolled joint was usually made with tobacco. John didn't care for the taste, and while it must have taken some courage to say 'No' in a flat filled with hippies grooving to *Sunshine Superman*, he was willing to risk their disapproval if it meant not throwing up down his expensive new kaftan.

John had dropped acid on two occasions, but never favoured large quantities of drugs once the 1960s had shrunk into the distance, unless you count vegetable korma as a narcotic, which he always did. His first experience of acid was pleasant enough, but then it was voluntary, which makes all the difference. He described it as like visiting Stratford-upon-Avon: having done it once he felt no pressing need to do it again.

On the second occasion, John was doing a gig at the Roundhouse in North London in 1969, and someone gave him an ice cream that had been spiked with acid. We were living together by this time, and I'd stayed at home studying. When he arrived back that night, he was making an awful racket, banging around and slamming doors. He stomped upstairs and kept saying to me that he'd crashed the van. I rushed out into the street to check the damage, but there wasn't a scratch on it. When I went back inside, he was still there, but he looked very faraway. And when he finally realised what had happened, he fought it, which everyone says is the worst thing to do. Whoever spiked him must have used some serious stuff, because for three or four days he was incapable even of writing his own name.

It was this incident that he discussed with each of the children when the time came for the Big Drugs Talk. They always knew when they were about to hear one of John's talks because two cars would arrive to collect them from the school bus. Alexandra and Thomas remember that on this occasion I took Flossie home in one car while John drove them out to a lay-by in the other. There they were told of the legend of the spiked ice cream and warned that while they might choose to experiment, they should remember that quality-control procedures do not generally pertain to narcotics. There is no kite-mark on a tab of E, unless you have an unusually conscientious dealer.

So, with John keeping his body as a temple, beer was off the menu for our first night out together. He rolled up at five, as promised, in his tatty Bedford Dormobile, and off we went. As soon as we pulled away, he said he had something to tell me. 'I haven't been feeling very well for a few days,' he mumbled, 'and I hope you don't mind, but I've got a doctor's appointment before we go out.' It was certainly shaping up to be a hell of a date. Five o'clock pick-up. No alcohol. A detour to the doctor. It would have been consistent with the pattern so far if John had been diagnosed with leprosy.

We went to the surgery in Fulham, and I sat in the waiting room. John came out eventually and said, rather forlornly, 'I've got to go straight to bed. I've got yellow jaundice.' It's funny now to think that I missed it, but he did look – well, there's no other word for it – *yellow*.

I said, 'Well, you'd better take me home then.' But he pleaded with me to come back to his flat with him. 'Don't go,' he said, 'I feel really sorry for myself, please come with me.' And I did. He lived at Park Square Mews near Regent's Park, and his home was something to behold. It was very groovy, and I say that as someone who loathes the word 'groovy'; there is simply no adequate alternative. Joss sticks were burning in every corner. To complete the picture, John's flatmate was an androgynous photographer called Beautiful Peter, whose gorgeous blonde girlfriend was always sashaying around the place.

It was such a different culture from the one I was used to. My friends Gerry and Terry were like me – one was from Halifax, the other from Barnsley, while I was from Shipley near Bradford. Not that John thought hippies were better than anyone else; he always maintained that dropping out was an essentially middle-class affair, a luxury not available to working-class people or anyone for whom money was scarce. From my experience of the hippies that we mixed with in the 1960s, I agree; they certainly felt like some kind of elite to me, and I always suspected that I wasn't quite up to their level. I was intrigued by them, but never entirely comfortable with them.

I had stepped out of my digs that night anticipating an evening of being wooed, if not wined, and barely an hour later I found myself in a scented hideaway tending to a DJ with yellow jaundice. It wasn't the most conventional start to a romance, but it was a nice evening: we talked a lot, and listened to records. He was incredibly gentle and kind, which appealed to me, and very handsome; I was attracted to him from the start. Perhaps we became close more quickly than we might otherwise have done because there was so much tenderness involved simply in me playing nursemaid to John. Not that yellow jaundice dampened his ardour. Whatever the symptoms, diminished libido didn't appear to be one of them.

Incredibly, John clambered out of bed the next morning, giving off this glowing yellow aureole – from the jaundice, rather than any kind of innate divinity streaming from his pores – and made it over to Radio 1 to do his Sunday-afternoon programme, *Top Gear*. I was shocked that he was going to do it despite being told to stay in bed, but it was an attitude I got used to over the thirty-six years we were together. John was one for soldiering on, even in the face of medical advice, common sense, earthquakes. He was unstoppable.

That never changed. When he had kidney stones, and was in so much pain that he was unable to drive, I took him into London from Suffolk to do his show, and then drove him back again. The BBC would have been perfectly able to find someone to fill in, but John didn't want that: he had to do the show. Similarly, there were those evenings during his years of broadcasting from his studio at home when I could see that all he needed was to get some sleep. I'd give him a meal, dust him down, and he'd go in and do the programme – and, invariably, do it better than ever because he was trying that much harder. There were occasions when even he had to concede that the show didn't have to go on, and that work was beyond his limits, such as when he was admitted to hospital in 2001 after it was discovered he was diabetic. But even then it was necessary to keep him under armed guard in his hospital room, with the windows monitored from the rooftop by snipers, in case he should try to make it to London on the milk train to do his show (though the snipers had been asked to aim below the knee if possible).

I went with John to the BBC on that Sunday afternoon in November 1968, and watched him do the show, which was then running for two hours from three p.m. I hadn't even known him for twenty-four hours by this point, but as I was sitting there, watching the engineers behind the glass and listening to Jimmy Saville doing the handover, I felt petrified on John's behalf – not because there was anything particularly terrifying about Jimmy Saville (no more than will be immediately apparent to anyone who meets him), but because here was this man I was becoming fond of, and he was poised to broadcast to the entire country. I was racked with nerves. John, on the other hand, was a picture of serenity, despite his poor health and disturbing hue.

Glancing back through his diary now, I see that he was petrified in the hours leading up to his first appearance on Radio 1, which came on the station's second day of broadcasting. Radio 1 was not running full-time at that point, but rather shared its transmission time with Radio 2. John had been hand-picked by the producer Bernie Andrews – who had relished his presenting style and choice of music on the Radio London show *The Perfumed Garden* – to be one of a number of co-presenters who would join Pete Drummond at the helm of *Top Gear*. Also on the rota were Mike Ahern, Tommy Vance and Rick Dane, but it was John whom Bernie had been determined all along to install as permanent presenter, despite the concerns of his Radio 1 bosses.

Robin Scott, then controller of Radio 1, has said that 'There was a feeling in-house that John was almost too much his own man to let loose.' But on the morning of Sunday 1 October 1967, John was anything but a livewire or loose cannon. 'Rather frightened this morning when I woke up,' he says, before noting that Bernie was 'in good spirits'. He goes on:

> Had an amusing rehearsal although Peter and I were both trying to cover our nervousness nervousness nervousness. At 1.15 we went and had lunch. I drank only coffee and was in an extreme nervous condition. On the air at 2.00 following Ed Stewart who sounded very shrill and panic stricken. Peter and I were a bit stiff though competent during the first half hour. After a news summary we settled down into a bit of a routine. It was by no means *Perfumed Garden* – I hope people will understand that that must come later. Had a few good lines I suppose. No big mistakes. It was certainly a strain on the nerves, though . . . We tired out after 4.30 and struggled a bit to the close at 5.00 . . . Robin Scott was there . . . I suddenly felt incredibly paranoid and just gathered my belongings and left. Walked down Regent Street and a bus driver yelled, 'Very good show, very good,' which was nice.

When he returned home that evening, John was comforted by Shirley, his first wife, while Bernie called to announce that the reaction had been favourable. But the tone of the diary entry is emotionally precarious, to say the least, and ends on a sad hint of the emerging discord in John and Shirley's marriage. 'Shirley very unhappy – poor tiny creature,' he observes, before adding: 'She'll understand soon.' The following morning, John was told that 'Tommy Vance thought the show was a drag,' but there was comfort to be found elsewhere, in a 'good notice in the *Daily Mail*' and 'overall critical acclaim for Peel'. The peculiarity of John referring to himself in the third person is explained by his next sentence, in which he responds to the positive reviews by confessing, 'I didn't really feel it was me.'

Bernie had a lot of faith in John, and though almost a month elapsed between his first and second stints co-presenting *Top Gear*, he was a regular fixture on the show from 29 October. From 12 November, he co-presented with Tommy, and eventually took over as sole presenter on 4 February 1968.

I saw John anxious or uncertain on many occasions, but he always exhibited a genuine ease at the microphone, even on that Sunday afternoon, just over a year after his *Top Gear* début, when I gnawed my nails to the quick watching him slog on through a two-hour broadcast. When it was over, he took me home and then, as far as I know, went back to bed and drifted into a wistful waking dream about me. Or possibly just put on *Piper at the Gates of Dawn* and lit another joss stick.

It was a long time before it occurred to me that John and I would be together. At first, our relationship was on a casual basis. I knew he was seeing other people, so I thought: Right,

I'm going to as well. That's why I'm amazed to read the letter that he wrote to Tom Robinson in 1968, in which he says that he has fallen in love with me. We were having fun, and I enjoyed being around him, but he certainly didn't appear to be in love.

However, I took him to meet my parents in January 1969, which was quite a big step. John had a gig in Bradford with a band called A For Andromeda, who were playing at the University's Great Hall – the very same Great Hall, in fact, where John received an honorary doctorate thirty-three years later. We travelled up there with the band; the weather was atrocious, and the van spluttered and strained through the thick snow. John and I stayed with my parents in Shipley. It was quite a culture clash. John was everything that they didn't expect. They had never met anyone like him – or anyone involved in the media, for that matter. I suppose you could say he was famous then. His visit to Bradford made it into the local paper, but maybe it was just a slow news week – no cats stuck up trees or price cuts at the Co-op.

My parents seemed a bit apprehensive, but John was incredibly nice. He was also extremely shy, and remained so throughout his life. I suppose it was quite cruel of me to tease him when he asked my parents if he could take a bath. I asked Mum to put the tin bath in front of the fire while I fetched some hot water, and John looked suddenly panic-stricken. He'd already used the lavatory, but the bath was in a separate room downstairs, so he had no way of knowing that I was joking. If Mum hadn't told me to stop being so horrid, I can't say for sure that I wouldn't have taken that prank to its humiliating conclusion.

For most of the evening, John sat cross-legged in the corner of my parents' living room. He never liked chairs: I think it was a hippy thing. He carried a portable record-player wherever he went, a tiny little number on which he would listen to singles, and he just sat there playing that and reading the paper. He wasn't being rude; his shyness was simply overwhelming, and it never really diminished.

In later life, we would arrive at parties and John would search immediately for some task that would excuse him from the awkward formalities of socialising. He just needed a job to do, and once he had found one he would take as long as he could over it. It was not unusual for John to spend three hours doing the washing up or making cups of coffee while the party raged in the other room. People would usually drift over to him, have a chat, and then drift away. Or else he would go unnoticed for the entire evening. He wasn't so bad during parties at our own house; I think he was generally happier playing home games than away ones.

Once he was ensconced in an environment, though, he really blossomed. For instance, he often mourned the fact that Radio 1 in the 1990s and beyond had become such a fragmented place to work; unlike in the 1970s, the DJs had very little to do with one another, and it wouldn't be until the Christmas get-together that you even got to meet some of your colleagues. John used to moan about Chris Moyles when he heard him on the radio. Perhaps that verb doesn't quite convey his initial misgivings. What he actually said was, 'When Chris Moyles came to Radio 1, I thought about strapping explosives to myself and taking us both out. I'm an old man now, it'll make little difference.' But when they met at one of these increasingly rare Radio 1 social gatherings he realised he rather liked him.

John Ravenscroft and Sheila Gilhooly
(Peel 'n' Pig)
invite you to the wedding of themselves.
This will take place (for reasons too complex to
explain here) at St. Paul's, Lorrimore Sq., London S.E.17.
at 1.00 p.m. on Saturday, August 31st. 1974.
You are also invited to a reception afterwards
at The Holme Bedford College
Inner Circle
Regents Park N.W.1.
R.S.V.P. as soon as possible

Costume should be comfortable
rather than formal

Above: John and Sheila's
wedding in 1974
Left: Alan, John and
Francis with their mother

I LOVE YOU HBILLIONS LIHLE PIG

A VERY BAD DRAWING OF US

Top: Sheila in Shipley, Yorkshire
Left: The note John sent the
night he first saw Sheila
Above right: John in bed
recovering from yellow jaundice
Right: A sketch by John of him
and Sheila

Would you call WEL 5847
on Saturday morning – about 11.30

Love.

*Opposite page, clockwise from
top left*: John as a lion in Kenya;
in Regent's Park; posing for
Yoko Ono's birthday album;
on a pre-wedding honeymoon
in Egypt; exhausted in Florence;
with his birthday cake at St
Stephen's Gardens

Festivals in the
late sixties and
early seventies

D.C.F.E. S.U. Presents

John*LIVE
Peel
+
33s DISCO
+
Felix Road Show
+
Loupgarau

At D.C.F.E.
Wilmorton

Main Hall
Sat 8th July

7.30. - Late

80p £1.00 At Door
BAR

With assorted friends and colleagues, including Teddy Warrick (second left), Dusty Springfield (third left), John Walters (centre) and Elton John (second right)

John with fellow Radio 1 DJs

Dancing with Alan Freeman

Hosting *Top Gear*

John falls off a donkey at a Radio 1 Fun Day

John loved going into the office because it was his territory: he belonged there. He had his own corner, and he'd sit there feeling like father of the office, really enjoying himself, especially when producers from other shows would come over and ask him to identify some mysterious remix or sample. It was all open-plan, like a giant telephone call centre, except that every seat had a stereo beside it. Everyone who worked in what was euphemistically called 'Specialist Programming' – the likes of Zane Lowe, Annie Nightingale, Steve Lamacq – was lumped in there together, and John loved the atmosphere. When he got tired, he used to lie down under his desk and sleep. The music and chatter would continue at the same volume, but even that couldn't wake him from his pretty slumber.

The same thing happened at Radio 4, where John worked on *Home Truths*. The show's senior producer, Chris Berthoud, was distinctly alarmed the first time he saw John lying down in the tiny office: he thought there had been an accident. In the early days, John would curl up on the floor; sometimes he would snooze under the desk in the studio if there were long breaks between recording links. Later he moved on to sleeping in chairs. Chris soon grew accustomed to showing people around the office and saying, 'This is *Home Truths*, and that person sleeping is John Peel.' John claimed that his ability to doze off anywhere was the result of having to sleep in the back of army trucks during his National Service.

At Radio 1 or Radio 4, he was in his element. But put John somewhere new, and you could watch him retreat into his shell, although he couldn't always recognise that shyness in other people. It bothered him that he was unable to elicit any response from Neil Young when Mike Willis from the record company brought Neil to John's house on the edge of Regent's

Park. A few years earlier, John had compèred a concert at the Orange Hall in San Bernardino, where Buffalo Springfield were at the foot of a bill topped by the Byrds (whom John regarded as so devastatingly unpleasant, because they refused to speak to him when he introduced himself before the show, that he had difficulty enjoying their work from then on). Neil had been relatively garrulous on that occasion, and told John backstage that it was the band's first proper concert, so his embarrassing silence later on was quite unsettling. Not that it dented John's appreciation of the music, though; we attended a superb performance by Neil and Crazy Horse at the Hammersmith Odeon in 1976, and we were for some time unable to drive anywhere if not accompanied by our battered eight-track of *Everybody Knows This Is Nowhere*, which John considered one of the ten greatest albums of all time (though this top-ten list contained anything up to two hundred albums).

I always maintained that John had read Neil all wrong that evening at his house, and that he suffered from the same intense shyness as John. But I'm willing to accept that John's assessment of Nico, whom he described in his 1971 diary as 'stunningly rude', might have been nearer the mark. 'Andy Warhol NY super cool rat shit,' he fumed when she walked out on him mid-conversation on 4th February.

On that first evening at my parents' house, my mum was feeding John like mad, trying to get him to eat another slice of cake, or drink another cup of tea. They thought he was a bit strange, but they liked him. Or rather they did until a week later. John and I had returned to London and got on with our lives as normal – John was gigging, I was back at college, going along with him to shows whenever I could spare a break from my studies. Meanwhile, my parents had opened the latest edition of their local paper, the *Telegraph & Argus*, at the tea table, only to read the splash on John and discover rather more about him than either of us would have wanted them to know.

The letter from my father came as a complete shock to me. There I was thinking the meeting had gone swimmingly. Admittedly, they might not have experienced ceaseless jubilation upon first clapping eyes on John. The sight of him can't have coincided too closely with every parent's idealised image of their offspring's prospective partner. They probably weren't, all things considered, expecting me to find lasting happiness with a man in a fake-fur coat, baseball boots and a pair of corduroy trousers. From the belt-loop on those trousers dangled a tiny plastic mouse – unzip this mouse and out would spill a pair of miniature maroon pyjamas made by Sandy Denny of Fairport Convention. I have them here in front of me on the kitchen table. They're beautifully stitched and would doubtless make some dapper young mouse look like the Noël Coward of the rodent world. But for all John's eccentricities, something had definitely clicked between him and my parents by the end of the evening, and I remember the contentment that I felt the next morning when John and I went for a walk in the park. The snow was packed densely beneath our feet, and it muffled every sound so that we seemed to be sealed off from the rest of the world.

Yet here was a letter from my father demanding that I break off the relationship and have nothing more to do with John. For some unfathomable reason, John had let slip in that newspaper interview that he had a wife from whom he was estranged. To the *Telegraph & Argus* it was probably the scoop of the year, but John was always very open about discussing his first marriage – and anything else, come to that. When he was writing his various columns, he would even invoke his unhappy matrimonial experiences to try to point impressionable young readers in the vague direction of sound judgement. 'My wife and I were very young when we married,' he once wrote, 'and I think we did so for all the wrong reasons. It wasn't a shotgun wedding or anything, don't get me wrong, just that we had differing ideals which perhaps weren't right. Marriage is a very serious thing to enter into. You must watch that you don't start to take one another for granted – that's one of the big dangers.'

All I can say is that, in our marriage, he stayed true to his word. Whenever he was away, he wanted to be back at home with the children and me. It could be difficult to wriggle out of his arms sometimes; he was rather unhappy when I started attending Spanish lessons in the village, because he wanted me to be at home with him. I invited him along, but I knew he wouldn't come because he had this strange aversion to being taught anything. He appreciated the value of knowledge, and hoarded information as obsessively as he did mementoes and keepsakes (there's a box somewhere in the house containing over thirty years' worth of my shopping lists). But he disliked immensely being tutored in anything.

As admirable as John's determination was, it did occasionally have its downside. We couldn't watch television for two weeks once because he wanted to decipher independently the instructions for the remote control. Then there was his laptop computer, which was bought for him by family and friends for the purpose of writing this book, but which sat dormant in his room for over a year. Thomas offered to show him how to use it, but John would always decline; he wanted to learn by himself, at his own pace, so that it was his achievement. That's why he took so long to write half this book. That's how we came to find ourselves in this pickle.

No-one in John's youth, apart from R. H. J. Brooke, made him feel especially important or worthwhile, and it's possible to interpret his stubbornness as an attempt to prove he wasn't so bad after all. When he overcame some technological obstacle later in life, it was his way of saying: I can do this; I can stand on my own two feet. It could be something as simple as sending a text message, which John spent an entire evening teaching himself to do so that he could text Flossie while she was at university. Or it could be his knack for unblocking the stream near our house. Whenever the road became flooded, he'd go out in his wellies, wielding a hoe or a rake or whatever came to hand, and he would set to work. Then he'd trudge back up the driveway, visibly proud of himself, ready for a pat on the back. He always felt inadequate about practical things because he wasn't a man about the house – it was me who did the painting and decorating, who fixed things around the house and garden, who bled the radiators.

Deep down I think he knew that his job carried its own value. In one of his columns from *Disc and Music Echo* in 1972, he outlines briefly the rationale behind his radio shows, in response to a reader who has written to thank him. 'Now this, frankly, is the motive behind everything I do,' John admits. 'The programmes with which I'm involved are aimed at turning y'all onto some musicks that you might not otherwise investigate.' It's so simple, but it's the essence of what John did.

The relationship he had with his listeners, from *The Perfumed Garden* through to *Home Truths*, was predicated on openness. There was nothing that was out of bounds to John, and his refusal to be embarrassed irritated some people. I was often asked whether I minded John revealing so much about our family on *Home Truths*. My answer was always that it didn't matter to me; what was so shocking about the fact that we had chaotic or strange or embarrassing things happening in our lives? Didn't everyone? Admittedly the children grew slightly uncomfortable with it, especially when their friends' parents would say, 'Ooh, I heard all about your exam results/moody introspection/embarrassing rash on *Home Truths* at the weekend.' But once the children had made their feelings clear to John, he agreed to be a touch more discreet when discussing them on air.

John's frankness could be alarming. In 1969, the BBC commissioned a programme about the epidemic of venereal diseases that was apparently sweeping the nation, and suggested to the producer-presenter, Tony van der Berg, that he should plug his work on one of John's Radio 1 shows, *Night Ride*. The unspoken subtext was that management believed John's listeners were more likely to suffer from venereal diseases than most. In the course of their on-air chat, Tony said that one of the problems health officials encountered in reducing ignorance about VD lay in the reluctance of anyone who was suffering from sexually transmitted diseases to admit it publicly. 'I believe I can help you with that,' John chirruped. 'I'm suffering from one now.' And he was: the symptoms are recounted in all their gruesome glory in his diary, with its references to having 'yer actual clap' and experiencing 'disagreeable sensations in the Peelian penis'.

The BBC switchboard lit up in the traditional manner after John's confession on *Night Ride*. Campaigners tried to get John taken off the air, seemingly under the impression that non-specific urethritis could be transmitted over the airwaves. The judge in the *OZ* obscenity trial in 1971, in which John was a defence witness, ordered a court official to dispose of a glass from which John had taken a sip of water, apparently believing that VD could be spread by sharing kitchenware.

For years afterwards, John suspected that his name was filed in retrieval systems under 'VD DJ'. Hardly a week passed in which he was not called by someone anxious to discuss the clap with him, but he had hardened his heart and passed by, as it were, on the other side.

Luckily this hadn't yet happened when John met my parents. And besides, it would have been small potatoes compared with their primary objection to our relationship. As staunch Catholics, they found it hard to accept that I was stepping out with a married man – albeit one whose sole contact with his wife occurred when she would call him asking for money.

But my parents weren't interested in what contact John had with his wife. They just wanted it to be over between us. Writing that letter asking me to break up with John must have been one of the hardest things my father ever did. He was such a gentle man, and the letter, for all its seriousness, was soaked in affection; I remember that it began with the words 'Well, my dear' and he signed off with a sincere 'Phew'. I don't have the letter any more. I couldn't bear to keep it.

It was especially difficult to read because, contrary to what my parents hoped, things were becoming serious between John and I. Not that there weren't other contenders in his eyes. But he said later that he had boiled it down to two candidates and that I came out on top. John would bump into this other woman from time to time, and he always remarked on how she seemed to have bounced back marvellously from what must have been a terrific disappointment.

In spring 1969, I had moved in with him at Park Square Mews. Beautiful Peter didn't appear to mind that John referred to the house they shared as 'Peel Acres', any more than I minded John christening me 'the Pig' right from the beginning of our relationship, on account of my snorting laugh. From our earliest days together, John referred to me as Pig, and his readers and listeners got to know me as that too. Someone he knew who was taking a jewellery course made a silver ring for me in the shape of the animal with which I found myself sharing a name. When John and I got married in 1974, John had an identical ring made for himself. Strange to think now that there are very few people around – perhaps no-one, in fact – who would refer to me as Pig.

I think the idea of Peel Acres was an expression of Wodehousian quaintness rather than a Neverland-style testament to ego. Certainly we never considered populating the garden with anything exotic like ostriches or chimpanzees, and while I must confess to harbouring a deer, this delicate creature – named Rose, after its first tentative meal of rose petals – was, in mitigation, rescued by us, as opposed to being purchased to increase John's eccentricity rating.

Peel Acres was simply the light-hearted title John gave to wherever he happened to be living. The children sometimes expressed discomfort at the general assumption, carefully fostered by John over half a lifetime, that we do indeed live at the rather grand-sounding Peel Acres, when in fact our cottage has its own name entirely unconnected to John.

This sentimental attachment to the idea of home probably grew from the anxiety John experienced over domestic upheavals in his own adolescence. He once wrote:

When my parents divorced I was about 16, and I think I regretted the loss of our home in Cheshire more than I regretted the divorce. People came and went, as they do, throughout our childhood, but the house was a constant and you learnt to play upon it as upon a stringed instrument. We valued not just the openness and the coolness but the darker corners, the skirting boards, the suspicion of damp, the infinite strangeness of the kitchen range.

When I first lived with John and Beautiful Peter at that particular incarnation of Peel Acres in Park Square Mews, we all seemed incredibly busy, but also very happy. The house was teeming with people. That had always been the case, right from when I first met John. While he was still suffering from jaundice, there was a day when the singer Melanie arrived on the doorstep wanting to sing John some of her songs. John had forgotten about the appointment, and asked Bridget St John, who was at the house with us that afternoon, to listen to the songs and talk to Melanie on his behalf. Melanie came into the room brandishing her guitar and sat on the end of John's bed – I say bed, but it was actually just a mattress in the middle of the floor. She strummed and sang her heart out, staring at us intently as she did so, until none of us knew where to look.

If musicians weren't calling round, they were sleeping over. You were always guaranteed to find one band or another staying in the house. If you made your way to the bathroom in the middle of the night and tripped over some unknown object in the centre of the room, then it was sure to be a bass player or rhythm guitarist who had fallen asleep wherever they happened to have collapsed.

I don't know if John ever turned away any bands, but I'd be surprised. I certainly don't recall him ever refusing to lend money – though I use the word 'lend' here in the archaic sense of 'give with no hope of ever getting back' – to any of the various bedraggled souls with outstretched hands who would turn up at Peel Acres and tell John that they'd written to Lennon asking for fifty thousand pounds, and to Donovan requesting an island off the coast of Scotland, but in the meantime could he lend them twenty-five pounds to see them through the night? Invariably, he would give them whatever he had.

The situation became so drastic that John's booking agent, Shurley Selwood, and I were forced to cut off all access to his own bank account, out of fear that he would render himself penniless. Not that he needed much money for the life he had chosen. The rent at Park Square Mews was negligible even when the landlord remembered to call round for it, which wasn't very often. Neither did John require much money for his social life – which was spent mostly at gigs where he was compèring or on the guest list – or for records, large quantities of which were sent to him anyway. Or for his diet, which didn't extend far beyond brown rice and tahini.

One of the bands that spent a lot of time at John's house was Forest – or, as John writes in his diary, 'the luckless Forest whose second LP is beautiful and almost certain not to sell at all'. They were a charming group of lads whom you could happily have taken home to meet your mother, just so long as she had lost all sense of smell. It would be kindest to say only that their musical prowess far outstripped their grasp of personal hygiene; at times the situation got so severe that John actually forced them to have a bath.

Forest were with us on the day that the house was raided by the police. Two years earlier, in 1967, John had seen some of his friends in trouble over drugs. 'Jeff told me that he and Paul, Cheryl, Zelma and Pete had been busted on pot charges,' he wrote in his diary on 19 September of that year. 'What a big drag. How can I help them. Feeling moody. Marc [Bolan] trying to cheer me up . . .' But until 1969, John himself had never been targeted. The drugs squad had been on a bit of a roll for a few weeks, however, turning up suspicious-looking cellophane packets in houses belonging to members of famous bands. Lots of people claimed that the police came with their own supply of contraband goods, which they would then plant surreptitiously in nooks and crannies. John had been expecting a raid for some time, though, and was meticulously organised when the knock came – or rather, when the knock didn't come, since they simply burst through the door.

It's amazing how calm and prepared he was, especially considering that the police had slyly scheduled the raid for just an hour or two before he was due on air. John assigned someone to accompany each officer, in order to eliminate the possibility that anything could be planted: every member of the drugs squad was shadowed by one of us. We knew from the start that they wouldn't find anything, because none of us were into drugs, but they ploughed on with quite remarkable thoroughness. They dismantled the hamster cages. They tore open the apple pie that I'd just finished baking, which was cooling in the kitchen. They marched John out to the Dormobile so they could rifle through that. And just in case anyone could accuse them of not having every angle covered, they had brought the press along with them; that evening there was a picture of John in the *Evening Standard* looking like an ill-tempered gnome.

I think the police were surprised at how tidy the place was – that and the towers of chemistry books piled high on the long wooden kitchen table, in preparation for my exams. They were not expecting such efficiency from John; you could sense their disappointment at not having caught him in the act of snorting crushed hallucinogens off the inner thigh of a top international model. When the house had been picked apart, the police filed out one by one, shaking hands with John as they went and saying, 'Thank you very much, Sir.'

But it didn't end there. For some time afterwards, every shopping trip was fraught with anxiety. We'd be ambling home with bags of groceries only for a police car to screech up to the kerb and disgorge a couple of officers, who would then search us and go through our shopping before driving off again. It happened so frequently, but it never stopped being humiliating.

I was preparing for my chemistry finals around this time, and my academic timetable didn't always correspond with John's social and professional one. I remember one night when I couldn't sleep because John was downstairs with Marc Bolan and they were playing an advance copy of *Tommy* by The Who over and over again with the volume cranked up; on that occasion I was the party pooper who had to keep asking them to turn it down.

Traditionally their late-night sessions revolved around a mutual passion for Scalectrix. John and Marc had set up a sprawling Scalectrix track that had begun to colonise the house, room by room, until almost every inch of carpet, every surface, was obscured. There was constant music in the house, but now this was joined by a new sound audible in the spaces between songs: the tinny crackle of toy cars negotiating complex slaloms. Each of us – John, Marc, Marc's girlfriend June, and myself – had our own car. Meanwhile, the track just kept growing, and the larger it got, the more power it required, until eventually John and Marc would embark on an emergency errand to buy more booster packs. They must have been quite a sight: two hippies dashing to the nearest toy shop for another fix of Scalectrix.

John and I saw as much of one another as we could without being on each other's backs. We took a driving holiday in Europe in summer 1969, accompanied by John's brother Alan, blasting out The Who and Leonard Cohen and Captain Beefheart on the superb eight-track cartridge system in the Dormobile. That holiday included our first trip to Venice. The Dormobile, sorely underpowered, had made a bit of a mountain out of the Alps, and we – and it – were dirty and exhausted when we arrived at the jewel of the Adriatic. As we drifted from one deliciously crumbling Renaissance palace to the next and scurried, rat-like, beneath masterworks by Tintoretto and Titian, the minds of all three of us were on but one thing – a sit-down toilet. Eventually we found one, hidden away behind a panelled wall in the Palazzo di Monteverdi della Santa Fiona, as John insisted on calling it, and, although it was intended for the use of staff only, we took turns to enjoy its superior, if illicit, appointments. Ah, sweet Venice: its beauties and mysteries are many, and its toilets are really something else.

Whenever possible, I went with John to gigs and recording sessions. Looking through his diaries throws up happy memories of the sort of things we'd go to together. On 1 April 1971, we were at the Paris Cinema in Lower Regent Street to see Led Zeppelin. The engineer Chris 'Wyper' Lycett was there as usual; he became a good friend of the family, and was always incredibly supportive of John, who wrote about that night:

> Talking to members of Led Zeppelin. They got ratty with Wyper Lycett, quite unfairly really as the BBC equipment is obviously a stupendous joke . . . Audience cold and unresponsive. Band good. Pig was only one bopping about at all in whole audience. Zeppelin played for 100 minutes – nice people too. After Robert Plant and Jimmy Page had made their usual promises to call, we drove home and had some good whipped hot chocolate. Straight to bed.

Rock 'n' roll with a hot-chocolate chaser – it doesn't get any better than that.

John was gigging most nights of the week all over the country. He also had to find time to help run Dandelion, the record label that he had founded with Clive Selwood of Elektra. He wrote in an advertisement:

> The half-witted, idealistic notion behind Dandelion and our other violent, capitalist enterprise, Biscuit Music, is that any profits, if such there be, should go to the artists, not to Clive nor myself. We want to record people whose songs and poems we like and whom we like as people. At the moment this means Bridget St John, Beau, Principal Edward's Magic Theatre and the Occasional Word Ensemble. If people like their records, and I honestly can't think of any reason why they shouldn't,

then we'll be able to record a host of other people you've probably never heard of either.

I'd try to find the time to go along to the all-night Dandelion recording sessions, which were tremendous fun. On some occasions my presence alone would earn me a credit – that's why some of the records bear the legend 'Produced by Pig'. The first releases were Bridget's single 'To B Without A Hitch' and her album *Ask Me No Questions*, which John produced. During one mammoth all-night session that I attended, he came up with the idea of putting layers of birdsong and church bells on the title track, weaving together sounds from the BBC library until it felt just right. After the album's release in August 1969, John used to get enquiries about the birds: people wanted to know where he had recorded them, since there were species singing together that had never been known to gather in the same habitat.

Sadly John never raised the funds necessary to finance the 101 Sharons, his pet Dandelion project for which he planned to gather together 101 women named Sharon, lock them in a studio and refuse to release them until they'd recorded an album.

But the quality of the artistes who did record for Dandelion varied greatly. One of John's favourite signings was the singer-songwriter Kevin Coyne. Then there was Principal Edward's Magic Theatre, whom John's producer John Walters and I both loathed. However, my dislike of them was not exclusively musical – though their twee compositions would have provided reason enough to take against them, even if they hadn't made a habit of borrowing John's Dormobile when they lived with us and then refusing to give me a lift when I was struggling down to the launderette to wash their bedsheets. They were rarefied rock stars. They were above such trifles as laundry.

Another Dandelion band, Stackwaddy, a gang of Mancunians whom John described as 'punks before punk was invented', were no-one's idea of shrinking violets. Luckily, John was never on the receiving end of their rather raucous brand of merriment, since he was their benefactor and the only person willing to give them the time of day and the money necessary to keep them in the drunken state to which they had become accustomed. But there are plenty of people who, if they were to hear the name Stackwaddy today, would have to reach for medication with a trembling hand. Like the plugger they said could ride in the van with them back to Manchester from London, before kicking open the doors halfway up the M6 and shoving him out on to the motorway. Or Jack Holzmann, president of Dandelion's US sponsors Elektra, who was over in London for a showcase gig at which John and Clive planned to impress him, and who witnessed Stackwaddy's singer urinating on the crowd during the band's opening number. Perhaps it was his idea of giving the audience that little bit extra.

I suppose the fun wore off when they started turning up on our doorstep in London in the early hours of the morning wanting to know what presents they could buy me, and whether or not I would like a sewing machine. I don't want to sound ungrateful, but their generosity was rather outweighed by the fact that it was three a.m. In the end, the spirit of Stackwaddy was best epitomised by the name of their album: *Bugger Off*. Yes, only their mothers could have loved them. Their mothers and John, that is.

*

Apart from the days when he had to be in London for his Radio 1 show, which varied as the years went by, most of John's evenings were spent ping-ponging around the country's polytechnics and universities, first under his own name and then, from the mid-1970s, as the marginally more highfalutin-sounding 'John Peel Roadshow'. How to encapsulate in a single sentence the essence of this phantasmagorical entertainment? 'It's John Peel and two boxes of records,' was John's way of putting it.

Until I win the pools, the John Peel Roadshow will continue to be me and those two boxes, one with the handle broken. I often wish it could be otherwise. I've never been a roadshow before. Previously we DJs just went out under our own names, nothing more, nothing less. Then some smart Alec thought of calling his equipment, and Doreen and Maureen the go-go girls he met outside Broadcasting House, a Road Show. Now we're all Road Shows, like it or not. Naturally I'd like to bring a circus with me at no extra cost. I don't know any circuses. If I could I'd bring go-go persons of some sort. Rosko or Johnnie Walker can call up serried ranks of go-go dancers at the flick of a finger or the pop of a Babycham cork. I don't know how they do it. They also have tons of equipment – '1,200 watts,' said Johnnie W., when I asked him. The moment they're due on stage, the stars arrive in their sharp Italian sports cars. Smiling modestly, they run through the autograph hunters and bound on to the stage, the night air heavy with the thud of swooning womanhood.

I did a gig last weekend at Middlesex Hospital and I had to get eight or ten would-be medics to push my car, which had broken down outside the hospital, backwards up a ramp so that I could unload my equip— my Roadshow. They didn't seem impressed. An hour later, with the stuff all on stage, I was covered with a thin film of sweat, mingled with dust, which was solidifying in a most interesting manner. I sat on the stage to contemplate the imponderables of life and a youth sauntered up. 'Er,' he began promisingly. 'When does John Peel get here?' Trouble is, I'm not an impressive presence. I try to hold my stomach in certainly – but sometimes, in the excitement, I forget.

Those gigs quickly became a staple of college and university life across Britain, as well as providing an opportunity for eager musicians to ensure that their demo tapes reached the one man in the music industry who could reasonably be relied upon not to throw them in the bin – or at least not without listening to them first. The boot of John's car was full to the brim with cassettes that had been presented to him by starry-eyed young lads and lasses in the grim car-parks of higher-education establishments the length and breadth of the country. If I went along with him, I would always be sure to take a carrier bag; without exception, it would be bulging with tapes by the end of the night. One evening, John's car was broken into, and a weird sort of insult was added to injury when the police went to the trouble of returning the demo tapes that the thieves had erroneously considered to be some kind of bounty.

One of John's regular gigs was at the Nag's Head in Wollaston, Northamptonshire, where he first appeared in spring 1970; the usual arrangement was that he would do a show, kip the night at the pub, then head into London for *Top Gear*, which was at that point going out on Saturday after-noons. The local DJ, 'Big Bob' Knight, had run a Motown club in the pub's upstairs room before he took over as landlord in

1968 and transformed the place into a haven for long-haired prog-rock types, attracting the likes of Wishbone Ash, Uriah Heep and John's own Dandelion signings, Medicine Head, as well as even more extreme, hard-rocking acts like Elkie Brooks. John became the pub's Friday-night DJ, performing hand-stamping duties at the door on occasion, and persuaded bands of his acquaintance, like the Faces, to put the Nag's Head on their tour itineraries.

He was soon gigging at another of Big Bob's venues, the nearby Blisworth Hotel. It was there that Ginger Baker's Airforce turned up to do a gig, with Ginger one high hat short of the full kit and somewhat the worse for wear. John and Bob literally carried him on to the stage, sat him at his kit, then carried him off again after he played. There was a similar incident at a gig in Birmingham with The Who, where Keith Moon collapsed on his drum kit. John helped to drag him off stage, where he was roused with a bucket of cold water in the face before being carried past me and plonked behind his kit again.

John's diaries from the late 1960s and early 1970s tell a pitiful story of slogging back and forth across the country for ready cash; on some pages, a succession of sums offered for gigs are crossed out, replaced by ever-decreasing figures, suggesting that John's value as a DJ was actually depreciating as the weeks went by. There was a rider, which sounds rather splendid, though nothing that could find its way between the covers of *Hammer of the Gods*. John's rider said something about providing a few beers and a vegetarian meal. These were seldom supplied, but you felt that the conventions had been observed.

Whatever else the evenings might have been, they were

usually colourful. John describes one gig in East London, during which a roadie for Spontaneous Combustion warned that the singer would kick John's records off the stage if they were still there when the band came on, as being akin to a slow-motion replay of a Fellini film. Other evenings were more redolent of *The Blackboard Jungle*. In October 1970, Clive Selwood, the husband of Shurley, John's booking agent as well as his Dandelion partner, was moved to write the following letter to an associate who had hired John for a gig:

> Thank you for your cheque in payment of John Peel's appearance for you some months ago. I'm sorry you feel that John did not earn his fee. I should have thought that being forcibly thrown off the stage by your 'security guards' as reported in the *Daily Mail* and being prevented from returning to the stage by the same guards, who threatened to mutilate his face and that of his lady companion, was earning a fee the very hard way . . .

The gigs were valuable, though, for bringing John into contact with many of the musicians whom he admired, and who would feature on his shows. He did a few gigs with The Jimi Hendrix Experience, for instance, and often argued that Hendrix had never been surpassed as a live performer. If you were really lucky, John might also have told you that he had had illicit carnal knowledge of one of the nineteen naked women on the cover of Hendrix's album *Electric Ladyland*, though he could never decide whether to reveal which one it was. While he reasoned that it would be unfair to say who had been unfortunate enough to undergo the John Peel Experience, on the other hand the remaining eighteen would doubtless have wished him to make it clear that it wasn't them, no sir, not even for a bet. It was a profound and resonant struggle that he never quite managed to resolve.

John also liked to say that he had been billed above the band, and he had, in a manner of speaking, at Southampton University, where the poster read, 'The John Peel Roadshow – with The Jimi Hendrix Experience.' On the page dated 6 October in John's 1967 diary, there are autographs from the band; Hendrix has written, 'To John and Shirley, the best of happiness forever.' On 8 October, John hosted a gig featuring Eire Apparent ('very poor'), The Herd ('very ordinary'), The Crazy World of Arthur Brown ('His act was most alarming – flaming helmet, rising through the floor and extraordinary clothes in myriad colours and flame effects') and Hendrix, about whom he wrote, 'The whole second half was a teeming, whirling, angry set . . . He was fantastic although seemingly a bit uneasy. Rather constrained humour.'

If Hendrix was uneasy, then John was even more so. Milling around outside before the show, he was approached by autograph hunters whom he had heard whispering, 'There goes John Peel.' 'Funny to think of me being asked for my signature in London,' he wrote, slightly unsettled. 'It seemed natural somehow in America but very alien in London.'

During John's last few years in the US, he had become something like the fifth Beatle. No, that was Pete Best. Perhaps John was the sixth, then. Or the understudy. Certainly the women who flocked to touch the hem of John's garment, or, failing that, the hem of anyone who had touched the hem of John's garment, were convinced that they had been in the presence of undiluted Liverpudlian greatness, and that John was on hairbrush-sharing terms with the Beatles. I'm sure that at some point he considered disabusing these adoring teenagers of their illusions, but perhaps he didn't want to risk shattering their dreams. Either that or he had grown accustomed to the automatic reverence and the menu of sexual favours made possible by an economical approach to the truth.

The John Peel of the early 1960s – or John Ravenscroft as he was then – sounds pretty similar to the man I met in 1968, give or take the hippy accoutrements and those long, flowing locks. In fact, John's hair had begun to recede when he was a coltish fourteen-year-old and at the time he was pleased. He felt it made him look older and would aid his boyhood ambition to resemble an Eastern European dissident, an ambition thwarted, perhaps for ever, when he started to gain weight. Latterly John remarked that his only consolation in this matter was that former Eastern European dissidents, now subsisting on a Western diet, were growing to look more like him.

He probably grew more resigned to putting on weight, though his diary from 1971 charts his infinitesimal gains and losses in meticulous detail. 'No matter how hard I try to discipline myself,' he wrote on 4 May, 'the waist of Peel moves inexorably outward. Eleven stone eleven lbs this morning – where will it end? "The Incredible Increasing Man." ' Later, weight became a particular issue between John and his friend and Radio 1 producer, John Walters. In one of John's columns in the music paper *Sounds* in 1973, he revealed the details of his ongoing rivalry with Walters:

I have not been slow to notice that the hulking Walters, previously a man of no little girth, has been surreptitiously losing weight and is beginning to take on the aspect of one of those warriors seen prancing about in an abandoned way in the woods of classical mythology. Just last week I observed him cooing over his reflection in a pool at the base of the Post Office Tower. What, I suspect, the comely little rascal has in mind is to continue shedding the avoirdupois (as the women's magazines so coyly have it) until the time comes when he can ask me, with an affected casualness, how much I weigh. When I reply ten stone eight (actually it's more like twelve stone but it wouldn't be good for my image for you to know that – any more than if you should accidentally discover that I am not, in reality, eighteen years old) he will announce, in a voice of burnished brass, that he weighs less than I do, and I will have lost the one advantage I have over him, unless you count the fact that he supports Crystal Palace, and even then supporting Palace has a certain cult value – like pretending that you think some Peruvian rock band is the best in the world. As Walters is always quick to point out, he is taller than I am, has some trumpery degree to my O-levels, tells stories better than I do and believes that his silly cat is better than our three majestic animals.

In the 1960s, when the collegiate look was in, John came to regret his early enthusiasm for incipient baldness; each morning he had to craft a Kennedy-style quiff from the remaining hairs and a lot of soap. He used to worry, he said, that he resembled a pedal bin, and that some swaggering bully would stamp on his toe to see whether his hair would shoot up in the air. When serious baldness first menaced John and his brother Alan, they put themselves in the hands of a Mr Luke, who operated out of a Knightsbridge salon. They spent a lot of money having their follicles stimulated by an electric device that spat out blue sparks, hurt a bit, and evidently had no effect whatsoever on the steep decline in the growth of John's mane. He always said he wanted more hair, and occasionally suffered sharp pangs of resentment towards those people generously endowed with the stuff who insisted on wasting it in fatuous haircuts – Michael Portillo, for example.

In the early 1960s, John lived on Potomac Avenue, Dallas, the sole occupant of a wooden shed that had formerly been servants' quarters – possibly even slaves' quarters – at the bottom of somebody's garden. In the evenings, spurred on by the *Playboy* philosophy that what women wanted was a sophisticated fellow who drank bourbon, drove a Maserati and listened to jazz, he sat on his bed and tried terribly hard to like records by Dave Brubeck and Shelly Manne and His Men, purchased from the Columbia Record Club. His economic plight meant that the bourbon and the Maserati would have to wait until he abandoned his career as an office messenger – he had been one for three years and his employers assured him that he had every chance of remaining one – and settled instead for medicine or architecture. Until then, it was Hostess Twinkies washed down with Royal Crown cola.

It would, by this point, be perfectly natural to be wondering what decadent experiences were waiting in store for John during his visit to a Mexican brothel with his friend Harry in 1962 – that was, after all, the point at which John's telling of his own story ended, in true cliffhanger fashion. But I have it on good authority – John's authority, in fact – that he was involved in this visit, and others like it, only as companion to Harry, and would loiter outside for him until the business transaction in question had been completed to the satisfaction of all parties.

The following year, John quit working for K. T. Martin, and was hired by Republic National Life Insurance, 3988 North Central Expressway, Dallas. His job there, filing card programmes for the IBM 1410, was so boring that he spent two hours a day reading in the toilet. His days must have been brightened, though, by the appearances he had begun making on Radio WRR, where he introduced the second hour of the R 'n' B programme *Kat's Karavan*. John had got the job, for which he was paid in glory rather than cash, after turning up at WRR boasting of his extraordinarily eclectic record collection. 'I started working there because I had records that they didn't, mostly LPs of blues and R 'n' B stuff that were only available in England or the Netherlands,' he said. WRR wanted to dip into his collection; John stipulated that if they wanted the records, they had to take him as well.

He liked to think they kept him on because of his extraordinary knowledge of music, as well as his high-calibre platters, but it was his vowel sounds, rather than his vinyl, that really impressed the Texans. Every Monday night from eleven until midnight, John would play Jimmy Reed, Lightnin' Hopkins and Brother Dave Gardner, until he had the temerity to ask to be paid, after which he was unceremoniously dropped.

Dallas was also the site of one of his brushes with the law, which, though infrequent, lent him a whiff of the outlaw. He spent a few hours in the drunk tank of Dallas County Jail in 1963 for traffic violations committed during a wildly exciting dash across Dallas, prompted by a call to his then-girlfriend that had ended suddenly when she exclaimed, 'My God – there's somebody in the house!' Those crimes included speeding, running red lights and something like failure to stop when called upon to do so by a duly authorised officer of the municipal authority. By the time he reached his girlfriend's house – it was the garbage collectors, incidentally, who had alarmed her – there were three police cars on his tail.

He hadn't even been drinking, but the custom was to lump together multiple traffic offenders in the drunk tank for a spell to teach them the evil of their ways. It was not a fun place to be, with most of its twenty or so occupants being still drunk or mad or both, and more interested than he would have wished in the smartly dressed Englishman who had arrived in their midst. Otherwise his reluctant cellmates seemed united only in their lack of enthusiasm for white folks, and as he was the only specimen of that genre in the tank, he felt keenly aware of this.

With the exception of such freakish moments of high drama, John's life in Dallas seems to have been one of enviable leisure, listening to music and cruising in his car, the whole *American Graffiti* routine. There were, though, some dramatic disruptions to this routine. On 22 November 1963, John was engaged in his usual pressing business at Republic National, catching up on his reading in the Gents. Suddenly a voice interrupted the Muzak to announce that word had come from downtown that the President had been shot. John ran out to the Chevrolet Impala that he could barely afford to run and tuned in to radio station KLIF. Five minutes later he was on the expressway, heading downtown.

Turning right on Elm Street, John parked up and made for the area near the station, where the shooting was reported to have occurred. As he was running, he suddenly realised he had no idea what he would do once he got there. But those fifteen or so seconds during which he had talked with Kennedy in 1961 had left such an impression on him that this didn't just feel like the shooting of the President; as John ran, he wanted to know why someone had shot his pal Jack.

Three or four blocks from the underpass, he came across a police barrier and, to his astonishment, a sobbing policeman. When he attempted to block John's path, John claimed to be a reporter for the *Liverpool Echo* in England. Presumably convinced by the accent, the policeman allowed him through. For forty-five minutes, John wandered about the area where Kennedy had been hit, never allowed near the roadway, but able to stand and watch agents combing the grassy knoll and the railway marshalling yards beyond. Eventually he got bored and drifted back to work. No-one had even noticed that he'd gone.

From the office, he called the *Echo* and told them his story. They printed a paragraph under the heading HESWALL MAN IN DALLAS, and were unenthusiastic when he suggested that he might investigate further and phone again.

That evening, John went driving around Dallas with his girl-friend, Nancy, and his friend Bob Cook, stopping at Charco's Drive-In for a burger and cruising out to the Dairy Queen in Mesquite for a Dr Pepper Icy. Nancy had to be home early, leaving John and Bob with time to kill. They went downtown. Outside the jailhouse, John did his *Liverpool Echo* routine, with Bob as his supposed photographer, and asked a policeman what was happening. 'They've got some guy,' he was told. 'In fact, there's some sort of press conference due.' Wearing his best seen-it-all, done-it-all face, John said, 'I guess I'd better get down there, then.'

Two minutes later, he and Bob were in the jailhouse base-ment, in a room usually reserved for identity parades, despite having neither a notebook nor a camera between them. The room wasn't especially crowded, not even when District

Attorney Henry Wade told everyone that the alleged assassin was to be unveiled before them, and a group of deputies in cowboy hats spilled in escorting Lee Harvey Oswald. John said that Oswald looked so convincingly bewildered that he was either a damn good actor or he was innocent. The boy didn't seem to have a clue what was going on.

John often said, when discussing his seven years in the US, and in particular that night in Dallas, that he felt like he was lying – that he hadn't really been there at all. It was both comforting and eerie, then, at Andy Kershaw's house one evening, when Andy called him over to the television to watch archive footage from that press conference. Sure enough, there were John and Bob, standing about five feet away from Oswald – and from a certain Jack Ruby, back when he was just another face in the crowd, meriting no special attention, no place in history.

Being an ocean away from the Mersey-oriented music scene meant that John never got to see any of the Merseybeat bands in action. It should be noted, though, that the Cavern played a major role in his various seduction techniques in those curious times. He was, he made it clear to anyone who would listen, so frequently in the Cavern that he might be considered part of the brickwork – and weren't the management contemplating mounting a plaque to alert the clientele to the exact hallowed spot where John could regularly be found sipping something non-alcoholic and nodding thoughtfully? Impressionable young Texans were, well, impressed by that line of chat.

The truth, of course, was rather different. John had been to the Cavern only twice, when he had flown home for Christmas. The first time, he saw the Spencer Davis Group, with a wet-behind-the-ears Stevie Winwood – whose autograph, along with those of other members of his later group Traffic, adorns a page in John's 1967 diary – and the second time the Richmond Group, a Rolling Stones sort of band who featured on a post-Merseybeat live LP entitled *Where It All Began*. The closest John came whilst in Dallas to any genuine link with the scene back home was through a fellow founder member of the Dallas County Cricket Club, whose brother, Pete Clarke, was drummer with the Escorts. John believed that their version of 'Dizzy Miss Lizzy' eclipsed that of the Beatles themselves, and considered their song 'The One To Cry' nigh-on indispensable.

The Dallas County Cricket Club, incidentally, was a minor phenomenon of its own. John co-founded it in 1962 and it lasted long enough to attract the attentions of Beatles fans fascinated by anything English. When the club played a match at Texas University in Austin, members of the university football squad felt sufficiently threatened by this alien activity to come and break up the game.

John was fast proving adept at bending the truth to his own advantage, as evidenced by the effectiveness of his 'I'm never out of the Cavern, me' routine. It was through bending the truth that he landed the radio gig that was to transform him from 'English chancer with a knack for being in the right place at the right time' to 'English chancer with a knack for being in the right place at the right time, with thousands of screaming girls offering to surrender themselves to his every whim and desire'.

After John made a call to KLIF, to correct Russ Knight, more commonly known as the Weird Beard, on some point of fact about Liverpool, Knight – or should that be Mr Beard? – hired him as the show's official Beatles Correspondent. John was, after all, from somewhere near Liverpool, so it stood to reason that he would be the first person that John, Paul, George or Ringo would call whenever they were in need of a confidant. John has pointed out that around the time when Beatlemania was beginning to take hold in the US, you couldn't turn on the radio without hearing someone claiming to be Ringo's cousin, so his own unmistakably English tones – which were, upon his appointment by KLIF, magically glossed with Liverpudlian inflections – were as near to the stamp of authenticity as anyone could ask for.

In his capacity as KLIF's voice of the Beatles, John would be called upon to answer whichever enquiries about the Fab Four the young Dallas audience saw fit to send his way, though there would typically be a record played between question and answer, to give John time to find out the name of Paul's pet marmoset, or how many sugars Ringo's Auntie Beryl took in her coffee. The pinnacle of John's career as an adjunct to the Beatles appears to have taken place at a Dallas department store, where the Weird Beard was holding a record giveaway, at which it had been announced that 'Our man from Liverpool' would be making a personal appearance.

John duly showed up, only to find several thousand hysterical teenage girls tearing the place apart, screaming and fainting and begging him to lay his divine hands upon their unworthy flesh. When some measure of calm had been temporarily restored, the Weird Beard conducted an interview with John and asked him how long he had been living in Dallas. John replied that he had been there for three and a half years. But as soon as he pronounced 'half' in his English accent, rather than as 'hay-aff' as the Texans have it, a riot broke out again and John and the Weird Beard were forced to beat a retreat out the back door in true *Hard Day's Night* fashion.

After that, John's life involved being mobbed on a regular basis in downtown Dallas by teenage girls, who would offer themselves to him in the mistaken belief that this would somehow bring them closer to the Beatles. That shed at the bottom of the garden on Potomac Avenue became a little hive of carnal activity. John wrote:

> It wasn't long before girls anxious for a Beatles surrogate started arriving outside my modest home. Being a thoroughly decent sort, I'd invite them in and, well, if they were anxious to sacrifice their virginity to a Man From Liverpool it was churlish, even unpatriotic, of me to refuse to cooperate. In the space of four months or so I built up a formidable catalogue of deflorations. I rarely knew their names – or cared – and I suppose, in a way, that what I was doing was a form of prostitution. Mind you, I never charged for my services. Those four months were among the most exhausting but gratifying of my life, and it wasn't until an irate father questioned me at gunpoint for about an hour that I decided the time had come when I should retire.

One of the girls who visited him regularly on Potomac Avenue was Shirley Anne Milburn, who was then fifteen, though their friendship was, at that stage at least, more platonic. Following his encounter with the business end of a shotgun, John left his shed and moved in with Shirley and her parents. From what John has said about Shirley, it is clear she was as insecure as any fifteen-year-old, and there appears to have been some kind of conspiracy of silence between her and her parents to get John to marry her without revealing to him that she was only fifteen. He was misled, he told me, by her entire family, who colluded with her in deceiving him about her age.

Soon after John moved in with the family, though, both of Shirley's parents died – first her father, in a car crash, followed by her mother, who suffered a series of heart attacks. John married Shirley, but later referred to this decision as part of a 'mutual defence pact', since Shirley was about to be packed off, in the wake of her parents' deaths, to live with an uncle she barely knew. 'The marriage ceremony itself was pretty depressing,' he said. 'We had to get a couple of kids off the street to act as witnesses.' Whenever John referred to his first marriage, it was usually in regretful tones. 'It was unfair on her,' he said, 'and unfair on me. She had a lot of changing to do. She married me because she wanted a more interesting life, but it was doomed from the start.'

Eventually John and Shirley left Dallas for Oklahoma City, where John had a new job lined up. They headed north in a '63 Chevrolet 409 convertible. With red metalflake paint so dark as to be almost black, and upholstery that *was* black, this was, he maintained, a seriously pretty machine.

After he bought the car, friends warned him that it looked ripe to be hijacked. 'Carry a gun,' they said. So he did. John could never remember what type of gun it was, but he was fairly sure it was big and mean-looking and that waving it about beneath the nose of any prospective thief would ensure trouble-free motoring. During the three or four months that he 'packed a rod', as he could sometimes be heard to refer to this brief period of armament, he grew so ill at ease when driving – expecting an OK Corral-style climax to every trip to the Dairy

Queen – that the pleasure of running the 409 threatened to evaporate. So he dumped the gun and learned to live again.

Once in Oklahoma, John teamed up with another DJ, Paul Miller, on *The Paul and John Show*, during which the duo, deprived of any control over the playlist, would ridicule the various advertisements, with John essentially playing straight man to Paul. The show became so popular that whenever John and Paul went to high-school football games the half-time show would be dedicated to them, and they would stride out on to the grid-iron to acknowledge the applause. Heady days, heady days.

Around this time John also branched out into managing, taking under his wing two groups – Dann Yankee and the Carpetbaggers, and Jay Walker and the Pedestrians – whom he would ferry to and from gigs on Indian reservations. It was during this period that John, as a man enjoying Permanent Resident status in the US, might have been liable to be drafted and sent to fight in Vietnam. Fortunately, having served with an allied army, he was deemed to have done his bit to make the world safe for rampant consumerism and was declared ineligible. But many of his American friends and acquaintances were drafted and shipped out to the jungles of South East Asia. When they came back – if they came back at all – it was clear they were deeply scarred.

One lunchtime in 1966, for example, John sat in a bar in San Bernardino and listened to a draftee describing, with no little relish and in some detail, the death of the first Vietnamese he had killed. John found the account as shocking as the change that had come over the raconteur. He had gone from being an amiable, liberal, laid-back sort of fellow to a bloodthirsty killer. Many, if not most, of the other people drinking in the bar would have applauded that transformation, of course, but John was horrified, and often wondered what became of that friend of a friend. Voicing dissent was no more advisable for John then than it would have been years earlier in Texas, when he had witnessed signs in Greenville warning blacks not to remain in town after sundown; in the prevailing climate of intolerance, he kept his opinions to himself. It was an intense time to be living in the US; during the Cuban Missile Crisis, the predominant feeling in the Lone Star State was that Americans were finally going to be given the chance to whip the Russkies' Commie asses all the way back to the Kremlin. John claimed he was at least as frightened by the Americans as he was by the Russians.

Despite having reluctantly left the hormone-induced frenzy of downtown Dallas behind him, the pressure was still on for John to maintain his image as Authentic Best Buddy of the Beatles, particularly as a DJ on a rival Oklahoma station not only had long hair but had also once spoken to the Yardbirds. John couldn't match that, of course, though he came reasonably close with a collarless suit that fitted in places and glistened like a slug when the light caught it. The David McCallum look helped too, though this illusion required industrial quantities of hairspray and could be shattered abruptly by a passing gust of wind. Whilst in Oklahoma, however, John was forced to admit publicly that he had never actually met the Beatles, after which his stock dropped sharply.

The station countered this shortcoming by sending him to Minneapolis to interview the Fab Four. Unfortunately, fifty other Friends of the Beatles had been sent along with the same objective, and what John did manage to get on tape sounded so ludicrous and garbled that he threw it away and told the station that the interview had been stolen by a jealous rival. As if that wasn't bad enough, John was then thrown down a flight of stairs by a friendly policeman at the Beatles concert.

He never did get to meet the group who had been instrumental in the creation of his own impressive US reputation – at least not as a complete entity, and not while he was still in America. He did, though, meet the Supremes, who joined the ever-expanding list of bands who refused to speak to him. Conversely, The Lovin' Spoonful went straight to the top of the then-meagre list of bands who not only agreed to converse with John, but even invited him to the cinema with them (they went to see *The Greatest Story Ever Told*, by the way).

It wasn't until John returned to England that he finally became acquainted with one of the musicians without whom his sexual adventures in Dallas might not have been quite so numerous. John Lennon and Yoko Ono appeared on John's show *Night Ride* in December 1968 to discuss their album, *Two Virgins*, which had been released that week. In the course of the show, Yoko read a touching poem concerning her recent miscarriage.

It was a month earlier that John had first met Lennon and Yoko. He had received a phone call from Lennon asking him if he would donate some blood to Yoko following the miscarriage. Lennon had left her bedside only to ring three people he liked enough to request such a favour. Feeling rather honoured, John dutifully went to the hospital, where he was informed after some preliminary tests that he wasn't suitable blood-donor material after all, what with his recent medical history being tarnished by yellow jaundice and the clap.

But John hung around the hospital for a few hours talking to

Lennon, and the pair really hit it off, occasionally meeting up for a drink over the next few years. John once overheard Lennon asking an assistant to fetch the papers so that he could peruse reviews of the latest Beatles single. 'Why would you want to do that?' John asked. 'I like to find out what our songs are about,' explained Lennon.

One afternoon when I was out with John, we made a detour over to Apple Records on Savile Row, because he said he had something to pick up from Lennon. We'd been sitting in reception for a while when Lennon popped his head round the door and asked us in to have tea with him and Yoko. The whole thing had been planned from the start, but John hadn't dared say anything to me because he knew I'd get so nervous – I was one of those girls you see in newsreel footage from Beatles gigs, screaming my lungs out at every shake of Lennon's fringe, every wiggle of Paul McCartney's hips. My hysteria was suppressed rather than extinguished over time, as John well knew, which is why he enjoyed it so much when Paul came over to speak to me after a gig in 1972, and when I walked slap-bang into the surprise tea party at Apple. On both occasions, I nearly passed out with shock.

It was a wonderful afternoon. Yoko had been getting a lot of bad press at the time, but she was a delight, pouring the tea and playing mother. I'd never met either of them before, though we had participated one year in Yoko's birthday present, when Lennon organised for lots of people he knew to be photographed individually in Yoko T-shirts. The photographer turned up one afternoon and snapped John and me in our T-shirts, then the pictures were put alongside countless others in an album that Lennon presented to Yoko.

We adapted that idea for John's sixtieth birthday, when

we had T-shirts made bearing the lyrics from one of his favourite songs, Roy Buchanan's 'The Lonesome Fugitive', 'I'd like to settle down but they won't let me', and then photographed friends and family wearing them. The BBC really went to town with the idea, and John's then producer Anita Kamath collared various bands to do their bit for John's birthday.

Lennon stayed in touch with us for a while even after he moved to the States; we'd sometimes get postcards from him and Yoko, from wherever they happened to be on their travels.

As undeniably impressive as John's Beatles non-scoop had been, KOMA decided, in the face of ratings that were slithering ever downward, that he was expendable. Or maybe it was just that his talent shone so brightly it was eclipsing the station's other employees. But when management started streamlining, John was streamlined out.

This was the third time in four years that John's employment with a radio station was terminated, and it wasn't to be the last. John hit the road with Shirley and headed for San Bernardino, California, where he had managed to hook the morning-show slot at KMEN. For the eighteen months between the autumn of 1965 and the spring of 1967, he changed fundamentally. You could even say he lost an integral part of himself: namely his 's'. It was that letter, sitting perfectly happily and minding its own business slap-bang in the middle of John's surname, to which his employers at KMEN objected, and so it was tweezered out. KMEN seemed to believe that this apparently innocuous consonant would cause some malfunction in the brains of John's listeners, who would never be able to remember such an unwieldy name.

So the 's'-less Ravencroft was assigned the role of the station's personable Mr Morning Man, chivvying the kids off to school and hubby off to work with a smile on their lips and a song in their hearts. In order to be firing on all cylinders and ready to commence rockin' at six, he had to tiptoe from the log cabin at four thirty a.m., grabbing himself a mess o' beans from the skillet on the previous night's campfire. (He assured me that this was how everyone used to talk, and I have no evidence to the contrary.)

KMEN itself was located in the middle of a field filled with cattle. The rival pop station – K-something else – had its offices and studios in a corner of the local Holiday Inn, so KMEN was immediately considered cooler by its target audience of high-school students, inland surfers, hot-rodders, citrus-fruit growers and honey-skinned blondes, all of whom warmed to a playlist that accommodated Canned Heat, Love and the Doors. Because it was only a small station, John was allowed to play whatever he liked, and in time he persuaded his bosses to let him initiate a British chart. They thought it was a great idea, though of course this so-called hit parade was actually nothing of the sort: John would simply choose whichever records caught his fancy that week, and afford them random placings in his rundown. 'The Nazz Are Blue' by the Yardbirds lingered in his British top five for an unfeasibly long time, despite never having been released as a single anywhere on earth.

During his spell at KMEN, John used his show to give exposure to numerous bands that he felt would blossom if only more people could hear their music. Radio playlists were as conservative then as they are today, but John regarded it as something like his civic duty to introduce listeners to an eclectic range of music, while downplaying his own part in any subsequent success that the musicians might enjoy.

But one band who could testify to the role that John played in their career was The Misunderstood, a psychedelic five-piece from the downtown Riverside area. He first saw the band when they made an unscheduled appearance between the Mystics and the North Side Moss at a gig to mark the opening of a new shopping mall in Riverside. John began to drift off round the mall during what he thought was the interval, when he heard the band tuning up. He later wrote:

> It was like one of your St-Paul-on-the-road-to-Damascus experiences. When they played, I couldn't believe what I was hearing. The shopping mall was filled with the roar and thrust of their music and the lead guitar of Glenn Ross Campbell tore strips out of the sky for us to walk on. They are prophets of a new order, harbingers of a brilliant, soft and alive dawn for mankind.

Well, it was the 1960s.

After they came off stage, John went for coffee with them and advised them that London might prove more receptive to their music than Los Angeles. Over the next few months, he grew close to the band, who came to regard him as their sixth member. Presumably this meant that John could no longer consider himself to be the sixth member of the Beatles. There has to be a limit, after all, to the number of bands in which a person can be designated sixth member at any one time before things start getting out of hand. These are the kinds of principle on which any sane civilisation must be founded.

John regularly brought The Misunderstood back to the apartment he shared with Shirley, and invited them to sample his record collection; the band members, who didn't even have a record-player between them, were inspired and influenced by what John played them, from the latest English imports to new West Coast bands like the Mothers of Invention and Love. He gave The Misunderstood regular plugs on KMEN, much to the annoyance of other bands. He would say, 'Here's one The Misunderstood will be playing tonight at the so-and-so,' before putting on something by another group. When it was finished he'd say, 'And remember – you can hear The Misunderstood play the same song ten times better tonight at . . .'

On one occasion, John became the band's guardian in a more literal sense. They had been hanging out at his apartment when a couple of the band members went across the street to get some beer. The man at the till was giving them a hard time, and calling them 'fairies' because of their flowing locks. When the band returned and mentioned this to John, he was fuming. 'You shouldn't put up with this!' he said. 'This is outrageous! We should go down and have a word with these people.' They all piled back down to the shop, John armed with good old British righteousness while the band favoured earthier weapons like switchblades and monkey wrenches. The store-owners, though, proved to be even better prepared, greeting John and the band with axe handles and metal pipes. Once they had reached the safety of the apartment once more, John seemed genuinely shocked by the speed at which the situation had escalated. He was expecting a nice sort of talking down, and hadn't realised it might get physical.

John continued to help The Misunderstood in any way he could. In spring 1966, he arranged for them to record in Gold Star studios in Hollywood, in order to produce something that he could play on KMEN. He arranged for his brother Alan to do some reconnaissance PR work back in England to locate some potential managers. He joined the group in an ambush on the Hollies at a Los Angeles hotel, where the young upstarts thrust their recordings into the hands of the more established band, whose disdainful expressions masked great admiration. Or possibly didn't.

Perhaps most charitably of all, John let the band's singer, Rick Brown, and his girlfriend Tanny use his bedroom when he was out. Rick would later write the song 'I Can Take You To The Sun' for Tanny, though, as the lyrics rather sadly report, it turned out she didn't want to go. Rick, on the other hand, did want to go. Following the break-up of the band in 1967, he fled the draft to become a Hindu monk in India. John even drove him to the airport.

Back in 1966, The Misunderstood were finally persuaded to try their luck in England when John promised that they could use his mother's Notting Hill house as a temporary base. That plan would have worked out splendidly if John had remembered to consult his mother about it. The first she knew of it was when she returned home after being away to find on her doorstep a gang of scrawny, long-haired, rain-drenched Californians who had arrived three days earlier expecting a warm welcome, steaming tea and hot buttered crumpets. They begged her to call John in San Bernardino, and after much apologising he persuaded her to let the band stay. It sounds like the basis for a rip-roaring seventies sitcom – which would, naturally, be called something like *Oops, Mrs Ravenscroft!* – and we can only speculate about what they all found to talk about when the tea and crumpets were eventually wheeled out.

John's brother Alan was living with their mother in Notting Hill when The Misunderstood arrived, and remembers it with a shudder. 'Since the house had been designed for a maximum of four to sleep in and we were already four-strong, this presented a problem,' he says. 'But our mother not only harboured Bohemian tendencies, she was very accommodating – she essentially kept an open house, which caused John and Francis to put a notice outside the door, on one occasion when we ourselves couldn't get near the food, proclaiming "Wagon Trains Catered For." The Misunderstood were new to London and frankly the town wasn't ready for them. They used all the lovely purple-glass Habitat wine glasses to make coffee and destroyed them. They were big Californians and "hung out" when this was an activity still in its infancy. And they practised. God knows they needed it, but we didn't, and nor did the neighbours.'

After three months, Alan hooked the band up with Nigel Thomas, an old school chum of his who had become a manager and was impressed by John's enthusiastic letter of introduction, and Nigel moved the boys out of chez Ravenscroft.

If the history books feature any mention of The Misunderstood, it is rarely as more than a footnote to a footnote. But the mutual respect and encouragement that existed between John and them is typical of the atmosphere that John cultivated. The world wasn't always in sync with his tastes. When The Misunderstood eventually had a single, 'Children Of The Sun', released by the Fontana label in early 1969, it was reviewed in *Melody Maker* by Roy Wood of The Move and later Wizzard. 'Terrible,' he declared. 'I don't know why they bothered. I don't think even John Peel would play this. Oh yeah, I like his show. It's quite interesting, but he does play some weird stuff at times.'

John's recollections of his life at KMEN were scattered, to say the least. He remembered that the station was regularly visited by whichever it was of Jan and Dean who hadn't been in an accident, and that his best mate was fellow DJ Johnny Darin. Johnny Darin wasn't really called Johnny Darin. In fact, John never found out what his real name was, as DJs tended to have names waiting for them when they arrived at the station, names that would be discarded when they moved on – hence the difficulty encountered by John in his numerous attempts to contact his old US DJ pals, a difficulty that the hardiest of *This Is Your Life* researchers found similarly insurmountable.

He did unearth some old copies of KMEN's news leaflet, the *KMENtertainer*. Here is a picture of John Ravencroft showing actress/singer Donna Loren how to run the KMEN control board. And here he is again with Buddy Budnik, Chuck Christensen, Mark Denis and the rest of the team, dressed in fetching figure-hugging outfits and poised for some white-hot basketball action. The *KMENtertainer* reports that they faced off against various girls' teams for some hilarious hoop antics. This rather baffled John, who was ready to swear on oath that he had never played basketball in his life. There's even a photo of him sitting on the floor and talking into four phones simultaneously. 'John Ravencroft taking a few of the many requests that are called in every morning,' runs the agreeably cheesy caption.

A Radio 1 colleague returned from San Bernardino a few years ago bearing maps from the area, designed to stir the embers of John's nostalgia. With a trembling finger, John located the street on which he had lived. It was, he recalled, a wooden house on the corner, but was the street really called Waterman Avenue? And was the Mojave Desert really that close? And the Joshua Tree National Park? If so, then why had he never bothered to visit them?

After an hour poring over the maps, the memories still resolutely refused to come flooding back. Called upon to imitate someone with a mothproof memory, John did his timid best – he failed entirely to recognise one of the guests wheeled on to bring a tear to his eye during *This Is Your Life*, but made a good show of cheerful affection all the same. The truth was that delving around in the past could be disorienting for John whenever his recollections failed to square with the documentary evidence at hand, or failed to materialise at all. His memory was selective. He could list every incarnation of The Fall on demand, but he couldn't always remember where his underpants were.

It was during John's eighteen months in San Bernardino, though, that he attended a gig that it would not be an over-statement to say changed his life. There were, it should be acknowledged, quite a few such gigs which John would speak about in hushed and reverent tones, and had he completed this book with his own hand, he would doubtless have offered up for inspection the Ten Best Gigs list that he had promised so tantalisingly to include. I can't say for certain what would have been on it alongside Eddie Cochran and Gene Vincent, but among the nominees would have been the following:

Dick Dale in Islington
The Four Brothers at John's fiftieth-birthday bash in our garden
PJ Harvey in Cardiff
The Misunderstood in Hollywood
Van Morrison in Finsbury Park

Roy Orbison in Ipswich
Pink Floyd in Hyde Park
The Undertones in Huddersfield
The Fall in – well, The Fall just about anywhere.

Then there were the Faces in Sunderland, where they played on the evening that Sunderland qualified to be in the FA Cup Final. That was the first time John met them, and he always said they were the perfect band to play that night: they came on and started booting footballs into the audience. It has even been claimed by keen-eyed observers that John could be seen dancing at the side of the stage in Sunderland. As John has already written in these pages, he was never the world's most willing dancer. What seems to have slipped through the cracks in his memory, though, is that he invented his own dance – a kind of energetic, springy, shuffling walk on the spot. We christened it the Westbourne Grove Walk because the first sighting of it occurred one day when he returned from Westbourne Grove and began performing it while he was telling me what he had been doing while he was out.

Those moves always resurfaced on special occasions. In his diary entry for 24 July 1976, John writes about compèring a huge outdoor gig in Cardiff headlined by Status Quo: 'Went onto the stage and introduced Quo. As it got dark, I stood behind the stage and did my Westbourne Grove Walk.' Fashions come and go, governments fall, wars are waged, and still the Walk endures. Anyone at Fabric not caught up in their own dancing when John DJed there in 2002 would have glimpsed for themselves the Westbourne Grove Walk when he broke into a few energetic steps in the DJ booth, his little legs going back and forth. He used to dance pretty hard in that booth.

Also near the top of John's ever-expanding list of life-changing concerts was the Rolling Stones in San Bernardino. He was something of a KMEN celebrity by that point, and so was entrusted with the noble task of loitering around the stage while the Stones played, fielding the numerous and eager young women who'd made their way round the side and were preparing to launch themselves at Mick Jagger. During the show, a lad battled his way on to the platform, seized a policeman's handgun from its owner/operator's holster, and fired several shots into the woodwork only a yard or two from Jagger's nimbly prancing feet. The general din was so great that the band played on, unaware that whole generations of innocent woodworms were dying particularly unpleasant deaths as they romped and stomped the night away.

But the show that really altered John's perception of what music could achieve took place at the Whiskey A Go-Go in Hollywood, where Van Morrison's Them were supported by Captain Beefheart and his Magic Band. John's admiration for Beefheart's masterpiece, the 1969 album *Trout Mask Replica*, never palled over the course of more than thirty years, so it's easy to imagine how gobsmacked he must have been that evening. He compared it to hearing Elvis for the first time. When he reeled out into the Hollywood night, he felt like nothing would ever be the same again.

An idiosyncratic but enduring friendship existed between John and Beefheart, which began with John's support of his music in the 1960s. When Beefheart came to London in 1967, shortly before he recorded a session for *Top Gear*, John drove him around the country; he was a rather enthusiastic chauffeur, in fact, later extending the same courtesy to the great guitarist John Fahey. With Beefheart in the back, John headed for the

Frank Freeman School of Dancing in Kidderminster, where Beefheart was playing a gig. The Captain was very excited about this show, and one of his band remarked on what an original and groovy name this was for a club, until John pointed out that, no, it really was a dancing school run by someone called Frank Freeman.

On the way back from that show, Beefheart asked John to pull over so that he could get out and listen to the trees. John wrote later:

> I've always thought that's a really strange thing to have done, but of course it could have been his way of saying that he wanted a pee – probably was. He might have said 'listen to a tree' because it rhymed with 'having a pee'. His thought processes were not like those of other men – you could well believe he wanted to listen to a tree. If anybody else had said it, I would have said 'stupid bastard' under my breath. But with Beefheart, you thought: Well, he knows more than I do and if he wants to listen to a tree, and I'm in a position to enable him to do so, then I'm going to give him a chance to do it, because it would be quite wrong not to. So he got out of the car and disappeared. It was one of those things where a plaque ought to have been put there. I'd like to say that I can see him silhouetted against a gibbous moon with his ear firmly pressed to a fine old elm, but I just don't know.

When I lived in London with John, telephone calls from Beefheart were a regular occurrence. But he used to hate it if he called and John wasn't in. He thought that people should know somehow when he was going to phone, and make sure they were in to take the call. If they weren't, he would get irritated.

The calls continued throughout the rest of John's life; they usually came in August, a few weeks before John's birthday, though I think the timing was a complete coincidence. And even though they might not have spoken for a year, Beefheart would always pick up the conversation as though it had only been interrupted the previous day, and they would just chat about whatever they'd been doing.

In John's diary entry for 1 December 1975, just over a month before William was born, he writes of a twenty-minute call from Beefheart: 'He was saying nasty things about the former Magic Band, dropping rather aggressive asides at his wife, being friendly but fraudulent. He ended by saying he hoped Pig "had a fine swine".' More recently, Beefheart would call to discuss matters of livestock, since both he and John kept chickens. Or he would offer John titbits of advice to pass on to the children – 'John,' he'd say, 'be sure to tell them never to swim in water that hasn't been pissed in.'

Before John and Shirley had left Oklahoma for California, their marriage had already shown signs of faltering. There was nothing confrontational in John's nature, but Shirley had grown increasingly violent with him, and took to waiting until he had fallen asleep at night before launching her assaults. On one occasion, he ended up in hospital in Oklahoma City after she hurled a stone frog at his head. He used to describe how embarrassing it was to be there with all these other men swapping stories about why they were in hospital, only for him to pipe up, 'My wife threw a frog at me.'

The violence seems to have increased, with the authorities being called to intervene at one point, but John's determination to rescue the marriage, and help Shirley, temporarily prevailed.

John and the children with Sheila's parents Denis and Eileen on the steam railway at Haworth in Yorkshire

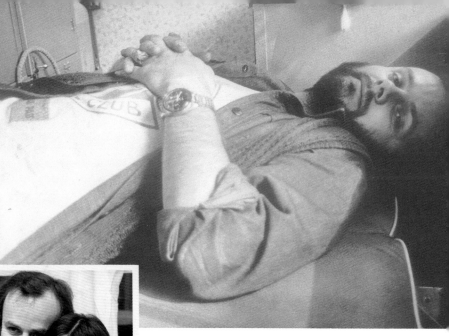

Above: resting in the Dormobile
Left: with William at two days old
Bottom left: asleep with Alexandra, William and Thomas
Bottom right: with Florence

Above: John at home in Suffolk, 1972
Below: The Youth Club on holiday in Cornwall, 1976

Right: John and Thomas,
before Ipswich play Liverpool
Below: Playing football with
Woggle, 1972

Above: John scoring at
Wembley in a Radio 1
football team, 1978
Right: Playing football at
the Phoenix Festival, 1996

LIVERPOOL FOOTBALL CLUB

LIVERPOOL
versus
CHELSEA

21st OCTOBER, 1978

ADMIT TO

PADDOCK

No 3206

This portion to be retained

Villa Park, Birmingham

F.A. CHALLENGE CUP   No 13375

Wednesday 3rd April, 1974

Semi-Final (Replay)

LEICESTER CITY v. LIVERPOOL

Kick-off 7.30 p.m.

PRICE
£1.00
Incl. V.A.T.

You are advised to take up your position
not later than thirty minutes before Kick-off

This portion to be retained

WITTON
LANE

BLOCK

X

TERRACE
STANDING

Left: John Walters in Room 318, Egton House – Radio 1
Background: John paddling in the fountain in Le Havre, 1979, after the Le Mans twenty-four-hour race
Bottom: John in the cage on *Tiswas*, 1980

FOX AT **GREYHOUND**
PARK LANE CROYDON
Sun. 20th Aug

JOHN PEEL
CAPABILITY BROWN

Licensed Bar   plus Rick Hawkins   7-00 p.m.

★ **ADMISSION ONLY 30p. with this ticket** ★

SUN. AUG. 27th TERRY DACTYL Brett Marvin and the Thunderbolts
SUN. SEP. 3rd HAWKWIND

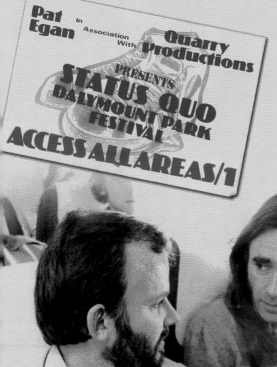

Above: The Rhythm Pals with Elvis Costello, 1983
Below: With Francis Rossi, 1979

At home in Suffolk. Left to right: Alexandra, Florence, William, John, Sheila with nephew Little John, and Thomas on his bike

When he left San Bernardino in March 1967 for London, where he hoped to continue working as a DJ, he brought Shirley with him. He always hoped that he could do more for her, but his diary entries once he returned to London tell a story of increasing tension and unhappiness. 'So worried about Shirley,' he writes on 19 September 1967. 'She grows more and more enigmatic. I don't really understand how I can bring her back into the fold. She doesn't understand what I want from life. Oh well.'

The situation had worsened by 24 October: 'Shirley very, very depressed. She's gained weight and was crying and feeling very helpless and unimportant.' Even once John and I were living together, she would still call, often to tell me some-thing like, 'I saw you at the Albert Hall with John, I was watching you both.' I didn't feel sorry for her then; I felt threatened. But as my relationship with John became more secure, I realised how sad her situation was.

When John and Shirley arrived in London, they moved into a flat in Fulham, and John began looking for work. One of his mother's neighbours, who used to place advertising with the pirate station Radio London, suggested that John talk to Alan Keane at the station. After an initial conversation, Keane put John straight on air without an audition – it seemed that John's experience as a DJ in America was impressive, not to mention exotic, enough to allow him to bypass any such formalities.

But before he began working for Radio London, John had to surrender a not inconsiderable portion of himself. He had already grown accustomed to having his consonants interfered with during his time at KMEN, when the objectionable 's' was expunged from Ravenscroft. But now the whole surname was for the chop. It was suggested that three syllables might be trimmed to one, which put paid to John's hopes of renaming himself Helen Llewellyn Product 19. The story as John always told it was that a secretary in the Radio London office looked up from her emery board and uttered those words that were to change a man, a name and a way of life:

'Why don't you call him "John Peel"?'

And lo, the clouds did part and sunbeams poured forth and it was decreed that, yes, John Peel had a certain ring to it. Many people would be grateful for this decision, not least the youngsters advertising for pen pals in the late sixties. 'During that extraordinary period when it was fashionable to be me,' John wrote, 'folk seeking companionship through the small ads of the *International Times* would describe themselves as "Peelites". I don't think I want my religion so personalised.'

Once John was Peel, he never considered switching back to Ravenscroft in his professional life. The downside of that for me was that I was forever being introduced as Sheila Peel. Whoever this Sheila Peel might be – and I always had strong suspicions that she was a stripper – she definitely wasn't me.

'Peel' was John's business name, then, but it brought with it other, unforeseen comforts. The name could provide unexpected solace or sanctuary in trying times. It was a kind of disguise that was permanently at John's disposal. If celebrity is, as John Updike maintains, a mask that eats the face of those who wear it, then John was lucky to escape that fate, and to strike instead a balance between fame and anonymity. In fact, Updike's proclamation was distorted slightly when John DJed at Chibuku in Liverpool in 2004, where many of the clubbers turned up wearing John Peel masks. It would have been hilarious if the effect of lots of Johns bopping away with youthful abandon wasn't so damn eerie.

You might say we kept his feet on the ground, but in fact he did a perfectly good job of that himself. It's hard to appear enigmatic or aloof when you've admitted on air that you have gonorrhoea, or made a public inventory of the detritus in your children's bedrooms, or climbed inside a pram on national television.

Because he was reluctant to succumb to most of the trappings of celebrity, he was always shocked whenever anyone appeared nervous to meet him. It didn't happen often, mostly because his own laid-back manner was usually mirrored in his fans. He was just being himself on the radio, so when people approached him in the street to shake his hand or talk about some obscure Scrotum Grinder track, they felt similarly at ease with themselves. But occasionally someone, usually a teenage boy or a nervous young couple, would be visibly shaking when they came to speak to John. He'd say, 'Why are they like that? I don't understand,' conveniently forgetting that when he came face to face with Kenny Dalglish for the first time, he could scarcely squeeze out more than an awestruck whimper. He couldn't comprehend, though, that anyone would feel about him the way he felt about Dalglish; he couldn't imagine being anyone's hero.

He remained eternally surprised that none of the listeners he invited to the house ever showed up. He wrote in 1978:

Do you realise that throughout the decade I have been droning away on British radio I have given my phone number and address to any correspondent living close enough to Peel Acres who sounded amiable, and suggested that they got in touch? And that during all that time only one person – a student in

Cambridge – has actually telephoned? We arranged to meet up with him but he never arrived.

But from his days with Radio London, it was clear that people were tuning in for more than just the music. It's funny now to listen to *The Perfumed Garden* – to hear John's delivery, as drily amused and stubbornly unwavering as it would still be thirty years later, in the days when it still retained a crisp upper-class crust. You could hear the traces of his education in the way he spoke, and the care he took over language. I think that's one reason why he was so incensed by Ludovic Kennedy's attack in 1973 on the inability of Radio 1 DJs to express themselves in articulate English. 'They have no respect for the English language,' said Kennedy, 'which they constantly mispronounce, and they have no vocabulary apart from grunts with which to narrate or describe. They seem wholly contemptuous of anything they do not understand – which in the case of most is a very great deal.'

The truth was more complicated than that, the class divide not so easily demarcated. John used to treasure, for example, the memory of an early meeting with someone in the upper echelons of Radio 1, who regarded with some displeasure John's kaftan and shoulder-length hair. John must have mentioned public school during the meeting because the fellow asked, with surprise, whether John had met someone who had attended public school. 'Went to one myself actually,' John shot back. 'Shrewsbury. Riggs Hall.' The pain lifted from the man's face. 'How's old Brooky?' he cried, and John knew that his Radio 1 contract would be renewed for another three months.

The Radio London ship, the *Galaxy*, was anchored just off the coast at Felixstowe, not too far from where John and I would live four years later, and John often spoke of how idyllic that summer on the ship felt to him; it sounded like something of a working holiday. One advantage was that it provided an escape from his home life, where his marriage to Shirley, who was still being violent, was in its final stages. John was on the *Galaxy* two weeks out of every three. He started out doing the afternoon shift, then volunteered for the midnight slot, which he quickly made his own when he realised that no-one at the station actually listened to it – everyone else was playing cards or watching dirty movies or sleeping.

This first became apparent to him when no-one complained about the various cock-ups he made. Later in his career, John would become notorious for these spontaneous errors; there was even an infamous occasion in 1973 when he played tracks from Robert Fripp and Brian Eno's *No Pussyfooting* backwards, though only Eno called to point out this mistake. John took it all in his stride, and these days you can find dimly lit corners of the internet dedicated to his various slip-ups. It was in the unorthodox nature of the music John favoured that songs would begin quietly, or end in protracted feedback. Someone called Stirmonster, which I would venture is not the name on his library card, writes: '"Fades in gently" became a catchphrase for me and my pals when we were teenagers. We were even going to start a band with that name. In almost every show something would "fade in gently'.'

Though the station only lasted for a few more months after he joined, before it was closed on 14 August 1967 by the Marine Offences Bill, *The Perfumed Garden* was like a sacred little corner of hippydom magically unsullied by commercial forces. The discovery that the bosses weren't listening gave John licence to make the programme his own. He stopped running the ads and the weather, and instead filled the airtime with the records that excited him. He played the début albums by Jimi Hendrix and Pink Floyd when no-one else would; he found space for The Grateful Dead and Country Joe and the Fish. And the first his employers knew about their station breaking new ground and showcasing artists who were ignored elsewhere was when they received a call from the Beatles' manager, Brian Epstein, who was raving about what a great programme John was commandeering.

It was while presiding over *The Perfumed Garden* that John first received correspondence from Marc Bolan. By the time John and I first got to know one another, he was close friends with Marc, who had by that time formed his latest band, Tyrannosaurus Rex. John had appeared on their début album – *My People Were Fair And Had Sky In Their Hair, But Now They're Content To Wear Stars On Their Brows* – reading one of Marc's fairy stories, a gesture he repeated sitting cross-legged on the stage of the Royal Albert Hall. In the days of his previous group, John's Children, Marc had written to John at the *Galaxy*. They connected initially through the music, but it went deeper than that, and by the time I started visiting John's flat, Marc was a regular fixture there.

I was out of place, to say the least, so I tended not to say much. I'd just marvel at this laid-back, hippyish atmosphere, where John, Marc, June, and all their friends lounged around talking about music, love and peace. No-one ever got agitated. Drinking was frowned upon, and there were no raised voices.

There was, on the other hand, an abundance of velvet. You couldn't have swung a dead chicken without hitting someone shrouded in the stuff. Not that there would have been a dead chicken handy if you felt like swinging one – everyone was vegetarian except me. And although I was fond of Marc's music, having listened to so much of it on John's radio programmes, it was quite intimidating to find myself in the middle of this very sixties vibe, or being dragged off to macrobiotic restaurants.

Possibly John didn't know the whole truth about my diet, at least not at first. His brother Alan remembers meeting me before a show that John was compèring at the Royal Albert Hall. 'To John's delight,' recalls Alan, 'he had found a girl who neither ate meat, drank alcohol or smoked. To my delight – so much virtue can't be healthy – no sooner had John gone on to introduce the next act than Sheila asked me, "Do you think we can get down to the bar for a sausage, a cider and a smoke before he comes back?"'

Gradually the group of friends became more streamlined until just Marc, June, John and I were hanging out together. They were our best friends, and those were very relaxed, carefree times we had together. John used to bring Tyrannosaurus Rex along with him whenever he was doing a gig and squeeze them on to the same bill. It really was that casual – 'Oh, this is a band I know, OK if they play?' The four of us would go out to gigs, or on day trips. We did a lot of the usual hippy things at weekends, pitching up at Stonehenge or in Glastonbury. And when John was away, as he often was with work, Marc and June would call round to the flat, knowing that I was on my own, and whisk me away to see a band for the night, or off to a festival for the day.

And then, in the space of one telephone call, it was over: we felt that Marc had simply erased us from his life. John had been overjoyed for Marc when he finally got the success that he knew he deserved, after years of knocking on doors and getting nowhere; there can't have been many people who were happier about it. There's a lovely diary entry dated 2 January 1971, in which John drives 'in frost and considerable cold down to Portobello Road . . . Bought a couple of lovely old children's books for Marc and June and also a set of swans for them to mark the success of "Ride A White Swan" which is back up to #4 in the charts.' Later that evening, John writes, 'Marc and June arrived with a WhizzWheels car thing for me and a horrifying kit for producing "sea monkeys" from crystals which sounds macabre.' When T.Rex got their first number one with 'Hot Love', John was listening on the car radio; he became so emotional that he had to pull the car into a lay-by and mop his eyes.

However, on 30 April, John hears 'disturbing stories about T.Rex drifting back from the States. Marc won't allow photos to be taken of the drummer and bass-player. He's being v. moody and playing the pop-star pretty heavily. Walks out alone at the beginning of each set and plays a long – and I should imagine, loud and boring – version of "Elemental Child" before Mickey Finn comes on. A side of Marc that was obviously there before but he's usually been able to suppress . . . Perhaps he feels he no longer needs to.'

It was towards the end of 1971 that our relationship with Marc and June collapsed completely. John had admitted on air that he was less than enamoured of the latest T.Rex single – 'Well, that was called "Get It On",' he said, 'but I couldn't wait to get it off.' He had, I think, imagined that his friendship with Marc was built on something more substantial than flattery, and that it would survive John's dislike of the occasional record that Marc made. Anything less would have been sycophancy. But Marc obviously saw things differently, and for him John had breached some kind of unwritten code.

In his diary entry for Sunday 19 September, John listens to T.Rex's new album, *Electric Warrior*, whilst eating his breakfast and observes: 'It's beautifully done but the worst side of Marc's personality seems to have been unleashed – we've not heard from them since "Hot Love" got to No.1. Very sad.' In hindsight, Marc's sudden success was the beginning of the end for him and John. It was clear that Marc was becoming not just famous but silly-famous: screaming girls, popping flashbulbs, all the things that have become clichés now. He had split from June when John finally decided to give him a call to see what he was doing one weekend. Someone answered the phone, and when John said who was calling, there was a barely audible voice in the background saying, 'I'm not in.' John was told that Marc would call him back. But of course he never did. In later years, John said that he had felt mildly offended, but I know that at the time we were both very shocked.

And John was exceedingly hurt. He had been around for long enough to have heard about this kind of behaviour, and he didn't lose sleep over it. But neither did he ever forget it. 'I was fond of the old Marc,' he writes in his diary on 9 January 1972, 'although I don't care much for the current Marc who is really causing riots wherever he goes. The *Sun* has printed pieces describing him as the new Beatles. That, regrettably, is Show-Biz.'

John knew that the same thing could easily happen if he befriended other musicians – one surge of success and he would be dumped again. Some people were surprised that he didn't always meet the bands who recorded sessions for his shows. I think ultimately the music was the only thing that mattered to him.

It was hard to know how to react, though, when Marc cut

237

us off. There was enough happening musically at that time for John to get excited about, and Marc had meanwhile moved on to stuff that wasn't quite John's cup of tea. But it's sad now to look over some of Marc's letters to John, and to see how close they had been at one time. Marc sent poems and drawings to John, and little reminders of how he felt about him. One letter from 1969 reads:

> John our freiend on the hills of Fame
> we'd walk with you what ere your name
> a trees is tall a babe is small,
> if nights are cold, you've but to call.

Another ends with the sign-off: 'King Arthur would have loved you as I do.'

But it's clear from a letter written in May 1969 that, even then, Marc knew he was prone to distraction:

> John,
> I hope your well, I've not been round lately, don't be sad. I've
> had strange wrestles with the gaolers of my destiny, causing
> much upset in my usauley sweet calm life, I thought of you
> often, your nice to know if your loney before I see you phone,
> if not when I see you, you wont be. Ozeons of love as a friend
> – Marc.

Marc and John did bump into each other again on 2 July 1976, just over a year before Marc's death, after a recording of the Radio 1 programme *Rosko's Round Table*. 'He threw his arms around me,' John writes in his diary, 'but he was v. much a stranger. He was somehow larger, looking disconcertingly like Gary Glitter. I was quite pleased when he went to the loo and I could escape.'

Naturally we were both saddened by Marc's death in a car accident in September 1977, but John felt he had lost him once already. Mulling over his temporary and thoroughly disagreeable role in the media as Former Friend of Marc Bolan during the weeks following the accident, John used his *Sounds* column to reflect upon this lost friend, and this lost friendship:

In the late 1960s Marc and June Child were as good friends as the Pig and I had. We climbed Glastonbury Tor together, together advanced frankly potty theories about the origins of Stonehenge as we mooned about the famed site, did most of the things that flower-children did together. When I did gigs Tyrannosaurus Rex went with me, all their gear crammed into the boot of a rented mini. We drove to Newcastle to share fifteen pounds between the three of us. Marc and Steve recorded several *Top Gear* sessions, and Marc and I spent too much time and too much money searching for old rock 'n' roll singles in junk shops in South London.

He told me once and with justifiable pride, as we left a shop somewhere in Tooting, how he had carried Eddie Cochran's guitar for a few feet sometime in the earliest sixties. It is certainly ironic that Marc should have died in much the same manner as Eddie the C., but, as a man only too aware of the considerable part played by legend in the history of rock 'n' roll, Marc would, I think, have approved the manner of his own passing.

When he made the transition from bopping elf and hero of the flower-folk to fully fledged teen idol and *TOTP* staple – a transition that he alone was able to make – he vanished out of my life too. I was sad then, as I am now, to see him go.

During his brief tenure at Radio London, John made other friends, as well as the odd enemy. Radio London also employed Kenny Everett, whom John was always quick to praise, and Tony Blackburn, whom he wasn't. John and Kenny used to regard Tony as the Anti-Christ, and would do whatever they could to disrupt his programmes. But John eventually mellowed in this respect, and was moved to think less harshly of Tony after overhearing him discussing with 'Diddy' David Hamilton the relative merits of various brands of hairspray. Their relationship was certainly rocky over the years, and their mutual hostility probably benefited each of them in different ways. We define ourselves as much by what we stand against as what we uphold, and by railing against Tony's presenting manner and musical tastes, John was defining his own style; I dare say Tony was doing likewise.

That must be why Tony took a break from opening a boutique in Wellingborough in the 1970s to tell the *Wellingborough News* that *Top Gear* 'spoilt his weekend listening'. 'I really think it should be taken off the air,' he complained, before condemning the kind of bands favoured by John as 'hairy, scruffy individuals, unsociable towards everyone'. It always seemed curious that such a laid-back presenter as John should prove so inflammatory. John even received a letter in the early seventies from a vicar who wrote that he should be castrated and deported, which seemed a touch un-Christian, indeed Jacobean in its excessiveness. Castrated *and* deported? Couldn't it have been one or the other?

There was always something rather absurd about the joshing

between John and Tony. Not that both men weren't being sincere in their dislike of one another. You can feel the irritation beginning in John's diary entry for 20 September 1967, just under two weeks before the launch of Radio 1:

> Read the new *Melody Maker* which contained the Poll Results. I was placed 7th in the DJ poll which I was pleased about as I'd only done 2½ months broadcasting at the time of voting. Jimmy Saville was first, then Simon Dee, Johnnie Walker (Caroline), Alan Freeman, Kenny Everett, Tony Blackburn, me, David Jacobs and Pete Murray. I do wish I'd beaten Tony Blackburn, who will be initiating Radio 1 at the end of the month.

John's disappointment was assuaged when he won the *Melody Maker* poll the following year, and most of the music-paper polls thereafter, but the prickliness between him and Tony rarely abated. On 3 April 1971, John teased Tony during the handover from *Top Gear* to Tony's new show, *Live at Five*, as he recounted later:

> Tony Blackburn now recovered from piles. In the handover I played 45 secs of his dreadful RCA single 'Is It You, Is It Me?' and said, '. . . Tony B with piles of former and current hits, take it away, Tony!' He was delighted!

The real joy of John's show *The Perfumed Garden* came from the level of fanaticism it inspired in its listeners. This audience wasn't getting the music it loved from any other outlet on radio, so understandably it grew protective of John. Here is someone called Monni, writing in the magazine

Gandalf's Garden of the show a year after it came off air:

John Peel spoke to his listeners kindly, lovingly. He urged them to communicate, to contribute to the programme, to write him letters, to set down their thoughts and feelings, hopes and fears, to send in poems, pictures, anything their minds had created. As much as possible of what he received he would read out, mention or describe over the air. And for all of us, the sense of participation, the sense of involvement with *The Perfumed Garden* was something very real and very personal, and added a new dimension to our lives.

When it became apparent that bureaucracy would force Radio London off the air, that the gates of our magical mystical garden would have to close, and the softly encouraging Peelian voice remain silent, we, the listeners, decided to continue *The Perfumed Garden* as best we could, in our own way, and to communicate with one another. We were not prepared to lose our newly established togetherness even if, for a while at least, we had to lose Peel. So one of our number began collecting names and addresses, and thus the famous *Perfumed Garden* list was born. One thing we are not is the John Peel Fan Club. John is our gentle philosopher, our beloved founder, our good friend. But we all care just as much about each other as we do about John. And this, perhaps, is the very essence of *The Perfumed Garden* and all that it stands for – we are people who CARE.

For his part, John valued the show as much as his listeners did. Here's an extract that he wrote from the same magazine, which evokes perfectly the mood of *The Perfumed Garden* for anyone who never heard it:

It was over a year ago now. In the studio the only light came from the tape cartridge machines and from the recording studio two Venetian blinds away across the hall. In a matchbox set on end, incense burned and the small room was soon filled with a sweeter smell than the beer and cigarette mixture the air recently carried. On the faded blue carpet sometimes sat Mad Engineer Russ Tollerfield, phasing his head, or Hermione Hawkins, the largest Australian in these threatened waters. Upstairs others, better known now and further away, played cards, watched the last agonies of an evening's television, or drank Dutch beer. The crew went to bed early on a lower deck and the guttural tongues faded. 'Someone sent me an acetate of Marc Bolan, he has a very strange voice and I don't know what to make of it, listen.' 'At last I have the Captain Beefheart LP, it's called *Safe As Milk* and I'm going to play "Sure 'Nuff" and "Yes I Do".' 'I got a nice letter today . . .'

Outside, the lights of Frinton were a reminder of another world, even, it seemed, another planet. In the swift current, a trail of debris floated off to join the moonbeams. The transmitter crackled alarmingly overhead. Kenny sat on windstained planks and listened for New York. 'That's some station in Yugoslavia.' Under the tyres the silver waves stroked uneven green paint.

The days marched towards sudden silence. Around noon the tender came and brought the world with it. The postmarks said Holloway, Liverpool, Oslo, Brentwood, Brussels, Utrecht, Chelsea, Newcastle – and meant it. The envelopes contained hearts and heads, and other shorebound envelopes carried love. There was no sadness because there was no room for it aboard. 'Liverpool two, Chelsea nil.' 'Where's Ed?' 'Clive sent me the new Doors single . . .'

This evening, as the sun set behind a shifting mist and colours slid across the calm sea, a lone seagull swooped and reeled between the veils of light. No-one misses it more than I do. I left something behind.

After the pirate stations had been closed down, there was a jubilant scene at Liverpool Street station as many of the DJs returned to a triumphant welcome from their fans. It was a big media event, packed with fans and celebrities and journalists, and John was there in his kaftan and bells and beads. All the DJs got off the train and made their way past thousands of people, none of whom looked twice at John. Just to make sure there hadn't been some kind of oversight, he strolled round to the back of the station and walked through the crowd again, and failed once more to attract anyone's attention.

John knew from the moment he joined Radio London that its days were numbered, and had taken the precaution of writing an eager-to-please letter to Radio 1 on 27 July 1967, a fact he conveniently forgot when telling people later that the station had approached him.

He had been at Radio 1 hosting *Top Gear* for just over a year when we met, and had proved immediately popular with audiences. Bands were already flocking to record the sessions that were fast becoming a staple part of the show, and to appear on the *In Concert* programmes sometimes hosted by John, which featured acts such as Elton John, Fleetwood Mac and Mott the Hoople. It was on one of the *In Concert* programmes that John inadvertently helped Pink Floyd come up with the title for one of their songs. They had written a new composition to play on the show, and were struggling with a title when they caught sight of a headline in John's newspaper: 'Atom Heart Mother'.

In a letter to John, written in 1969, David Bowie requested just such a booking on *In Concert*:

> I think I should stay out here [Bromley] for most of the
> summer, and come into town just for the gigs and the one
> or few friends that I know. Do you think we could do your
> Strand place soon? It would be nice to work so close to
> Charing Cross as my last train leaves at 12:15.

It's interesting that what began as a means with which to fill dead air – Radio 1 being restricted in its early days to the amount of hours it could devote to playing pre-recorded music (known as 'needletime') – soon grew into an indispensable element of John's format. He loved the immediacy and energy of the sessions, just as he cherished those same qualities in live broadcasting, which is why he resisted pre-recording his Radio 1 shows, even as his schedule grew increasingly punishing. John would do unprecedented things on *Top Gear* – unprecedented, that is, since the days of *The Perfumed Garden*. He would clear swathes of airtime to broadcast entire albums: he played all of Stevie Wonder's double-album *Songs In The Key Of Life* and Mike Oldfield's *Tubular Bells*, and broke the unwritten rule that records of more than four minutes in length would not be given airtime, which was especially good news for bands like Led Zeppelin and Soft Machine, for whom brevity was an alien concept.

Top Gear was the venue for some inspired one-offs well loved by listeners, such as the Christmas 1970 carol concert, at which all the usual suspects – the Faces, Marc Bolan, Ivor

Cutler, Sonja Kristina, John Walters, Robert Wyatt, and myself – squeezed into the studio to contribute our own idiosyncratic versions of 'Silent Night', 'Away in a Manger' and 'Good King Wenceslas'. In recent times, the Christmas carol concert was resurrected and became the centre of some raucous get-togethers, first at Maida Vale, and later at home. One year when John was broadcasting from the house, we had a Welsh-themed concert, with the likes of Melys and Gorky's Zygotic Mynci joining the children and me around the piano in the living room, while John contributed vocals by dashing madly back and forth between the piano and his studio at the other end of the house.

Three years after that first carol concert, John persuaded Elton John to mark Christmas by coming in for a rowdy 'pub singer' set. He wrote:

> He reacted with enthusiasm to the whole idea of playing Christmas favourites and pub singalong stuff, and he played them just as they should be done. A trio of the more sensitive Dylan songs was cheerfully butchered and then he led a gaggle of rapscallions and n'er do wells in a hideous drunken shout along of 'Your Song'.

Top Gear was popular with audiences, less so with the Radio 1 establishment. Like most of the station's management until the arrival of Matthew Bannister in 1993, there was the feeling that John catered for undesirable elements in society, and that as such he should not be indulged any more than was strictly necessary. At one meeting, the former controller Derek Chinnery even referred to John's audience as 'unemployed yobbos'. *Top Gear* was bounced around the schedules until its disappearance in 1975, but John continued to present what was in effect the same programme with his own name as the title. He also presented *Sounds of the Seventies* – billed as 'adventurous contemporary sounds' – from 1971 until the end of 1974, and hosted *Night Ride* from 1968 to 1969, as well as *In Concert*.

These changes would, by and large, be but minor disruptions to his routine compared with a change of personnel on *Top Gear* in April 1969, when Bernie Andrews was replaced as producer by John Walters, a former trumpet-player with The Alan Price Set who had made his name in radio working with Jimmy Saville on *Saville's Travels*.

John didn't like Walters at all when they first met. He was used to Bernie's way of working. Bernie had always been very serious, even reverent, about music, and their approach to putting together *Top Gear* was fairly regimented. John would often go to Bernie's house in Blackheath, where Bernie had an amazing record collection, and they would get the programme ready: they would go through the records together into the early hours, then John would sleep there. I sometimes stayed over too, but Bernie wasn't too interested in me being there, and the three of us never socialised together, the way John and I did eventually with Walters and his wife Helen. But that was just Bernie's style, and it suited John fine because they shared a very ordered, pedantic approach to compiling the show.

When Bernie was moved from *Top Gear* to work on other programmes and Walters stepped in as producer, John was not happy. From the first time they worked together, on 27 April 1969, he found Walters to be oafish and abrasive. He recalled:

I greeted his posting with the sort of enthusiasm that would have followed the news that King Herod had been chosen to supervise the crèche. Very early in our working relationship I ventured the notion – on air – that clouds were, if you like, poems in the sky and he greeted this outbreak of loveliness with spluttering disbelief. Here, I felt, was a singularly crass man.

The BBC surely couldn't have found a more jarring replacement for Bernie, but with hindsight it was exactly what John needed. His relationship with Bernie, and the whole atmosphere around *Top Gear*, had grown rather intense: it was a fine programme, but there wasn't much laughter when John and Bernie got together. I think John, and *Top Gear*, really needed the rude upheaval provided by Walters. He didn't put up with any nonsense, he said whatever was on his mind, and was baldly disparaging about much of the music favoured by John. He reserved particular opprobrium for anything even vaguely hippy-oriented; he sneered at Marc Bolan for singing like Larry the Lamb. Bernie, on the other hand, was swept along by John's enthusiasm for Marc, and had been persuaded to let Tyrannosaurus Rex record a session – the first unsigned band to be afforded that honour. Worst of all, in John's eyes, was that Walters liked going to the pub.

I warmed to Walters before John did, but in time John thawed out and grew very close to him too. After a while, they both realised that they had more in common than had first been apparent. Chiefly they shared the same sense of humour: they both idolised WC Fields, and a tremendous rapport built up between them. It was a joy seeing them together, listening to them sparking off one another. And just as John always said he prized me for telling him what a daft bugger he was, in the midst of all these ditsy girls with flowers in their hair who were hanging on his every pronouncement, so I think he valued Walters for providing a similarly salty dose of reality.

Their relationship became more harmonious as they learned how to accommodate one another. John never liked any fuss or noise in the studio while he was doing his show, and at first Walters was always in there, bothering or irritating him. We both agreed that the show usually went better whenever 'Petals', as Walters was known, wasn't there. And as they became close, the programme would usually run itself. By the early eighties, when John was doing his show four nights a week, Walters sometimes didn't even come in; he'd just stay at home and phone John during the show to check everything was going smoothly.

That was just what John wanted – a producer who would help organise the show, booking bands for sessions and whittling down John's list of records to provide a running order, but who knew how to be hands-off when that was required. They still had their occasional arguments – in his diary entry for 14 January 1971, John reports that 'Petals . . . launched into a long character assessment of me, very rude and harsh. Said my fall would be rapid. Quite hurt and retired to bed in confusion . . .' There was always an element of antagonism between them, even at their closest, but such upsets never lasted very long.

Some bands that John wanted and ultimately got for the show weren't any more to Walters' taste than T.Rex had been. He tolerated bands he didn't like because he respected John's opinion and knew that it would be for the good of the programme. And Walters made his own valuable contributions when it came to suggesting bands for sessions – it was he who rushed into work on 7 May 1983 to tell John that they had to book the Smiths, whom Walters had seen the previous evening at a show in London. John had never seen him so excited.

Walters, like Teddy Warrick before him – the assistant head of Radio 1 praised by John as 'a heroic figure to whom I owe a great deal' – and Matthew Bannister after him, proved to be a valuable ally whenever general opinion at the BBC suggested that John's days there might be numbered. John used to worry about whether or not he would be remembered, but Walters argued that John was the only thing about Radio 1 that would ultimately endure.

Socialising with Walters and Helen was always a riot. We had a ritual that we observed most weekends from back when we lived at Park Square Mews, right up to when we got married. In those days, the television schedules weren't saturated with films, so the midnight movie on Saturday night would be quite an event. We took it in turns to cook dinner for one another most Saturdays, and the rule was that the meal had to be connected in some way to the movie that was on television that night.

When the film was *The Asphalt Jungle*, the menu consisted of rock cakes, berries and some kind of 'jungle juice' – a rather lethal punch, if I'm not mistaken. For *The Three Musketeers*, an assortment of vegetables and baked potatoes were skewered on to a fencing rapier. *Where Angels Fear to Tread* was accompanied by, among other things, angel cakes and Harp lager, while for a film about drugs, the name of which escapes me, Walters and Helen cooked up a *pot* roast and then wheeled it in – at great *speed*.

Walters and Helen provided the most ingenious movie dinner

on the night when *Ice Cold in Alex* was being screened. Their flat in Croydon was unusually hot that night, since Walters had cranked up the heating to provide an authentic replication of the film's desert setting. Soon after, we were treated to a viciously spicy vegetable curry that left us gasping for a drink. Obviously lager was out of the question, at least until that famous moment in the movie when John Mills is rewarded with his own refreshing pint, so John asked if we could have a glass of water. 'Sure,' Walters piped up, 'help yourself.' John rushed to the sink, turned on the tap, held out his glass expectantly and waited. And waited. Walters and Helen began chuckling to themselves, which was when we realised that our hosts for the evening had become our tormentors: they'd turned off the water supply.

As our family grew, we socialised less with Walters and Helen, though of course John remained close to Walters, and worked with him into the nineties. Although they saw less of one another in the last few years before Walters' death, John remained terribly fond of him. They had a closeness that was quite touching to observe. John frequently characterised their relationship as being like that of a man and his dog, but with each plainly believing the other to be the dog. Walters came up with his own analogy, likening John to Eeyore from A. A. Milne's Winnie the Pooh stories. 'Everybody's having honey while he's in some damp corner of a field, alone and ignored, with nothing but thistles,' noted Walters. 'If I call to remind him that he has a programme on Bank Holiday, it's: "Everybody gets a holiday but me." If I say he's got the day off to make way for some sort of Radio 1 special, it's: "They're trying to get rid of me." Either way it's thistles and I suspect he finds them rather reassuring.'

John used to love the fact that Walters would feel compelled to ring him the instant he saw something on television that he thought would tickle him. The phone would go, usually on a Sunday morning, and if one of the children or I answered it, Walters would drawl, 'Is the man they laughingly call "Daddy" there?' Or else he would feign irritability and declare, 'No, no, I don't want to talk to him, just tell him: turn over to BBC2!' You can almost imagine it as a split-screen in a movie, with Walters and John like Rock Hudson and Doris Day in *Pillow Talk*: Walters on one side of the frame, dialling, and John lying in bed on the other side, answering.

'Hello?'

'Peel? Right. BBC1. *Now.*'

The obsession with the famously infant-phobic WC Fields went some way towards explaining why Walters didn't set foot in our house once William was born – or so John believed. But the children have fond memories of visiting Walters and Helen at their house. William was obsessed with elephants as a child, and Walters used to greet him with an enthusiastic impersonation of this favourite animal, much to William's delight. And when Thomas was learning the trumpet, Walters would goof around with various household objects, using each one in turn as a mute to discover the different sounds they created.

As with any friendship, Walters and John had their ups and downs. I know that John was upset by his friend's very public hostility towards *Home Truths*, which Walters rarely missed an opportunity to disparage. But when Walters died in his sleep in 2001, John was distraught. 'Today I feel as infantrymen in the trenches must have felt when the man beside them was hit,' he wrote in his *Radio Times* column.

The pair of them had always assumed that John would be

the first to go. Indeed, it was a running joke between them that Walters had resolved to outlast John in order to deliver the eulogy at John's funeral, detailing his faults in meticulous and whimsical detail before sending him on his way with Roy Harper's 'When An Old Cricketer Leaves The Crease'. In the event, it was John who got to play that song in a tribute programme to Walters: he scheduled it as the last track on the show because he knew he would be unable to speak by that point. Just over three years later, Andy Kershaw in turn played the song on Radio 3 at the end of a tribute programme that he recorded shortly after John's death.

John wrote in 2001:

I owe Walters more than I owe any other person in my life. He taught me that there was nothing shameful in getting things wrong from time to time, provided you remained true to some sort of ill-defined but genuinely held principles – and popped around the corner for a beer if time permitted. Whenever I have received an honorary degree or similar tribute, I have known that no more than a third of it was really mine, with a third going to Walters and a third to Sheila.

Barely half an hour before John died, he was thinking about Walters. We were having a drink in a bar in Peru when suddenly John went into a whole speech about his old friend. 'I miss him, you know,' he said. 'I miss him ringing up when there's something on telly. I haven't got another friend who does things like that. I wish I'd spent more time with him before he died.' I find that almost unbearably ironic. It was completely out of the blue.

*

Had John been more aggressive in the area of self-promotion, not to mention more slick in his presentational style, his television career might have taken off sooner than it did. In truth, he had no desire whatsoever to appear on television, at least in the sixties, and it's tempting to wonder if he didn't botch his first *Top of the Pops* appearance, back in early 1968, on purpose, rather in the fashion of someone who fluffs dinner so that they won't ever be asked to cook again.

After introducing himself as 'the one who comes on Radio 1 late at night and plays records made by sulky Belgian art students in basements dying of TB', he was supposed to say 'And here's the latest happening platter from Amen Corner' – or words to that effect. But nothing came to mind, least of all the band's name; he had gone blank. As John tiptoed towards the exit after the show had finished, the producer spotted him, stamped over and hissed, 'I'll make sure you never work in television again.' These were among the most wonderfully thrilling words John had ever heard, since he had no desire to set the world of television aflame with his talent.

As literally several people across the nation mourned the fact that John Peel Television Superstar was not a phrase ever likely to enter the popular lexicon, at least not in the late 1960s, John was busy with two radio programmes. As well as *Top Gear*, he started presenting *Night Ride* in March 1968. This was a more conversation-based show that attracted its share of controversy. The show had some notable run-ins with the government and the media. On 6 November 1968, John interviewed the satirist John Wells, author of Mrs Wilson's Diary in *Private Eye*, who made some bluntly critical remarks about the then Prime Minister, Harold Wilson, claiming that Wilson was not interested in the Nigerian war because it would cost him votes, and that he had lied about the airfield in Biafra being unusable to avoid supplying aid to that country. In the face of complaints from the government, the BBC was forced to issue an apology.

Hosting *Night Ride* helped to ratify John's position as a figure in the satirical counterculture embodied by the likes of *OZ* and *Private Eye*. He was one of a number of defence witnesses called by the editors of *OZ* – Jim Anderson, Felix Dennis and Richard Neville – in the course of their scandalous twenty-six-day obscenity trial in 1971. The trial centred around *OZ 28*, an issue of the magazine labelled 'School Kids' Issue' and featuring ribald and shocking work by twenty contributors under the age of eighteen.

The Crown rigged the trial from the start, since it was the establishment that was being challenged by *OZ* and the establishment that needed to triumph. John was expressing severe worries about the outcome a few days before the trial was due to begin. He writes on Friday 18 June:

> The *OZ* obscenity trial starts on Monday. They have no QC and today went down to apply for a week's delay in which to brief a QC. They were refused, thoroughly searched and Jim Anderson had his eye-drops confiscated. If ever anyone was convicted before they started . . . really believe this trial is the start of a period of considerable repression and nastiness. They could easily be imprisoned and then deported. Outrageous. Right-wing backlash starts here.

The following Tuesday, John took part in the march through London, from Lincoln's Inn Fields to Smithfield Meat Market, in support of *OZ*. 'Were you leading the march?' he was later asked by the prosecution. 'No, I was at the very back,' replied John with a smile, 'pushing a bicycle.'

The proceedings were a joke. The defendants were persecuted – their long hair forcibly hacked off at one point by prison guards whilst in custody awaiting sentencing – and it was clear from the off that this was a show trial. John was called, along with other defence witnesses including Marty Feldman and George Melly, to assert that there was literary or artistic merit in *OZ 28*; in particular he was asked to defend the line 'I'd love to meet a chick who could fuck like *Led Zeppelin One*, but she'd wear me out in a week.' But like everyone who appeared at the trial in an attempt to arrest this sabotage of free speech, John was doomed before he began. The court saw his long hair and T-shirt, and heard the prosecution's efforts to discredit him because he had discussed on radio his own experience of venereal disease, and that was very much that.

On 28 July, as Anderson, Dennis and Neville were waiting to be sentenced, John writes in his diary:

> Man from *Daily Mirror* interviewed me for 1½ hours – believe he was trying to be fair – re: *OZ* trial and my testimony . . . he thought they'd get 3 years. Judge very hostile indeed. Total cultural clash. He also thought Richard would be deported. What a country. Government by wankers for wankers. Very depressed by this.

In the end, Neville got fifteen months, and the judge recommended his deportation.

John's fears for the country had been realised, and his idealism dented somewhat. In court he had given a thoughtful speech about the changes he had seen since returning from America. 'In 1967,' he said, 'there was a period when we were optimistic; I really thought there was likely to be a lot of social change. People were starting to think more about one another instead of just acquiring property. Unfortunately, this has obviously turned out not to be the case, except in the area of music. Here, bands had broken away from the control of people in show-biz who manipulate everything. For example, I now have a very unsuccessful record company of my own; we have made about twelve or fifteen LPs and lost something to the order of eighteen thousand pounds. Yet we have found people whom I thought merited the attention of the public and who had something to offer. Although this has proved to be economically disastrous, we have made some nice records. But nobody's bought them.'

The following year, John notes that Neville has gone to New York to sell the musical rights of the trial to some Broadway producers. 'I hope that I get some good songs when it comes to the stage,' muses John. That idle dream may not have come to fruition, though we did watch the television dramatisation of the trial many years later, and William was impressed to see John's part being taken by Nigel Planer, who played the über-hippy Neil in *The Young Ones*.

Night Ride was as short-lived as it was inflammatory, but John was still plugging away on *Top Gear*, where he and Walters had discovered to their glee that it was surprisingly easy to be provocative: all you had to do was play songs that your listeners had never heard before. Despite John's reputation for airing new music, those audiences who clutched him to their collective bosom in the late sixties and early seventies often reacted with depressing hostility and snobbishness whenever he played something other than rock. When John included for the first time in his Radio 1 show a Jamaican record, Andy Capp's 'Pop A Top', and an African one, Sipho Bhengu's 'Tickey Dopies', he wasn't prepared for such a negative reaction. He had, his core audience claimed, sold out. But to whom, exactly? Unperturbed by this response, John and Walters programmed more reggae and went on to record BBC sessions with Bob Marley and the Wailers in the seventies.

One of John's favourite acts was the reggae band Culture, fronted by Joseph Hill, a man John considered to have one of popular music's greatest voices and a ripping line in visionary asides. Culture recorded two sessions for John's Radio 1 show and, had they so desired, would have been welcome to do hundreds more. When John curated the Meltdown Festival on the South Bank in 1998, he was especially proud about the inclusion of Culture, who played a storming gig at the Royal Festival Hall at his invitation. Indeed, reggae was probably the one ingredient that remained constant in John's shows over the decades. This despite the fact that the titles were often written in patois and John's attempts at reading them were little short of hilarious.

His inclusion of Jamaican music, along with sessions from such blues giants as Son House and Arthur Crudup, funk band Cymande and reggae kings Misty In Roots (whom he chose as one of his *Desert Island Discs*), so exercised racist elements that he received the occasional death threat. He kept one, in fact, postmarked Walsall. The correspondent, clearly a newcomer to hate mail, began 'Dear John' before getting down to some serious threatening. John was rather touched by that, but he took police advice nevertheless, since the sender had been careful to point out that he knew where our children went to school. There was also the time when a box of turds arrived for

John in the morning post from another listener outraged that his ears had been besmirched by black music. Exactly whose turds they were we never bothered to find out.

These incidents used to come to mind in later years whenever some ill-informed hack, trying to generate a bit of controversy, would accuse John of playing only white music, temporarily forgetting his passion for reggae and hip-hop. Perhaps his critics had selective or age-withered memories, and were recalling the punk era, when music was made predominantly by white boys and girls. John countered:

> Frankly, I listen to music with no concern whatever for the race, colour, religion, preference in breakfast foods, height, shoe size or whatever-you-like of the music makers. The only footling prejudice I do permit myself is this: musicians I suspect of supporting Everton or Arsenal have a bugger of a time getting their ponderous tripe on to the programme.

By the time of the OZ trials, John and I had fled London. We had been living at Park Square Mews until summer 1970, when we decided to start saving for a place of our own. This plan involved moving into my student flat at St Stephen's Gardens in Westbourne Grove with Terry and Gerry, where we lived on the money I was earning from teaching at a comprehensive in Tufnell Park, and put John's wages towards a house. The flat in Westbourne Grove was pretty grim in retrospect, though it didn't seem so at the time. But still, we felt faintly insulted when it turned up on television years later as a fine example of sub-standard housing stock, making the grimmest of slums seem beguilingly quaint.

A year earlier, John had received a letter from his father. John hadn't spent much time with him since returning from the States, though he spoke with genuine fondness about the time his father visited him over there and they drove around New England together.

When I first met John, he had little contact with his mother either. They had a rather fraught relationship. John was always very wary of his mother, and I could see that she was nervous of him too. She never knew quite how to take him. I think that was true right from when he was a boy; he was her first child, and she had been quite a naïve young mother. They got on better later, if only because I made an effort to organise things for birthdays and Christmas, whereas John had never bothered before. But there remained a lot of tension between them. Whenever she came to stay with us, she would always prepare herself to go home a good few hours before John was ready to leave. She'd be up early doing her hair and make-up, terrified that John would suddenly announce he wanted to get going and she wouldn't have her face on.

She was, as John had led me to expect, a rather formidable woman, but she was also a lot of fun – very flamboyant and theatrical. When John was working, my friend Gerry and I would sometimes call round to see John's mother. She could be great company. We would spend the afternoon drinking, gossiping, looking through old photos, drinking, laughing. Did I mention the drinking? Eventually I'd roll home even later than John.

'You're in a state,' he would say. 'Where have you been?'

'With your mother,' I'd reply. That explained everything.

When I was pregnant with William, she took me to one side and said, 'Darling, you must make sure – and this is terribly important, it's really the only thing I would stress – you must make sure that your toenails are painted before you go into hospital. There's nothing worse, darling, than giving birth and then staring down to be confronted with an awful set of unpainted toenails.' I have made a point ever since of passing on that advice to anyone I know who is pregnant.

While John's mother could be entertaining, there was also a cruel side to her that I glimpsed one evening when we were hosting a dinner party. She may have been rather chilly towards John throughout his childhood, but favouritism never really came into it – John's father was in Africa, and she was tucked away reading in what John referred to as 'the withdrawing room'. But she did give voice to her preferences, quite callously, over dinner. Fuelled by a prettily chosen Chardonnay, she broke into a pause in the conversation.

'Alan was always my favourite son. Then Francis and then . . .' She fixed John with a basilisk stare. '*You.*'

'Gee, Mom, thanks,' John said with an airy laugh. But it hurt.

John did manage to get closer to his mother in the years before her death; he would stay with her a lot when he was working in London, and by the time she died in July 1992 the fissures in their relationship had been reduced, if not quite repaired.

John also managed to make peace with his father. When I first met John, his dad had recently retired and moved to a beautiful house in North Wales. Sadly he wasn't there for more than a few months before he discovered he was dying. After John got the letter in which his father revealed that he had cancer, we started visiting him regularly. From what John had told me, I was expecting someone terrifying, but he wasn't like that at all. Maybe he had mellowed a lot, but the fellow I met was terribly sweet. He told John that when we got married – which, unfortunately, he didn't live to see happen – we should take on my family name, Gilhooly, rather than Ravenscroft, since he insisted that Gilhooly was the superior name. That was how he referred to me: Little Gilhooly.

But it was strange to see him and John together. There was a stiffness and formality about their relationship that had obviously been cast in them over the years, and which they were powerless to eschew, despite the fact that John's dad didn't have long to live. There were no kisses or hugs, not much contact at all, in fact, between this father and son. You could see that John was still frightened of his father, and that he remained desperate to impress him with stories of what he had been up to.

We stayed a lot with John's father and stepmother. When John and I slept at my parents' house, we didn't sleep together out of respect for their values. But John's stepmother went further than that. Although John was thirty at the time, she forbade him from sleeping in the house when I was there. I got the bedroom. John had the caravan in the garden.

When John's father became more ill, he stayed with John's stepsister, Carol. I think that was when the feelings of guilt and regret really hit John. For a long time after his father died in 1970, he would say how he wished he'd spent more time with him; he longed for this unattainable closeness. And those feelings profoundly influenced his attitude towards his own children. He never wanted them to feel that they hadn't spent enough time with him. Not that there can ever be such a thing as enough time.

What I remember most about the funeral is the laughter. I travelled there with John and Alan, and we were laughing so much in the car. Perhaps it was just nerves, or the close proximity of laughter and tears. But we joked all the way up there, and John was even tittering during the service.

In 1972, John returned to Liverpool for a football match, but it was a very different place from the Liverpool of his child-hood, and this helped reinforce the fact that his father, along with his past, was truly gone. He wrote on 5 February:

> I thought I'd drive around in Everton and try and find some of the places I used to know when I was going to the Shrewsbury Boys Club. The whole lot had been torn down . . . the whole of the city centre was entirely different with one-way systems and massive fly-overs and other devices. Finally found my way to the old Cotton Exchange and the entire front of it had disappeared. Being around there and thinking of my Dad made me very sad . . .

After that realisation, a kind of retrospective warmth towards his father kicked in unexpectedly. John had dug out and re-read many of his father's letters, and was beginning to see them – and his father – in a new light. Where he had read them originally as being quite detached in tone, he now under-stood that there was a subtle desperation about them. In many of the letters, his father was expressing a desire to see him more frequently, which John had overlooked on his first reading in the late sixties. John's 1975 diary contains an entry, written five years after his father's death, which crystallises his slow-dawning feelings. On 25 March, John and I went with some friends for dinner:

> As usual it fell to me to do all the ordering and I was being either witty and suave or a smart-alec depending on how you look at it. 'Just like your father,' said Pig, and whereas I'd once have been mortally offended at such a remark, I was rather

flattered. Would love to have had father stay with us down here. Always get angry and frustrated when I think of his death, rather than sad – angry that I never knew until it was far too late what a nice man he was. Although I hardly believe in an afterlife, the best aspects of such a thing would include being reunited w. Dad . . .

*

The idea of escaping London came initially from John, who, having been raised in the country, was yearning to get back there. And there was a sense that city life was becoming too intense for either of us. One night, we found a man on the balcony. He was naked and carrying an axe. That's the sort of thing that will make up your mind; to call it the straw that broke the camel's back doesn't convey adequately the sense of terror that we felt.

Actually, it was the last in a rich and diverse collection of straws. The joy of having a different young man appear at the door each night clutching a demo tape was also starting to pall around this time. What did it for John was when an entire band – America, in fact, who went on to achieve that all-important number-three spot in the charts in January 1972 with 'Horse With No Name' – turned up on our crumbling doorstep at two in the morning, bursting to sing us a selection of their songs. John was uncommonly forthright in expressing his determination to return to bed with their bleatings unheard. So that was it. Goodbye, London.

However, things didn't quite work out the way we intended. We had been looking at houses in the counties near London since before John moved in with me at St Stephen's Gardens, but we didn't have much money, and we realised that we could only afford places some distance away. I was concerned about this because I didn't want to be isolated from all my friends. And in London I could still be very involved in whatever John was doing – going along to gigs, or to his programmes.

Over the course of about eighteen months, we looked at hundreds of houses, spiralling out across the country in ever-increasing circles in John's Dormobile. I'd be teaching all week, then we'd get all the paperwork from the estate agents and drive round for the whole weekend looking at these wretched houses. We'd sleep in the Dormobile, then travel back to London on Sunday night feeling shattered.

On the weekend that we found the house we wanted, we only had three properties on our list, and the one we ended up taking was the last. We were very near to going home without even seeing it, since we were a bit put off by the fact that it was owned by a major and his wife. Then we decided it was silly to have come so far without at least taking a peek. The house was comprised of a pair of labourers' cottages knocked into one, and though it was more money than we'd bargained on paying, we decided we liked it enough to overstretch ourselves.

Everything was slotting into place nicely. John had even proposed to me, though in terms of romance the occasion probably ranks just below our yellow-jaundice evening. He came in late from his show one night in 1971, snuggled up in bed with me and said that he'd had a chat with his brother Francis over lunch.

'Oh yes?' I replied.

'Yes,' he said. 'And he thinks you and I should get married.'

'You what?'

'He told me he thinks we should get married. For financial reasons.'

I was flabbergasted. I demanded that John propose to me, on

one knee, in the conventional romantic manner. He never did, though, and I wonder now how I let him get away with that.

Somehow his businesslike proposal was allowed to stand, and we booked a date for our wedding – 1 April 1972. In his diary, John writes of breaking the news to my parents, who were at that stage still less than ecstatic about the idea of us being together:

> Pig and the rest of the gang went off to Mass, and I got up and read the papers for a bit and wondered how I was going to broach the subject of marriage. Did the washing-up and sat around a bit more. When everyone got back I sat there in the hope that I'd get everyone except the Pig's Mum and Dad out of the room . . . Finally I said, 'I think I'd better tell you that Sheila and I are planning to get married.' At first neither of them reacted at all so I said it again and the Pig's mother just said, 'Are you?' Eventually we settled down to discuss and they were very amiable about it – as I'd forecast – with Mr G. being a bit more flexible than Mrs . . . They were really quite nice about it – they admitted they'd been expecting it all for some time anyway – but could hardly be expected to be bursting with glee and huge enthusiasm.

After we'd passed that hurdle, there was an even bigger obstacle waiting for us. Shirley had written to John saying that she had decided to withdraw her signature from the divorce papers. John had no inkling that this was going to happen. He was absolutely heartbroken, and it took him an awfully long time to get over it. But in the end, it worked out better that we married two years later, on 31 August 1974 (the day after John's birthday, thereby minimising the chances of him forgetting our anniversary). By then, the rift between John and my parents had been comprehensively mended, through their systematic and prolonged exposure to the Peelian charms. My father was therefore happy to give me away at the wedding; perhaps he thought of it as not so much losing a daughter as gaining a hippy with a plastic mouse dangling from his trousers.

A rather touching friendship developed between John and my father, which felt all the more remarkable and precious given that they had got off to the worst possible start. John wrote in 1999:

> I was amazingly lucky in my in-laws. Sheila's dad, Denis, is the only person I've met who genuinely thought about other people before he thought about himself. I knew from the moment I first saw them together as a family that his death would be the darkest event in our lives. Sheila's hardly sombre, but she's a much more serious person since her dad died.

I'm just grateful that my father walked down the aisle with me: I never dreamed, during the years when things were frosty between John and my parents, that this would happen. So in one sense, Shirley did us a favour. Not that it felt like that at the time. To make matters worse, when Shirley did eventually consent to the divorce, she took every penny John had. She was in Holloway prison at the time, and had been allowed out for the day to come to the hearing. John and I had been naïve. We'd lived on my money and saved his, whereas we should have done it the other way round. I felt sick when John's money was turned over to her. But John didn't. He was just relieved that it was all over. He said, 'She can have everything. I don't care.'

In his will, John's father had left each of his sons around five thousand pounds, and in the wake of Shirley's court victory over John, this money secured us the house in the country that we would otherwise have been unable to buy. We took the place on as a risk, believing that we'd probably need to defer on the mortgage eventually, and lived here at weekends while keeping the flat on in London. For a long time there was no furniture, tea chests everywhere, nothing in the bedroom except a mattress. It wasn't until Christmas 1971 that we both admitted to each other that we hated going back to London every Sunday night. Just before we left on that return journey, we'd both get a bit sulky, knowing we wanted to live in the country. We had put down our roots.

John has said that he knew then that he wanted to remain here for the rest of his life. 'You should move every four or five years to gain maximum economic benefit,' people would tell us. And then, once the children started to arrive: 'It is broadening for them to experience living in different parts of the country.' 'That's interesting,' we would reply, completely uninterested.

We decided I should stop teaching, since John was earning enough by then for us not to need my income. We weren't wealthy, but we didn't have the children, and our overheads were low. It wasn't quite paradise at first – not for me, anyway. In fact, I came to hate it. I couldn't drive, I was on my own throughout the middle of the week, I'd never lived in the country before and I didn't know anyone. The village was populated largely by people born and bred in Suffolk. They weren't used to strangers, let alone strangers who had long hair and sex out of wedlock – or perhaps it was long hair out of wedlock they disapproved of – and we had to become accustomed to their strange behaviour as much as they had to ours.

I used to sit in at night watching television on my own and think: What have I done? I was missing out on all the excitement in London, and I thought I'd made one hell of a mistake. But by the following summer, we had got to know people, and suddenly we were having a good time, going to the pub, enjoying our harmonious new life. John wrote a sweet article in January 1973, perfectly capturing the flavour of what had been our second Christmas in the village, but our first as part of the community:

The Mighty Pig and I had one of our best Christmases ever. We seem, in some miraculous way, to have landed in one of the nicest villages in the British Isles. On Friday the 23rd we went up to the pub at the top of the road to celebrate what our mate John had declared to be the Start of Christmas. On Christmas Eve the pub closed at ten thirty. Now a country pub like this isn't one of those sombre places where morose men sit in pools of watery beer and drink themselves insensible. It's more of a community centre where you go to see your old friends and make new ones. At weekends, because there is no knowledge or understanding of rubbish like generation gaps here, Pig and I play Snip Snap Snorum with some of the wondrous old men who use the pub. Sometimes another old fellow plays the harmonica and everyone sings the old songs he plays. It is a genuine joy to escape from the horrors of London to a place like this and we count ourselves very fortunate.

As I said, on Christmas Eve the pub closed at ten thirty and thirty or more of the customers came down to our cottage to see in Christmas Day. We talked and drank and danced until after four o'clock and during that time there wasn't a voice raised in anger, no-one became obnoxiously drunk, not a single glass was broken nor were any cigarettes trampled out on the floor. Small things, yes . . . but the sort of small things that make this a lovely place to be.

We also became close friends with the artist Laurie Self, who was the most idiosyncratic and, for a while, feared resident of the village. Laurie had transformed his house into a kind of hippy commune cum artists' hangout, and for that reason he was regarded with wariness by some of the other villagers. But John and I considered him and his wife Ashe to be excellent company, and John really looked up to him. Laurie was a big, bright fellow with a rumbling voice; he was also an inspired artist, if somewhat reluctant to sell his work. Whenever he did, it was at a price that John usually couldn't afford. But we do now have some of Laurie's paintings hanging in the house. John even arranged to have Laurie's work on display in the foyer of the Royal Festival Hall during his two-week Meltdown Festival.

The pair of them used to go cycling together on epic expeditions, during which Ashe, the children and I would drive on ahead and wait for them at the pub. After these spectacular exertions, John and Laurie would usually collapse on the sofa at home, to be discovered by the rest of us curled up together like slumbering bears.

It was such a blow for John when Laurie died at the end of 2001. It would have been upsetting enough at the best of times, but he was still grieving from Walters' death six months earlier. With two of his most beloved chums gone, John felt increasingly paranoid that he didn't have any friends. I feel sad now that in preparing to write this book, John had failed in his attempts to trace some of his old friends from the US. Failed is perhaps too harsh a word – one of his former colleagues did write back, though regrettably the letter only reached the house a few months after John died. As someone who felt as if his time in that country had been a dream, I'm sure it would have pleased John to know he had left some footprints in the US, and some kind of mark on the people he met there.

Once we were more settled in the village, things improved immeasurably. I was still going to London with John as often as I could. Since the unhappy end of our friendship with Marc, we both felt wary of socialising with musicians, but it was hard to resist the Faces, with whom we were always guaranteed to have a great night out. They were what can only be described as real good-time lads. They can also share joint credit, along with John Walters and myself, for getting John back into drinking again. He didn't touch drink at that point, having been through a stage of getting smashed on bourbon every night when he was in America and having resolved to clean himself up.

But after a few years of abstinence, he was ready to enjoy alcohol again. He would see the Faces and realise that they were drinking and having fun, and he wanted to be part of that too. They never went anywhere without a few crates of Blue Nun. That's one of the memories I have of the time John and I flew with them to Rotterdam for a gig – it was just us, the band, and Blue Nun.

The Faces actively cultivated that atmosphere of bonhomie; it was what they were about, as musicians and as people. We became very friendly with them. John would go to Rod

Stewart's for dinner, and one time they attended a match at Millwall together. To avoid autograph hunters, Rod had a scarf wrapped round his face, with his nose protruding over the top of it like Concorde. He climbed out of the car and the first lad who walked past called out, 'Hi, Rod.'

The band did various programmes for John. There was the Thursday night *In Concert* show recorded at the Paris Theatre in Lower Regent Street. After the sound check we all went with the band to the pub round the corner, The Captain's Cabin, while the audience were queuing up. After a few drinks, Rod insisted on standing up and singing at the top of his voice, but received short shrift from the landlord.

'You'll have to shut up or leave,' the fellow warned him.

'Don't you know who that is?' someone piped up. 'He's Rod Stewart!'

'I don't care who he is,' replied the singularly unimpressed landlord. 'I haven't got an entertainment licence.'

Rod later dragged John along with him to *Top of the Pops* for the famous performance of 'Maggie May' for which John was required to mime playing the mandolin. The Musicians' Union was livid about this: John had to guarantee that the band hadn't offered him any payment, and the cameramen were ordered not to get John into shot. When Rod Stewart heard about this he made sure that he was always capering about behind him, so that if he was on screen then John would be too.

At the end of John's 1971 diary, he writes of being at my parents' house over Christmas and turning on the television to see a repeat of his big moment. 'Turned over to see myself playing mandolin with the Faces on *Top of the Pops*. Very funny to sit and watch it again. God bless them for giving us such joy during 1971.'

In March 1973, the band invited us to the playback of their album, *Ooh La La*. John wrote in *Disc and Music Echo*:

> At the door comes Ron Lane, kisses the Pig and throws his arms around us with much shouting . . . Various Faces run hither and yon debating the track order for the LP . . . More bottles of wine appear, the Pig and I discuss Manchester United with Ron and watch Kenny teaching his tiny baby the rudiments of drumming . . . I'm busy angling for an invitation to a forthcoming Faces gig in Holland and miss a lot of the music. 'You can come if you promise not to introduce us,' says Mac . . . Through the uproar the Pig and I recall hearing two excellent Lane songs and some astonishing moments on other things we never got round to identifying. No-one seemed entirely sure of any of the titles anyway . . . But as far as we can remember, *Ooh La La* is as good an LP as Liverpool are a football team – and, as you know, you can say no more than that.

John's friendship with the band was important to him, possibly because they made him feel like an insider, like part of their gang. One thing he dreaded was being regarded as just another music-business leech. That might explain why he took it so much to heart when the Byrds blanked him, or when the Mothers of Invention failed to let him in on their peace-pipe pow-wow. ('They were all smoking and didn't offer young Peel any,' he writes on 21 September 1967. 'Enraged. Just walked in and one of them said, "What's he doing in here?".')

On 20 October 1967, he visited the Arts Lab in Drury Lane, and wrote in his diary:

Many creative people there, so I felt my usual pangs of inferiority coming on. In the presence of so many talented, creative and constructive people on the underground scene I feel that I'm regarded as something of a hanger-on and bore. I hope this is not so because I want people to realise that I'm doing as much as I can in my foolish way to further their several courses.

The same concerns are palpable in a piece that John wrote for *Disc and Music Echo* in December 1972, detailing his adventures on tour with the Faces. The article begins in quite a rambunctious manner, but soon John's fears about the way others view him start to emerge:

In all the years I've been involved with the glamorous world of rockaboogie, I have had an unholy dread of being thought of as a hanger-on. For this reason I stay well out of the way of my heroes, cower when confronted with them and, even when I have their home phone numbers, would never dream of calling them. However, the Faces are different and for the first time I thought I'd try to attach myself to a tour so that I could (1) spend time with them and (2) enjoy their excellent music . . . They all assured me that I wasn't, as I believed, being a massive pain in the arse by inviting myself along. Having lost a lot of mates to the giddy whirl of show-biz over the years it was quite gratifying and in a way quite touching to see that the Faces have managed to remain generous and down-to-earth.

By the time the band's gig in Blackpool reached its raucous climax, John had become quite overwhelmed by the sense of occasion and, I think, by the band's enthusiastic acceptance of him.

Backstage a mass of Blackpool's finest had suddenly materialised, but even the presence of the law couldn't blunt the energy that was being generated . . . It was a real pleasure to feel again that feeling that comes only when a band is really hitting it right, when it seems as though some unseen hand is reaching right down inside you and dragging out all the hang-ups and inhibitions in there and flinging them away . . . Being an over-emotional sort of twerp and being a dark, whirling mess of inhibitions myself, I was dancing quietly in the corner of the backstage area with tears streaming down my cheeks and an idiot grin on my face.

It seems such a stark contrast to the way Marc Bolan eventually made John feel – which was, in a word, disposable. After Marc, he was very careful about the friendships he had with musicians. Beefheart was long-distance, and so required little investment. John was friends too with Viv Stanshall, who did frequent sessions for him, first as part of The Bonzo Dog Doo-Dah Band, then later in the guise of Sir Henry. I think there was a wild, outgoing quality about Beefheart and Viv that John really wished he possessed.

Viv would do outrageous things, like showing up at the London club Talk of the Town in a collar and tie and bare chest, having adhered pedantically to the dress code, which demanded only a tie. It might not sound too outlandish by modern standards, but there was something about the straight-faced aplomb with which Viv would execute these stunts that made them very striking. John would have loved to be like him. He gravitated towards those kinds of people – Viv, John Walters, Beefheart. He hated the fact that he had no confidence. As a couple we were both pretty pathetic – we'd always be the ones hiding in the corner. John sometimes couldn't even cope with visiting a restaurant for the first time; he'd push me in, and then shuffle in behind me.

The one exception was when he entered record shops – he could go into any one, anywhere in the world, and feel immediately at home. In those instances, I was the one who had to be dragged in, and who couldn't wait to leave.

He was often asked about his roster of celebrity friends by interviewers who apparently laboured under the misapprehension that he was forever going ten-pin bowling with George Michael or helping Courtney Love with those difficult interior-design decisions. Nothing of the sort. John was resolutely unstarry in his choice of chums, which is not to say that he wasn't occasionally dazzled by the floodlight-beam of celebrity – he could be heard grumbling about his own foolishness in not having asked Muhammad Ali for an autograph when he found himself alongside him at the studios of Thames Television (though Damon Albarn did eventually get John a signed photograph of Ali). And there was the time when we went to dinner with Nick Mason of Pink Floyd, though in all honesty the evening didn't show us at our best. John and I were terribly nervous, we couldn't understand what our fellow guests were talking about and weren't sure how to eat the excellent fondue and artichokes we were served.

John would probably have accumulated more celebrity telephone numbers in his Rolodex if only he'd learned to do some proper bowing and scraping. But his attitude towards celebrity ranged from amused to disparaging. It could have been so different. John might have enjoyed summers eating skinless grapes on yachts anchored off remote Caribbean islands, or winters sipping cocktails on the slopes at St Moritz, if only he had bothered to interrupt the phone conversation he was having with me the day that Mick Jagger popped his head round the door at Radio 1. Mick was apparently livid to find that awestruck worship was not forthcoming from John. So livid was he, in fact, that he stormed out of the BBC. It's quite big, so it takes a fair bit of storming from. He must have stormed for a good five minutes or so to get clear of the building.

Perhaps it's just as well John didn't mix with too many high-flying types, since when he did get round to talking to them, he could usually be relied upon to put his foot in his mouth. Sue Lawley, who had interviewed John on *Desert Island Discs* in 1989, once took him under her wing when he was getting in a tizzy about attending a heavy-duty BBC lunch. She allowed him to shadow her until he developed enough confidence to strike out on his own, and she introduced him to some of the grandees clustered about her. Later, as they sat down for a slap-up feed, John felt brash enough to turn to a somewhat ascetic-looking chap alongside him.

'Hello,' he said cheerfully. 'I'm John Peel.'

'I know,' the fellow replied. 'Sue Lawley introduced us five minutes ago. I'm still John Birt.'

Not everyone was so cool in the face of John's warmth. He was much taken with Courtney Love, and thoroughly approved of Alexandra's efforts in her late teens to actually turn into the Hole singer, though he did express mild concern at her habit of affecting a Courtney-esque lack of clothing when she sought fun in Stowmarket. John was introduced to Courtney at the Reading Festival by Kat Bjelland, singer with the wonderful and much-missed Babes In Toyland. 'John,' said Kat, 'this is my best friend, Courtney,' after which John got a fleeting impression of lots of lipstick and giggling and bare flesh.

The following year, he was leaning coquettishly in the VIP area at Reading with Alexandra and Flossie, hoping to catch Courtney before Hole took to the boards. When she came into view she appeared to be in an advanced state of intoxication. She spun and wheeled and stumbled about until she caught sight of the three of them. 'Hello, Mr Peel,' she cried respectfully. 'Hello, Courtney,' said John, ever the master of the snappy riposte. 'These are my daughters and they would like very much to meet you.' With that, Courtney grew suddenly calm, squatted with them on the grass and wrote them each little notes, more letters than autographs, in which she wished them well and advised them to miss her band and pop off instead to see Pavement, who were playing on another stage and whom she considered to be the far superior outfit. Then she smiled, stood up and carried on spinning, wheeling and stumbling, knocking over an adjacent rubbish bin as she went. It is no exaggeration to say that John felt oddly protective of her after that.

The assumption that John had 'Friend of the Stars' printed in the 'Occupation' box on his passport was shared by our insurance broker. John was maddened by this, particularly when it stopped him from being insured on his fourth 1963 Chevrolet Impala, which slept in the shed. The general view, it seems, was that he went everywhere with the car laden with top stars – 'Hiya, Madonna. Fancy a spin? Do you know Metallica? Move over lads and let her in' – and that if he so much as reversed over a woodlouse, everyone would sue everyone else. Many were the nights when he would wonder how footballers driven half-mad with money, cocaine and testosterone could get insured on Ferraris while he was forced to do nothing more reckless with his Chevy Impala than caress its inviting contours.

And how, come to that, did his former Radio 1 colleague Dave Lee Travis get insurance for his muscular Dodge Hemi Charger with its DLT1 numberplate and pictures of the Hairy Cornflake himself emblazoned tastefully on the doors? When John asked him about it, Dave did admit that it got vandalised a lot. 'I'd vandalise it myself if I thought I could get away with it,' John said. Dave thought he was joking.

John tried explaining to the broker that the longest journey he had planned was the fifty miles or so to the Denver sluice in Norfolk, and he was only doing that so if anyone asked he could say without fear of contradiction that he drove his Chevy to the levee, but it made no difference to stony-hearted non-insurers. He even mentioned that the most famous person who had ever been in one of our cars was Loudon Wainwright III, whom John had driven the short distance to Stowmarket station. 'Loudon Wainwright III?' he was asked. 'Who are they?' Sorry, Loudon.

The family has stayed in touch with Loudon since the 1970s, and we remain huge fans of his music, not least the album *T-Shirt*, which features this splendid couplet from 'At Both Ends': 'Who needs love, who wants romance/ I want to eat your underpants.' At their first meeting, John behaved like a bumbling oaf in Loudon's presence. In 1976, he wrote:

I've met Loud – as we who know him intimately call him – several times before, and have always been faintly appalled by my own inability to make anything remotely approaching normal conversation with him. As it is with people whose work I admire, I find myself saying things of quite breathtaking stupidity to him, wondering the while why it is that I am standing with my feet pointed inwards and why I have tried three times to lean against a wall that clearly isn't there. Afterwards I sit dumb-founded in whichever racer I have brought down for the day, trying to discover why it is that I do these things. You may have heard the often comical consequences of this rather special weediness when I have been compelled to discuss their new albums with the great on Radio 1.

That particular evening ended with John attempting to give Loudon the benefit of his wisdom: 'I told him that the wisest course was to change his name to Cat Sick and get into punk, but I think he may well ignore this fatherly advice.'

Someone else who has been a constant friend is Robert Wyatt, formerly of Soft Machine. Like Walters, and for a time Rod and Marc, Robert was one of those buoyant souls around whom John and I felt at our happiest and most relaxed. Even his terrible fall in 1973, which left him confined to a wheel-chair, did not dim greatly his spirits, as attested by John's memory of visiting him at Stoke Mandeville hospital mere weeks after the accident:

When I first trotted north to peer at Robert in his hospital bed I was rendered almost inarticulate by the circumstances of his accident. What sort of light conversation do you have with someone who is that seriously injured? The fact that Robert has been a friend for a number of years seemed to make it even harder. Curiously he seemed less affected by the whole business than I was.

There's something about Robert – a sort of questing, wide-eyed-innocent-abroad quality – that has always made the Pig and I feel very protective towards him. Supremely silly, really, as he's invariably shown a capacity for coping with and adjusting to traumatic changes of circumstances much better than I could. As a result I'd decided by yesterday that his adjustment to the fact that he can no longer walk or drum stemmed from some mystical inner power to rationalise to the point where his incapacity became merely interesting.

When I rather condescendingly trotted out this weighty tripe he quickly disabused me by observing that much worse things had happened to him in his life and his sole philosophy as far as his accident went was 'hum, bloody typical!' He's a man for whom the Pig and I have a considerable respect and affection. Therefore it's good to know that his scaly little head is sizzling with musical notions and schemes, and that the chances are good that some of these latter will be translated into vinyl.

And they were, with spectacular results. In September 1974, less than ten months after John visited him in hospital, Robert kicked off his solo career by recording a four-song session for the programme that included his now-legendary stripped-down take on the Monkees' 'I'm A Believer'. Perhaps, though, it is the song he wrote about our house which will always mean the most to me.

Robert and his wife Alfie remain among our dearest and most loving friends, and John respected Robert enormously. When he arrived for my fiftieth birthday party, the field was so muddy that his wheelchair didn't have a hope of making it across, so Thomas and his pal Nick carried him, neither having any real idea of the identity of their cargo until John crept up behind them and said, 'Do you realise you're carrying one of the greatest men alive?' John demonstrated further his admiration for Robert by making him one of only two people whose photograph has pride of place on the kitchen wall. We have a large framed picture of Bill Shankly hanging there, into the corner of which John has inserted a snap of Robert, staring out sagely from behind his generous beard.

By 1972, John and I felt so much a part of village life that we established a youth club for the various degenerates, wastrels and cutpurses who were milling around dreaming of one day finding some paint that they might be permitted to watch drying. In fact, we provided that very opportunity, when we got them to paint the back rooms of the village hall, where we had been allowed to hold the youth club. Not that we called it anything as commonplace as a youth club. The ambition and grandeur of our undertaking was announced by the name we gave it: Great Finborough International Airport.

The kids chose to paint it black. The colour scheme was brightened a little with the introduction into those back rooms of a pool table, an old jukebox, table football and a dartboard. We joined the Suffolk Association of Youth Clubs and made it all official, after which we had a programme of activities and outings that I'm betting wasn't matched anywhere else in the country. Who else can say, for example, that their youth club gave them occasion to put on their body glitter and stack heels for a concert by Sparks? In recent years, John showed a stubborn reluctance to use his celebrity status to acquire freebies, but back in the days of organising nights out for the youth club, he would ring up the record company and ask if he could bring some people along to the show with him. A Plus-1 is a common demand in the music industry. The press offices of London's record companies can't have fielded too many calls, though, requesting a Plus-25.

Parents were initially dubious about allowing their children to be exposed to our idea of entertainment, but there weren't any voices of dissent once we were up and running. We had our own football team – I'd be there first thing on a Sunday morning, marking out the pitch, and we'd play away games all over the county. There would be gigs at the village hall – Be-Bop Deluxe played there on one occasion, with me on the door as bouncer.

All things considered, the youth club was a spectacular little enterprise. We took the kids away on some adventurous camping trips, possibly our most ambitious being in 1975, when we took them to the former Yugoslavia while I was five months pregnant with William. We had bought our own minibus for the youth club, but we didn't think it would survive to the end of the holiday, so we hired one, which was driven by Phil, a friend of mine from my teaching days, while John and I took our Range Rover.

We headed down through the Alps, with the majority of the children in the minibus and the overspill following behind in the Range Rover with John and me. There were lots of hairpin bends, and when we stopped in a lay-by, Phil said that he felt uncertain about the bus – it didn't seem to be driving right. We all expressed concern about this, but no-one seemed quite sure what to do. We had to press on, after all, so we climbed back into the vehicles, albeit rather more reluctantly than before.

John and I were still driving behind when we saw that the kids in the back of the bus were waving at us. This seemed puzzling until we noticed that they looked terrified: they were frantically trying to get our attention. The distance between the bus and our Range Rover was increasing steadily before we realised that something was very wrong. That's when the problem hit us. The brakes on the minibus had failed.

The bus was quickly gaining momentum, and John made a few courageous attempts to overtake it. I don't think he was sure exactly what he was going to do, but he knew he needed to get in front of it. He was impressively calm as he slammed his foot on the accelerator and managed to manoeuvre the Range Rover alongside the bus, before swerving it into Phil's path just as another nasty bend came into view. John then slowed slightly, allowing the bus to nudge against our bumper. The first few times it made contact, the impact was so dramatic that John almost lost control of the wheel; I felt the back wheels wobble and skid, and dug my nails into the seat.

But John steadied himself, toyed judiciously with the brake and began drawing the minibus to a steady crawl. Eventually John led the bus over into a lay-by and suddenly we were at a standstill again after what felt like hours. It took a moment for us to catch our breath, and for it to hit me just how brave John had been. I climbed out of the car in time to see Phil leap from the minibus, ashen-faced, and throw up.

Another youth-club trip, to Wales the previous summer, took place just three weeks before our wedding. I should have been putting the finishing touches to the placecards at that point. Instead I was in the middle of a field, listening on a tinny radio to the news that Nixon had resigned, and then to John's show, for which he had driven back to London for the night. Meanwhile my old flatmates Terry and Gerry were staying at the house, looking after our sheepdog Woggle and posting out all the wedding invitations I'd made. It was a big wedding, but I can't say honestly that it was meant to be that ambitious.

Looking back on it now, it seems to have happened with scarcely a whisker of planning on our part. I know I ordered the cake – in red and white, of course, with a pair of pigs on top – only a week before the wedding. Our friends Teddy and Peggy Warrick organised the venue and the catering. In fact, there wouldn't have been a wedding – at least not one as lovingly organised as it was – without Teddy and Peggy. As well as being one of John's staunchest defenders and allies at Radio 1, Teddy was also a very dear friend of ours. He and Peggy spent a lot of time at our home over the years, and the children always thought of them as an extra pair of grandparents.

We were married at St Paul's Church in Lorrimore Square, near the Oval. It might seem like a strange choice of venue, given that the Oval had not figured prominently in either of our lives, but in the end it came down less to where we wanted to get married than where we would be allowed to. John had had some rather heated theological debates with the Bishop of Ipswich and St Edmundsbury about whether, having been married to Shirley, he would be permitted to marry again. Perhaps the Bishop had reached breaking point when he blurted out finally that, yes, John could get married, but not in his diocese. 'Ah,' replied John, 'so it's a matter of geography rather than theology?'

It was becoming too troublesome to wed in our neck of the woods, so we turned instead to Henry Morgan, the assistant vicar at the Oval, with whom John had been friends since coming to Cambridge to give a talk when Henry was still training. The only stipulation in this arrangement was that I had to pretend that I'd been living in his vicarage for a certain number of months before the wedding. Choosing a venue for the reception was also a matter of requesting favours and pulling strings. Since everything had been left until the eleventh hour, Teddy asked his sister, who worked at Bedford College, to arrange for us to have the reception there; such things were only countenanced for relatives of employees, so Teddy's sister pretended that I was her ward of court, and the do went ahead. It was a gorgeous building, with the grounds rolling away towards the river; it couldn't have been any more wonderful.

Between them, John, Teddy and John Walters sorted out the wine and catering. John also arranged for fifty people from the village, including members of Great Finborough International Airport, to travel down to the wedding on a bus, which he had generously stocked with a crate of champagne to ensure they were in high spirits by the time they hit London. On the way to our St Paul's, they stopped at St Paul's Cathedral, which was, as far as I know, an example of impromptu sightseeing rather than a mix-up.

We stayed with Walters and Helen at their home in Surrey the night before, then Helen and I went to Peggy's house on the morning of the wedding. I arrived at the church in Helen's Volkswagen Beetle – late, of course. The place was packed. Aside from family, there were a few select colleagues from Radio 1 like Johnnie Walker, Alan Freeman and Terry Wogan. Robert Wyatt and Ivor Cutler were there, and Roger Chapman from Family. There was our good friend Fachtna O'Kelly, a very kind and amusing fellow we'd met in Dublin in 1970 when he was working for the *Irish Press*, who remained a regular visitor to our home. Fachtna went on to manage the Boomtown Rats and Sinead O'Connor, though these impressive achievements were arguably dwarfed by the sterling job he did of hacking through the undergrowth in our garden when we first moved in.

All of the Faces came to the wedding, with their families. The cine film shows Rod Stewart spending the whole time talking to John's Aunt Ailsa. We never did find out what in God's name they were nattering about. John's mother was wearing a dress that looked like a deckchair; he made a point of telling her that too. And our dog Woggle was our bridesmaid. She had stayed with my friends Phil and Janie the night before, and they'd groomed her and dressed her in red ribbons.

John wore a suit of Liverpool red, and I wore a white dress with red trimmings, and carried a bouquet of white lilies and red roses. Walters was best man, and countered the Liverpool theme by wearing black and white in honour of Newcastle. It seems incredible now as I look through a battered suitcase of mementoes from the wedding, but we made the front page in several newspapers. Not just *Sounds*, which slapped us on the cover that week, but the *Sunday Express* and the *East Anglian Daily Times*. The report that accompanied the snaps in some of the papers had John's editorial fingerprints all over it:

Mr Peel is the secretary and self-confessed 'labourer' of the Great Finborough and District Youth Club, while Miss Gilhooly is the treasurer. A reception for 150 guests, held at The Holme, Regent's Park, London, included 50 guests from Great Finborough, who travelled down that morning in a bus. The bride's travelling clothes were a pair of blue jeans and an *OZ* 'Obscenity Trial' T-shirt. Their honeymoon was spent at the home of the best man in Wallington, Surrey, watching *Match of the Day* on television. Mr Peel, who describes himself as 'The World's Most Boring Man', has been voted Britain's top DJ in a poll run by a magazine for seven years, while Miss Gilhooly, a former teacher in London, is described as an enthusiastic mountaineer.

The service itself was an exceptionally tearful affair. It was emotional enough having my father there to give me away, which is what I had wanted so badly. He was a very wise and sensible man, but I could see he was quite overwhelmed by the size of the occasion. He just looked at me before we began our walk down the aisle and said, 'You look lovely, lass.'

During the service, John got up in the pulpit and read from one of his favourite passages, St Paul's Letter to the Corinthians – and cried as he did so. Then we left to the sound of 'You'll Never Walk Alone' booming out on the organ. It was incredibly moving, and I was so nervous throughout that I hadn't given any thought to what might be waiting for us as we came down the steps of the church. There were banks of photographers there, and all you could hear was the clicking of their cameras. I was flabbergasted. I didn't know how to handle it, so I just smiled and clung on to John. This wedding that had started out so low-key was suddenly nothing of the sort.

We had decided beforehand that we didn't want the reception clogged up with lots of speeches, so Walters was the only person who delivered one, and then everyone just partied into the evening. Most of the guests got pretty wrecked; some of them were careering down the green and leaping into the Thames. It was a beautiful day, and a golden evening; the sun was striking the side of the college, and warming the riverbank. I was so happy.

The finale was an evening with Walters and Helen, who had devised an ambitious theatrical 'happening' with which to entertain us on our wedding night. We had already had our official honeymoon with them, four months earlier in April 1974, when the four of us had spent a fortnight in Egypt. That was a wonderful holiday, though the moments that linger in the memory are notable mostly for their oddness. In the absence of vegetarian alternatives, John and I subsisted on endless meals of toast, eggs and cheese, arranged in various permutations, while Walters and Helen didn't seem to enjoy their grander meals any more than us, since they spent most of the time wondering if they were tucking into roast camel. John and I were always useless on holidays – at least those that weren't BBC trips with itineraries and properly informed tour guides – which may explain why a journey into Cairo to experience the true nightlife of Egypt ended with us all drinking Nescafé in a faux-French restaurant. Of course, one of the highlights for John was exploring the local record shops, which he made certain he did on our first morning there. A few of the singles he picked up by local musicians even found their way on to the show back home.

That was the first honeymoon. The second honeymoon was spent in the company of Walters and Helen at their Georgian-style townhouse in Surrey. For some weeks before our wedding, Walters had been dragging Helen out of bed every morning at seven, insisting that they rehearse what became known internationally as 'The Wedding Night Pantomime' before they both travelled to work in London. All I can say now is that it was well worth the effort.

John and I were furnished with wine and nibbles and seated at the far end of the sitting room, while the other end was lit by some kind of badly rigged spotlight. Dressed in an assortment of garish colours, Walters and Helen staggered through their big song-and-dance number called 'Another Opening, Another Show'. A costume change – Helen in rollers and pinny, Walters in high-waisted baggy trousers, vest, belt and braces – announced the start of 'the Geordie Sketch', for which they dragged out a table covered with a red gingham cloth, a teapot and a pair of cracked mugs, and grumbled their way through an extended Pete-and-Dud-style exchange. If a Broadway producer had happened to be passing through their living room that night, Walters and Helen would surely have been signed up for a career of opening nights, bouquets and champagne, for the pleasures came thick and fast: a jolly trumpet solo from Walters, various comedy sketches, and a climactic rendition of 'We'll Meet Again'. Even the interval was a performance in itself, with choc-ices served on a stainless-steel tray by Helen with a paper doily clipped to her hair.

The rest of that sublime evening was spent talking and laughing while the wine and champagne kept flowing. Finally we retired to bed. Within two minutes, there was an insistent knocking at the door. It was Walters, shouting, 'Have you done it yet?'

Life might not have changed overnight once we were married, but our circumstances were transformed as we thought about starting a family. Until then, our only child had been Woggle, upon whom we lavished untold affection. She was, to put it mildly, a spoilt brat. When John read that David Bowie had started fan clubs for his wife and son, he briefly considered founding one for Woggle – the 'Woggle (A Dog) Fan Club', which would entitle members to a piece of paper on which Woggle (A Dog) had recently stepped, an irregular bulletin on her dietary habits, and hospital reports on the local children she had bitten or knocked over.

Then there were the members of Great Finborough International Airport, who were our extended family. The youth club lasted until 1978 under our watch, but by then we both had too much going on in our lives to devote the necessary time to it. Our own family, which had begun its steady progress, was keeping me busy. Our first daughter, Alexandra Mary Anfield, more commonly known as Danda, was born in December 1977, a few months before we left the youth club; our son, William Robert Anfield, was nearly two years old by this time, having edged his way uncomfortably into the world in January 1976.

He had been William long before he was born, chiefly due to our affection for the *Just William* stories, which had been banned at John's school, but which I used to read to him when we were curled up in bed at night. Looking back at John's 1975 diary, it's clear that neither of us entertained seriously the possibility that we might have a daughter. On 11 May, when we were not yet certain that I was even pregnant, he writes:

> I'm quite sure that Pig has a William building inside her, have been for some time in fact. What we'll do if she has a girl I don't know. You can hardly call a girl William Anfield and hope to retain her undying love and devotion.

William was a difficult birth for me, and I had to be rushed into theatre during labour. John had a nosebleed on the way up, and after I'd come round, before I even knew whether we'd had a girl or a boy – or, for that matter, if it was alive or dead – I asked John: 'Are you all right, darling?' That was the first thought that popped into my head.

The first time I saw William, he was in an incubator, and I'd been taken up to intensive care in a wheelchair to see him. John wrote in the *Sounds* column dedicated to William:

What with one thing and another, he was steered out with a pair of pliers whilst his mother was unconscious, and sped straight away into an incubator from the doctor's gore-stained workbench. However, both parties seem to have recovered from the ordeal pretty well, although the Pig walks with circumspection, and William still looks rather more like Edward G. Robinson than either me or her. I have spoken, privately, to some of our more observant neighbours and they have all assured me that they haven't seen Edward G. loitering around the area at all, at least, not during the past twelve months.

So far William has refrained from speaking to me personally, although he has responded to a delicately posed question seeking his views on my radio programme by evacuating his bowels on to my forearm . . . The result of earnest father/son deliberation has been, to date, poor. I have ascertained that he is an anti-fascist, that he will not be drawn on the matter of Eric Clapton's guitaring, or say whether in his view Neil Young's *Zuma* is better or worse than Dylan's *Desire*. I have played him quite a few LPs over the weekend ranging from that by the reconstituted Quicksilver Messenger Service to *Natty Cultural Dread* by Big Youth. His reaction to each of them has been to continue sucking with a dedication and fervour which – and I'm being uncommonly frank with you – indicates to me that the seeds of fanaticism have already been sown in his tiny pointed head.

I won't go on any further this morning about William Robert Anfield, his life and times, and I will do what I can to ensure that he doesn't crop up in these columns too frequently. There is, as my friends, particularly red-faced and bullying Radio 1 producer John Walters, reaffirm at hourly intervals, nothing worse than a man who goes on and on and on and on and on and on about his child. On the other hand, I am glad the little blighter's here . . .

Despite the Edward G. Robinson factor, John was ceaselessly sentimental about William, to the extent that he was temporarily unable to speak through his blubbing when he announced his birth on the radio. But I wasn't in the clear even once I was discharged. When William was ten days old, I collapsed after starting to haemorrhage; they told me afterwards that my blood pressure had dropped through the floor. I had only been at home for three days at this point. John was back in London doing his show, and a friend of mine was staying with me at home, when I had to be rushed back into hospital. When John finally got to the hospital to be with me, the doctors told him that if I'd got there half an hour later, I would have died.

It took a long time for me to recover from that. My parents came to stay with us for a while, as I was incredibly weak and vulnerable. Shortly after I was released from hospital, I received a phone call from a friend of mine, Sue, who lived down the road. She said John had called her and asked if she would pick him up from Bury St Edmunds station: apparently he'd been on the way back from London and had had trouble with the Range Rover. He'd asked Sue if she could bring me along too because he thought it would do me good to get out. I was very resistant to this because I felt so frail. It was a very bleak winter, with snow piled everywhere like mashed potato. Finally she persuaded me that the fresh air would be beneficial, so I went along.

As we were nearing Bury St Edmunds, I saw a red Morgan zooming in the other direction and I almost swooned. 'Ooh,

I've always wanted one of those,' I said. A few minutes later, it overtook us and raced on, having obviously turned around. I thought that was a bit odd, but it wasn't until we pulled into a long lay-by ahead that I realised something was going on. The lay-by was full of people I knew. There were friends from the village, members of Great Finborough International Airport, even Terry and Gerry were there from London. We got out and I saw John walking towards us. 'What the hell's going on?' I spluttered.

Then I noticed there were bottles of champagne and glasses lined up in the snow, glinting in the sunlight. John took my hand and led me to the front of this long line of cars, where the Morgan was waiting for me. I was speechless. Considering my health at the time, it's a wonder I didn't collapse on the bonnet. We drank champagne, then climbed into the Morgan and sped home. It was terribly romantic.

We had three more children after William, though sadly there wasn't a new car waiting for me after each one. Luckily the births of the two middle children went smoothly, give or take the high-speed dash to the hospital in which John mounted the pavement, much to the horror of the pedestrians of Ipswich, in order to circumnavigate the rush-hour traffic that would otherwise have caused Danda to be born in the car.

He commemorated the occasion in his *Sounds* column, which offered a rather more relaxed interpretation of the events of that morning:

At eight fifty-five a.m. he draws up outside Heath Road Hospital and assists the Pig, now in considerable pain, into the building. He hardly notices the admiring glances of the trainee nurses as he manfully summons the lift. Forty minutes later he stands in the delivery room, clutching to his chest his spanking new daughter, the girl who will one day be the toast of all England.

Danda might have been born in haste, but she was named at leisure. As the first female Ravenscroft in over sixty years, there was pressure to choose a name that was just right, so for some weeks she was referred to simply as 'Child B'.

John also imposed his own brand of drama on the night in February 1980 when our second son, Thomas James Dalglish, was born. John was in London for his show when he got the call from the hospital to say that I had been admitted. He rushed to my bedside, but then excused himself just as the contractions were getting worse, so that he could ring the studio and promise to let them know before the end of the evening whether I'd had a boy or girl. I heard Mike Read, John's stand-in for the night, give out this little teaser on air and I thought: Hang on a minute – I think I may be married to a man whose priorities are a bit skew-whiff. And it put additional pressure on me to squeeze out Thomas before the stroke of midnight, just so that Radio 1 listeners could sleep easily in their beds. But I did it. Thomas was born at eleven fifteen p.m., and John was thrilled – not only to have had another son, but also to have done so within the constraints of his radio slot.

There would likely be a greater smattering of junior Ravenscrofts in the house if I hadn't suffered so much during the final stage of my pregnancy with our last child, Florence Victoria Shankly. Before she was born in April 1982, I contracted whooping cough, and also lost a lot of weight – it was falling off me when I should have been gaining. I was terribly ill in the weeks leading up to her birth, so much so that I had been scheduled to go into hospital to be induced. I was coughing so loudly and regularly that John was forced to bed down elsewhere in the house, just so that he could get a night's sleep. When the contractions finally began, I was grateful not to have to be induced – but I was still terrified. John and I were convinced that something would be wrong with the baby; the pregnancy had been so difficult it seemed inevitable.

I woke John in the early hours of the morning and climbed in next to him on the ledge above his room, where he had been sleeping. He put on Rachmaninoff's second piano concerto while he went to make some drinks, and when he returned with our mugs of tea we lay together talking until we were certain the contractions were real. The dawn light was starting to reach across the room. A short time later, we heard my parents, who had been staying with us, getting William and Danda ready for school; Thomas, who was only two, was tottering around in the kitchen. The house was slowly coming to life with noise and bustle. John and I readied ourselves and set off for the hospital.

We later confided to one another that during the drive we were nursing the same awful fears. Neither of us was saying anything, but we both thought that things were going to end very badly indeed – that either the baby or I would fail to emerge from the experience unscathed. Thankfully, Flossie and I were both fine, but the pregnancy was traumatic enough to thwart for good our plans to expand the family still further. John had always wanted to have six children. With some reluctance, mingled with relief that the children we had were healthy and safe, we halted at four.

The birth of our children inevitably changed our lives, but John seemed particularly ill equipped. I was better prepared for the noise and chaos of a full house; the arrival of one child after another represented a more dramatic disruption for John.

A diary entry for 13 January 1975, just a year and a day before William was born, shows this uneasiness surfacing in our relationship for the first time. John had expressed a genuine desperation to have children. I was nine and a half years his junior, and at thirty-six he felt the urgency more keenly than I did. But hints of ambivalence came through in an encounter with Mile, a puppy we had at the time:

> Mile knocked the sugar on the floor, and I got really ratty and yelled and then Pig went all quiet and melancholy on me. Got to bed around 1.00 and Pig was still very sad. I wasn't at all sleepy and I spent some time trying to figure out why. Eventually she explained that my yelling at Mile for knocking over the sugar indicated that I was not prepared to have my life disrupted, and thus that I will never want to have children. We discussed this for a good hour. I tried to convince her that I'm not really opposed to the idea of having children, just worried about it.

It took a long time for John to come to terms with having children around the house. One of the biggest shocks for him after William was born came with the realisation that, after commanding my full attention for over seven years together, he was going to have to share me. We'd gone everywhere together, and been virtually inseparable. Now things would have to change, and he found that incredibly difficult.

We both had a fairly equal hand in raising the children, though we occasionally employed people to help out. John once placed an advertisement in *The Lady* when we were looking for someone. In the same issue, Stirling Moss was also advertising a similar vacancy. His ad read something like: 'Must be willing to spend three to four months on French Riviera; own car supplied.' John, on the other hand, wrote: 'Help wanted with children at country house three miles from nearest disco. View of dead tree from upstairs window.'

He continued with his gigs and radio programmes and festivals, and spent most days in his long room next to the kitchen listening to records for the show, but he also put aside time to be with the children. He spent countless hours playing football in the garden with them, and used to take off on late-night or early-morning expeditions with William to spot combine harvesters, which were a one-time obsession of our son's, once the appeal of elephants had begun to wane (combine harvesters were a more common feature of the Suffolk landscape than elephants, which was a bonus).

I had an opportunity to return to teaching once our children were all at school, but I passed it up. A voice inside me said: Everything's going so well here, with John and the children – why would you want to jeopardise that? It was my own decision in the end, though John confided in me that he was glad I had made the choice I did, so that we could spend more time together.

Family life was very satisfying for me. But I saw how difficult John found it all when it didn't fit with his expectations. I had looked after my sister Gabrielle, who is ten years younger than me, quite frequently when I was growing up, so I knew what to expect. But John wasn't primed for what parenting entailed. He didn't reckon on the sleepless nights, the chaos, the tantrums, the repetition, and those occasional days that are just wretched from beginning to end. He liked the noise and frenzy sometimes, and there was plenty to go around. The house was never empty; as well as our own children, we had Gabrielle, and later her son, Little John, living with us for eleven years, and friends were always dropping in. But John liked the chaos on his own terms – when he was ready for it.

I often told him that life wasn't like a Kellogg's Corn Flakes advertisement or a Disney film all the time, with perpetually smiling faces crowded around the breakfast table. It could be a struggle for him to appreciate that.

Occasions when John's needs didn't square with those of the children were particularly tough for him. One afternoon he took William and Danda with him in the car to meet someone from whom he was collecting a demo tape. They hadn't got further than the end of the lane when William said, 'I don't want to come and neither does Danda.' John asked Danda if she wanted to come with him and she shook her head. So John dropped them both back at home and then set off on his own in floods of tears.

Even once his grandson Archie was born, he was still harbouring the same unrealistic expectations, and recoiling with the same injured look when they failed consistently to be met. John would cuddle Archie, and Archie would crane his neck looking around for Danda. That was enough to incur John's disappointment. 'He hates me,' he would grumble. I had to tell him to give Archie time, and sure enough, when John backed off and stopped advertising his affection, Archie came to him. Whenever he crawled into John's room to see him, John was made up. That was all he wanted. And they eventually became very close. When John and I were in Peru, John kept saying how much he was looking forward to returning home and holding Archie in his arms again.

*

By the time William was born, John was doing an hour-long show at eleven o'clock each night from Monday to Friday. A few weeks before William came along, John had amused himself on the programme by engineering a conflict with Radio 1's rivals, Capital Radio. On 6 January 1976, he writes in his diary:

> Petals had heard Nicky B. Horne on Capital saying they had a British exclusive on the new Dylan LP, *Desire*, and he phoned CBS to check it out. We could hardly believe our luck when Lewis of CBS told us he had a white label on his desk and would send it round. When it arrived, I hurtled down for it before they decided we shouldn't have it, didn't even dare call for recording info lest they discover they'd made an error. Timed it and it was marvellous – also 55 minutes long.
>
> Started the programme tonight by saying how fed up I was after hearing that another station had an exclusive on Dylan tomorrow night. 'Now that,' I concluded, 'really is annoying', and played the whole LP. Played a reggae record, 'Dreadlocks Came To Dinner', while I turned it over, and that was the only other record in the programme.

The next day, John was evidently pleased with himself. 'Capital were still claiming this morning that Nicky B. Horne was due to play Dylan exclusively so I gave the album to Johnnie Walker to further deflate 'em.'

1976 turned into a ferociously exciting year for reasons that had nothing to do with John making mischief with Capital. Punk made its first incursions into John's show in spring 1976 when he was struck by the lightning bolt that was the

Ramones' first album. He likened the experience to that of hearing Little Richard for the first time, and proceeded to scatter Ramones tracks liberally throughout his show after playing 'Judy Is A Punk' at the end of his programme on 19 May 1976. Once again, this caused loud complaints from his core audience – or rather those parts of it that hadn't been frightened off by reggae – though the band would doubtless have been disappointed to learn that the village postman brought us no turds in honour of their singular racket.

Most objections that John received, whatever the year or era, stemmed largely from the fact that he refused to play the bands that listeners already knew and liked. A spirit of searching and adventurousness drove his shows, and more often than not he would be proved right in his instincts, though it could take some time: Pulp, for instance, did not enjoy massive success until about twelve years after their début session for John.

And with punk, the audience took some budging. Initial reactions to John's punk-spattered playlist bore this out. Despite the furore caused by the 10 December programme, when John gave over the entire show to tracks by the Stooges, Richard Hell, Television and the Sex Pistols, listeners weren't ready to hack off their hair and burn their old albums quite yet. In the inaugural Festive Fifty poll that year, Led Zeppelin's 'Stairway To Heaven' came out on top, with the likes of Derek & the Dominoes, Pink Floyd, Bob Dylan and the Beatles dominating the rest of the chart. Two years later, punk ruled the poll.

Back in August 1975, John had written in his diary of the increasingly turgid experience of choosing records for his show:

The pile of records I've ploughed through this week is really drab. Awful formula disco stuff . . . third-rate drivel . . . Making my list up today, I kept thinking, 'But this isn't any good.'

With his own show reserved for artists he was enthusiastic about, John vented his spleen about the state of mainstream music in his singles reviews for *Sounds*. He wrote in an abrasive review of 'Jambalaya' in 1974:

Lots and lots and lots and lots of people think the Carpenters are just as neat as neat can be. I think they're revolting and they sing this righteous old country raver with all the verve and passion of a cadaver in an advanced stage of decomposition. They make the soundtrack of *Oklahoma* sound positively depraved. Such blistering wholesomeness is not a digestible commodity. Bring me my commode of burning gold.

Even the music respectable journals were raving about didn't always find favour with John. On 18 November 1975, exactly six months before he fell in love with the Ramones, he attended a gig by the up-and-coming Bruce Springsteen,

. . . who is being hailed as the saviour of rock music. His first few numbers were a trifle theatrical, like off-cuts from *West Side Story* . . . Don't think he is, as *Rolling Stone* have claimed, the future of rock 'n' roll, but rather a summary of its past. Vocally Van Morrisonish and I thought he rather overdid the street punk routine.

John's general disapproval, and his reluctance to play Springsteen's records on his show, obviously cost the singer

dearly in record sales, as it did other acts whom John spurned
– U2, say, or Dire Straits, who might have ended up playing
stadiums, winning awards and selling millions of albums if
only they had found favour with John.

It might dent his reputation to reveal this, but John had a
soft spot for the Dire Straits song 'Sultans Of Swing', and we
both sang it at the top of our voices when we were driving to
Niagara Falls. John sprung many surprises on me in the course
of our marriage. There was the time when he sent me a
bouquet of flowers every day for more than a week leading up
to my birthday; each morning the florist arrived and said,
slightly apologetically, 'I've tried to vary them a bit today.' But
one of his most spectacular treats was when he took me
on that surprise weekend to Niagara Falls in 1978. He
managed not to let on all the time he was planning it; I didn't
twig until I learned at the airport that we were flying Air
Canada.

There had been nothing but rubbish on the radio all the way
from Toronto airport, so we were both pathetically grateful
when Dire Straits came on, since it was the only thing we could
sing along to. After seeing The Falls, we stopped at the café
nearby, where John was slightly unnerved to find a gang of men
staring at us. We tried to carry on drinking our coffee, and pretended not to notice them, but it was hard to shake the
suspicion that we were about to be robbed and murdered and
dumped in The Falls where no-one would ever find our bodies.
Then one of the men approached John. 'John Peel?' he said.
'You are John Peel, aren't you?' John had to admit it was so.
'We thought it was you! We're Dire Straits.' And what nice lads
they were too. We had a drink and a chat with them and concluded that they were not at all the sort of people who would

have robbed and murdered us before dumping our bodies in The Falls.

With British music mired in prog rock, punk gave John the first thing he could really get excited about since Bryan Ferry had sent him a Roxy Music demo in the early seventies. By the end of 1976, his playlist was drenched in punk. 'We're not playing any of this punk stuff, are we?' the then controller of Radio 1, Derek Chinnery, asked John Walters in a phone call on 6 December 1976. Walters replied that John's last few programmes had contained little else, and that he was about to record a brand-new session by The Damned. The letters of complaint came thick and fast, but these were outshone by a sweet dispatch from the mother of one of the band members, who thanked John for 'helping Christopher with his career' – 'Christopher' being better known as Rat Scabies. Correspondence from proud parents was all too rare, though John was always pleased to receive letters from PJ Harvey's mum, who expressed her gratitude towards him for giving so much airplay to young Polly Jean.

On 26 October, John had played The Damned's 'New Rose' on his show, having come directly to the studio from a gig where he had introduced them. He writes in his diary:

> I had at first imagined that I was supposed to be officiating at the New Vic, but when I got there I discovered that Showaddywaddy were appearing, and I had to buy a *Time Out* to find where I was in action. Into pub and The Damned were on first: most enjoyable, uncompromising, heads-down punk rock. The audience didn't seem too taken with them, apart from a small coterie of dedicated followers, who booed me when I introduced the band. At the start of the final number Rat

Scabies grew dissatisfied with something, kicked over his drum-kit and left the stage alone. Despite the cries of the remaining Damned, he never returned ... Took the tube back to B.H. [Broadcasting House] to do the programme and it was a pretty fair one. I think I must do something to make the programmes more interesting in 1977.

The Sex Pistols' 'Anarchy In The UK' made its début on John's show shortly after, on 19 November. The BBC were refusing to accommodate it in its daytime schedules, a situation that was repeated the following May when John played 'God Save The Queen', which had been disparaged by the BBC for displaying 'gross bad taste'. On 1 December 1976, the Pistols made their infamous television appearance, goaded by Bill Grundy into saying lots of horrid words, and three days later John drove to Derby to see them play on a bill that also included The Clash and The Damned. He had gone to see them before this, at the 100 Club on 11 May, but had left halfway through the opening number because they insisted on being dreadfully naughty boys and not starting until late, by which time he had to hotfoot it over to Broadcasting House for his show. On that night in Derby, he was also unlucky because the gig was cancelled; he thought this was splendid, and much more in keeping with the spirit of punk than if it had gone ahead.

John was all the more appalled, then, when the band announced in the late nineties that they were re-forming for a comeback tour, though in truth what relations he had with the band had soured before they had even split up. He was highly principled when it came to choosing records for his show, and he wasn't about to play a sub-standard song just because it was by a band he usually liked. So when his opinion of the Pistols started to drop, he inevitably stopped including their new material in his playlist, much to the chagrin of Steve Jones, who accosted John and called him a 'cunt'. John was shocked by this display of aggression, though not by the insult. After all, didn't he himself happily attend festivals in a T-shirt that bore the legend 'John Peel is a Cunt'?

The origin of this can be dated back to a rainy Saturday in August during the 1976 Reading Festival. John, as festival compère, did his best to console the crowd, who had just endured a downpour that caused the sound to cut out during Manfred Mann's set. He suggested that everyone should focus their attention on him and purge their hostility by shouting 'John Peel is a cunt!' 'This they did,' John notes in his diary, 'with considerable verve at once and several more times during the evening. There were apparently complaints from over four miles away. Made me laugh hugely.'

Two years later, it wasn't quite so funny. 'This year the choruses of "John Peel is a cunt" seemed distressingly sincere,' he wrote in 1978, noting that someone even threw a rock at him on stage. 'I thought of the Pig, William and Alexandra at home, decided it wasn't worth being slain to demonstrate what a splendid chap I am, and resolved to complete my stage chores as unobtrusively as possible.' Still, the T-shirt was printed up, and John wore it with a pride bordering on sentimentality. I never objected to him having that slogan on his chest. But I refused to let him leave the house, years later, in the Cradle of Filth T-shirt that read: Dead Girls Don't Say No.

Different stories abound as to why the Sex Pistols never recorded a session for the programme. Walters blamed himself; he felt guilty about imposing on the unsuspecting BBC engineers a band that raucous. John thought that the Pistols had turned down the offer. Whatever the reason, they got away, as did The Clash, though in that instance John was happy to let them go.

> They actually got as far as recording the backing tracks, but then they were so out of their heads they couldn't finish it, and decided the BBC's equipment wasn't good enough. It was one of those things where you thought: How do you argue with stupidity on this level? Not a very punk attitude, I thought.

However, there was plenty he did approve of. We both relished our first punk gig, at the Roxy in January 1977, where we saw Generation X perform through a shower of phlegm. John also admired hugely the unshackled energy and DIY spirit of the Slits, whose singer Ari Up was just fourteen when the band recorded their first session for him, and whose drummer, Palmolive, greeted John in the Vortex club by banging his head against the head of the man with whom, until that very moment, he had been engaged in polite conversation. John reported later:

> Being a well-bred Gent, I merely smiled and continued my conversation. Come to think of it, we are shortly to record these Slits for Radio 1. I think I will take several of my friends and lie in wait for the brazen creature outside the studio.

1977 wasn't only important to John for being the year that punk exploded – and our first daughter was born. It was also the year that Elvis died. John always believed that Elvis could have been saved from himself simply by choosing to vacation with us at home in Suffolk (he later claimed that the same remedy would have cured whatever was ailing Kurt Cobain). A few weeks of 'Come on, Elvis, you can help with the shopping. Just pop to the village for some dog food, there's a pet. Don't forget the speech-and-drama run at seven thirty. Oh, and Elvis, the dog needs washing again . . .', reckoned John, and the King would have been back on an even keel.

The night that the news came in, John was playing Culture's 'Trod On'. The white light on the studio wall flashed. John picked up the telephone. 'Hello John,' someone said, 'this is the newsroom. We've had unconfirmed reports from America that Elvis Presley is dead.'

And as he lined up the next record, the Fabulous Poodles' single, John wondered what he was going to say. He thought back to the first time he had heard Elvis Presley, early in 1956, when 'Heartbreak Hotel' was played on *Two-Way Family Favourites*; the next day he had walked out of Liverpool's Central Station and crossed the road to Cranes to buy the record. Forty-eight hours earlier he'd been in there buying a 78 by Petula Clark. He never did anything like that again, not after 'Heartbreak Hotel'. That, along with early records by Fats Domino, Little Richard and Bill Haley, changed his life and, for better or worse, made him who he was.

'We've had as-yet-unconfirmed reports from the United States that Elvis Presley is dead,' he told his listeners. 'It must be emphasised that these reports are unconfirmed, and as soon as we have any further details they will be passed on to you at once.'

Then the phone rang again. This time Tony Wilson, Alan 'Fluff' Freeman's producer, was at the other end of the line. 'ITN have just announced that Elvis is dead,' he said. Then, after a pause, 'They finished the news by retracting the story, though.'

There seemed little point in sending runners to the library for Presley records with which to saturate the airwaves, although several listeners later called the duty officer to ask why John had not done this. One or two other radio stations gave the rest of the night to Elvis, but, in all honesty, Elvis and rock hadn't had much in common for quite a few years, and John maintained that this sort of overreaction always smacked to him of necrophilia:

> I prefer to remember those who have died, whether relatives, friends, rock stars or a combination of the three, in their proper context, filling some greater or lesser niche in everyday life, rather than distorting my memory of them in a welter of terminal sentiment. This is why we never did anything extreme when Jim Morrison died or Paul Kossoff died, not even when Hendrix died. We (John Walters and I, that is) still play their records on air from time to time – always will, I hope, thinking of them in the same sort of way that I sometimes think of my Dad.
>
> And death, for those who live on, is the ending of a chapter rather than the end of the book, and although the dead may have no more part to play as characters, their influence may continue right through the story. Presley's certainly will, for he was the first person we met on Page 1, and although his records later became irrelevant to all but the diehard Presley devotees and his private life seems to have plumbed new depths of nightmarishness, nothing can ever take that away from him.

While some timid souls might have taken cover from punk that year in the sentimental outpouring of Elvis-mania, John believed that the cultural explosion that the Pistols triggered, in the manner of a firework setting light to surrounding grass and woodland, made them at least as influential as Elvis or the Beatles. You could see their influence even on people in our village shop in the 1990s, who would deny any link with punk, but whose clothes, haircuts and attitudes tell a different story. John never really had the figure for punk, would have looked preposterous in bondage trousers, and was already too old anyway, but the exuberance of it all enveloped him like nobody's business. Especially when the second wave of punk bands – Buzzcocks, the Undertones, the Lurkers – arrived. With no art or fashion background, these were groups of rowdy youths battling to burst through the door kicked open by the Pistols.

While the punk revolution made 1976 and 1977 culturally significant, 1978 was probably more life-changing for John, since it heralded the arrival of what were to be two of his favourite bands. John Walters had caught The Fall at the Croydon Greyhound in May 1978, where the band was supporting Siouxsie and the Banshees, after a recommendation from Danny Baker. Walters wrote to Mark E. Smith: 'You don't know me but I know you,' and offered the band a session. It was recorded on 30 May 1978 and broadcast a few weeks later.

From that moment, The Fall were part of our lives, and the lives of John's listeners. John said that the band were like me. He didn't mean I was abrasive, experimental, confrontational and prone to fisticuffs on stage. At least he didn't say so. He thought we were alike because we were always different, but always the same. From 1979, when 'Rowche Rumble' scraped into the lower reaches of the Festive Fifty, The Fall always had at least one song in John's end-of-year poll, finally reaching

Number One in 1990 with the beautiful 'Bill Is Dead'. The year before that, John had chosen their song 'Eat Y'self Fitter' as one of his Desert Island Discs; it sounded even more otherworldly than usual being introduced by Sue Lawley, and played alongside Handel, Rachmaninoff, Roy Orbison.

The strange thing is that John and Mark never exchanged more than a few words over the years. Their friendship involved little more than a mumbled greeting and an occasional punch on the shoulder or squeeze of the arm. That was all John needed from Mark; if he got a punch or a squeeze he would be chuffed. 'Aw, that was nice of him,' he'd say. Mark wrote to John too, and John treasured his letters, especially the typical sign-off: 'Your mate Mark.'

As if further proof were needed of the esteem in which John held The Fall, it should be remembered that he kept all their records separate from the rest of his collection. Tens of thousands of albums are squeezed on to John's shelves. But only The Fall have their own special VIP enclosure, away from the hubbub, like religious artefacts with voodoo properties. There's also a framed photograph of Mark E. Smith in our hallway, and another picture of him pinned to the wall in John's room, gazing across at where John used to stand listening to records. It's as though Mark was keeping watch over him.

I heard Mark was upset that the band was never invited to our home when John started broadcasting sessions from here. In truth, I think John would have been over the moon to have them here. What a session they would have done! But the producers pretty much vetoed it; they knew they wouldn't be able to take responsibility for what happened if Mark was here, given that some of his performances tended towards the volatile. When John died, though, Mark was very kind and considerate to me, and offered to do whatever he could to help. I thought that was a lovely gesture.

Two months before we left for Peru, John had broadcast the latest session from The Fall – their twenty-fourth in twenty-six years. There was simply no other band that excited him quite so much. He once said, in a documentary made by the BBC to mark his sixtieth birthday, that he didn't want to die yet because there would be another Fall album out soon; we even chose that comment to play at John's funeral. What I can't quite come to terms with now is that there will be Fall records that John will never hear.

1978 was also, for John at least, the year of the Undertones. 'Teenage Kicks', his favourite record, was pure, undiluted fun. It was on 12 September of that year that he played all four tracks from the Undertones' *True Confessions* EP, before remarking: 'Isn't that the most wonderful record you've ever heard?' Over the next fortnight, John played 'Teenage Kicks' four times on air; for the rest of his life, it was the song that could be relied upon to give him a fillip after a day of un-inspiring new records.

Shortly after those first airings of 'Teenage Kicks', John stumped up the cash for the Undertones to record a session in a Belfast studio, which he then broadcast on 16 October. When the band came to London the following January to support the Rezillos, they did another four songs for John, this time at Maida Vale. 'People sometimes ask me what I do this show for,' John said. 'I don't do it for the credibility or the cool. I don't do it for the major record labels. I don't do it for the music industry . . . I do it for people like the Undertones.' There was, he would say frequently, nothing that could be added to or subtracted from 'Teenage Kicks' to make it any better than it already was. When he later heard Peter Powell playing it on daytime radio, he was so thrilled that he burst into tears.

I can still remember when John played that song at home for the first time. That was how he spent the majority of his time – tucked away in his long, thin room that stands parallel to the kitchen, with the door open, listening to record after record, all day long. There are family photographs on the walls; a stack of old *Private Eye* magazines reaching towards the roof and back through the decades; a BBC first-aid kit on the shelf; a training shoe secured to the ceiling, its laces dangling, from the day John nailed it there to illustrate to William the concept of Surrealism.

Most of the time John would be standing in that room, noting down the exact timings of every song, adding little comments to the label attached to each one, doodling asterisks according to how much he liked it, then tapping away at the typewriter compiling the playlists for his programmes. There are tens of thousands of vinyl albums, twelve-inch singles, seven-inch singles and CDs shelved around the house and in our shed, and John processed every one in this way. You can pull out one at random and find out what he thought of it. A Bhundu Boys album, for example, might have fifteen or sixteen asterisks. The Libertines' first album has an asterisk next to the song 'Time For Heroes', which, John notes approvingly, contains a lyric consistent with his own beliefs – about how upsetting it is to see English men wearing baseball caps. It was always his contention that the decline of European culture could be attributed solely to the burgeoning popularity of the baseball cap.

One asterisk means 'might play'. Two means 'should play'.

Three means 'must play'. John endeavoured to restrict himself to three asterisks, but if he got really carried away he might put four or even more. 'Teenage Kicks' got something like twenty-eight asterisks, though it would be a solemn soul who claimed it didn't deserve every last one of them.

When John played 'Teenage Kicks' at home, he asked me what I thought; he knew he liked it but I think he wanted a second opinion. And I raved about it to him – I thought it was wonderful. Between me enthusing about the Undertones and presenting 'Pig's Big 78' on John's show in recent times, and Thomas sifting through the sackfuls of jungle, drum and bass, and happy hardcore white labels and weeding out the best ones for John to play (introduced on the programme as 'Tom's Tip'), it should by now be clear that John was little more than a neat beard and a pleasant voice.

Music filled the house when John was at home. From around eight in the morning until late at night on the days when he wasn't at the BBC, he was in that room playing music. It was as if he wanted to be here and also not here. He would complain if I was cooking and smoke drifted into his room. But he would hate it even more if anyone closed the door. He was rarely happier than when he was in his room listening to music, but could still see and hear us all gathered in the kitchen, talking and laughing and arguing, and he knew everything was ticking over nicely. That way he had his music and his family at the same time.

He liked having people over for lunch, and one of his favourite things was to sit at the head of the table with a glass of red in one hand, telling some convoluted anecdote using silly voices. But it would get to the point, after an hour or so, when you could see him physically itching to get back to work. We might have guests over, but still the time would come when he would stand up, shuffle off in the direction of his room and say, 'I hope you don't mind if I crack on . . .'

Even on Christmas Day, he couldn't wait to get back to his records. At about ten a.m., once everyone had opened their presents, he'd be in there again and the music would start up. Then we wouldn't see him until I called him for lunch. He spent so much time in there because it was work, and because he loved it. And despite all the hours he spent listening to music, he never got the chance to hear everything that was sent to him.

Part of the problem for John was that listening to records was something that he could neither delegate nor accelerate. A record takes as long as it takes, and these days it takes much longer than it used to. Whereas, say, Eddie Cochran's 'C'mon Everybody' runs for one minute and fifty-three seconds, a single released today can be augmented by five remixes and last an hour. The original track may be only three minutes long but the remixes, two by thin boys from Germany, two by voguish New Yorkers and one by someone from Japan or Belarus, will be much longer.

No matter that he was listening to that thin-boys-from-Germany remix of the latest Schlammpeitziger single, John could still hear what was going on in the kitchen: you'd be having a conversation and he would suddenly appear in the doorway to interject or just to say, 'Right, what's going on?', with the music still thundering away in the background. 'Christ, there's nothing wrong with your hearing, is there?' I'd say to him.

We were all accustomed to the constant music. It didn't seem strange to the children that they would wake up to the sound of whatever John happened to be playing that morning. If it was something they liked, they would go in and ask him what it was. There were certain bands where the whole family seemed united in their opinion. We used to go together to see The Wedding Present play, for instance, and we all went crazy for Sonic Youth and the Pixies. That was one of John's regular battle cries – everything would be quiet and then you'd hear him booming from his room, 'Who's got my Pixies albums?'

Nirvana enjoyed the same distinction of being adored by every one of us, and though John usually shied away from using his position as a poptastic Radio 1 DJ to land special privileges, he did manage to get the children back-stage when Nirvana headlined the Reading Festival, so that they were as close to the band as you now are to this book. When Kurt Cobain committed suicide, John met the children off the school bus and broke the news to them in much the same manner as if it had been a close family member who had died.

If John extended his goodwill and airtime to a band, it was never with an eye on what might become the next big thing. In fact, when his taste and that of the general public and music industry did coincide, he expressed surprise. He is said to have broken bands in this country like Nirvana and the White Stripes, but he would argue that he was only giving them some exposure slightly sooner than they might otherwise have received it.

With so much music at their disposal, the children really had no need to build their own record collections, preferring instead to forage around in their father's room and gather scraps before returning hungrily to their own stereos.

Sometimes William might discover a new band and rush to tell his dad about it, only to discover that John had played their first EP months earlier.

Once the children left home, John would sometimes dispatch rations – care packages, if you like – to their respective universities. A typical parcel might comprise a stash of CDs, each bearing a handwritten label. One might read, 'Here's one I think you'll like.' Another would be, 'Here's one I think you should like.' Inevitably there would be one marked, 'Here's one you should pretend to like to annoy people.' (It was usually German hip-hop.)

Now the mood in the house is very different. When the children come across something they think John would have enjoyed, the feeling is likely to be one of emptiness. Thomas heard some tracks by Ergo Phizmiz recently, and felt sure John would have loved them. He was frustrated that he couldn't play them to his dad.

These days, there is obviously less music in the house. When Flossie comes down in the morning, she'll switch on the radio to fill the silence. The children have told me that they aren't as aware of new music as they were when John was here. When Thomas spent the weekend in London, he wanted to see a band. Whereas in the past he would have phoned John, who'd rave about such-and-such a band that was gigging at this or that club, this time he just stared at the music listings. None of the names meant anything to him. I wonder how many other young people feel the same way.

Punk was brief and bilious by nature, but there was no short-age of musical innovation following in its debris-strewn wake. British music in the late seventies was dominated by ska, and this was as well represented on John's programme as punk had been before it, with The Beat, Madness, The Selecter and the Specials all recording Peel Sessions in 1979. At this time, John was broadcasting Monday to Thursday from ten p.m. until midnight. In January 1979, his shows had been cut from five nights to four for the first time since 1975. While he was moderately placated by the addition in 1980 of an extra hour on Sundays (titled *John Peel's Rock Requests*), he would never again broadcast five nights a week.

The timing of his shows throughout the 1980s meant that he would leave the house for London at around the time the children came home from school, returning long after they had gone to bed. He made the effort to get up early enough to see them off to school in the morning, but he wasn't in peak working condition at that time of day, and communication between John and the children was pretty minimal, with John sitting in the kitchen with his head in his hands trying to remember which child was which.

Something had to give. Towards the end of the eighties, John started cutting down on gigging, which had begun to take its toll on him, before ceasing altogether in the nineties. He did, though, accept more voiceover work, something he had been doing on and off since recording a Bird's Eye commercial in 1970. In 1980, he was briefly the voice of the Marmite Baby, before being supplanted by Willie Rushton. Since then he took it upon himself to murmur apologetically on behalf of stout, fizzy drinks, chocolate bars, toilet paper and tinned fruit, as well as a lawn treatment which, he was informed by a platoon of hostile correspondents, contained an ingredient banned under the terms of the Geneva Convention.

He had one particularly gruelling Christmas when every

commercial break would throw up one of three ads he had recorded only to be replaced before transmission by Griff Rhys Jones. 'Wasn't this one of the ones you did, Dad?' the children would ask. From then on, whenever Griff appeared on screen John would snarl, 'That's the man who snatched the pudding from your lips and emptied the toys from your stocking.' The children had probably got over it by then, but John couldn't stop. *Wouldn't* stop.

For John, the voiceover experience was fraught with healthy liberal guilt, since he knew it was a well-paid doddle compared to air-sea rescue or brain surgery. It could also be a source of real anxiety. He wrote of the experience:

When you arrive all of a fluster at the studio, you are shoved, after a delay timed to remind you of your place in the scheme of things, into the presence of the people responsible for the commercial. You are, for an hour, their hireling, and they know it. There are never less than six of them; often there are more. They are invariably beautifully, if casually, dressed, bright, amusing, attractive and haven't seen each other since . . . was it Grenoble? I am none of these things and have never been to Grenoble.

After a round of introductions so intimidating that you remember not a single name, although you think one of them might be called Piers, the advertising dreamboats prod you into the ill-lit booth in which you are to work. As the door closes, you can hear them laughing. After your first tentative stab at reading the daft words they have been crafting for the best part of a week, you can see them arguing through the glass that separates you from them. They are saying, 'Whose idea was it to hire this twerp?' Alone and near to tears in the booth, you realise that you're not even sure which country Grenoble is in.

Eventually the advertising executive delegated to speak to the staff will press the talkback button and say, 'That was fantastic John, but . . .' In the language of advertising, fantastic is very, very bad indeed. After an hour of this, you emerge giddy with self-loathing but knowing that little William or Danda or Thomas or Florence can soon have some new jeans.

He also began to dip a few more toes in the shark-infested waters of television, a medium which he had largely avoided since what was known as the 1968 Amen Corner Disaster. The producers with whom John had crossed swords on that occasion had predicted that the nation's TV screens would be Peel-less, and he was right, at least until the early eighties, when John started cropping up again on *Top of the Pops* at the suggestion of the producer Michael Hurll, who believed correctly that John could inject some irreverence into the format. John appeared regularly on the show throughout the eighties, and would perhaps have continued into the nineties if he hadn't been so uncomfortable with the attention he got in the street in the days following a broadcast.

One of his first appearances on *Top of the Pops* since that ill-starred début was in February 1982. He writes in his diary:

To TV Centre in a highly nervous condition. Assigned to a dressing room and shown how I should do the chart rundowns. Did this without much trouble, only having to retake one of the four sections. Was reassured to learn that Mike Read once took 14 takes on a chart section. Down to make-up and Bryan Ferry came and sat next to me. Had a typically idiotic non-conversation. Him: 'Hello, how's it going?' Me: 'Oh, keep soldiering on, you know.' Wonderfully profound.

I was rather thrown when I saw how many kids there were in the studio. I was introduced to them and left to say amusing things – which I was quite clearly incapable of doing. This rattled me. I messed up takes 2 and 3, completely forgetting the spontaneous drolleries I'd been working on for months, and started sweating unpleasantly. Take 4 was rather rigid but OK and we pressed on with me gaining confidence. Lots of girls interested in me as a device by which they could be seen on TV, but they were amiable, and one of them perked me up by saying, 'You're not a poser like all the others.'

With Kid Jensen, John formed the Rhythm Pals, their speciality being extravagant costumes and dodgy gags. When they went for their costume fittings before each *Top of the Pops* appearance, it was a challenge as to how absurd they could be. They appeared as gladiators, centurions, the Blues Brothers; whatever it was, they were extremely lucky to pull off the links straight-faced, since Kid tells me it was common for him to have stomach-ache by the end of recording because John had made him laugh so hard.

John's speciality was mocking the day-glo, happy-clappy atmosphere favoured by the show's other presenters. It was a joy to witness his sense of humour seeping into *Top of the Pops*. 'That was the best song I've heard since – oooh, tea time,' he said after a Duran Duran video, before adding, 'Mind you, I had a late tea.' Aretha Franklin may or may not have been sobbing into a nearby Kleenex after John followed her duet with George Michael by declaring, 'You know, Aretha

Franklin can make any old rubbish sound good, and I think she just has.' And when Janice Long introduced David Cassidy by saying, 'Ooh, I used to have him on my bedroom wall,' John replied, 'That was very athletic of you, Janice.' He introduced Queen as 'those Sun City boys' – a reference to the fact that they had broken sanctions by playing to wealthy white audiences in South Africa – and said that Big Country were 'the band who put the "t" back in "country".' Sometimes the joke resided in John's expression alone. When he asked viewers, 'Isn't it great that Billy Joel has two records in the top ten?' his face indicated that, in his opinion, this state of affairs was considerably less appealing than a jab in the eye with a red-hot poker.

Given John's limited enthusiasm for Noel Edmonds, it was a surprise to find him hosting outside-broadcast segments on Noel's Saturday teatime programme *The Late, Late Breakfast Show* in the early eighties. But that didn't last long. One evening in 1983, John was introducing a stunt in which the driver Richard Smith attempted to break the world car-leap record live on air, only to flip the car over. For some bizarre reason, John seemed to get the blame for the incident, and was subsequently dropped from the show; possibly he was thought to be a jinx.

It was a terrifying experience for the children and me, all huddled around the television at home. The last thing we heard was John shouting, 'Oh my God! Oh my God!' Suddenly the screen went white and the camera cut to a rather disturbed-looking Noel in the studio. He quickly recovered his composure, though: the thought of a colleague being dead didn't throw him in front of the camera. I tried to calm the children and put them to bed, though inside I was in turmoil.

I tucked them all in and promised them that their daddy would be home very soon, to which Thomas replied, 'No he won't, he's dead.'

Noel Edmonds served much the same purpose for John as Tony Blackburn had done previously. John often found colleagues he could rail against, and at Radio 1 in the eighties there was no shortage of candidates. With the advent of today's specialist music shows, which represent most genres no matter how far they may seem from what is perceived to be mainstream, it's easy to forget precisely how pitiful much of Radio 1's output was at that time.

Those bands that were genuinely invigorating and innovative could rely only on John, and later Kid Jensen, Andy Kershaw and Janice Long, to be heard. More sessions were recorded in the eighties for John's programme than for all the shows broadcast on Radio 1 since its inception. It was such a fertile time for music. Cocteau Twins, Cookie Crew, Echo and the Bunnymen, Half Man Half Biscuit, The Jesus and Mary Chain, the Men They Couldn't Hang, Microdisney, New Order, the Pogues, and We've Got a Fuzzbox and We're Gonna Use It were some of the acts that cropped up regularly on John's playlist.

Billy Bragg also made his début on the show in 1983. He had already posted his single, 'Milkman Of Human Kindness', to John when one evening, playing football with a mate, he heard John say on Kid's show, 'I would murder someone right now in exchange for a mushroom biryani.' Billy's immediate thought was: '*Yessss!*' He bought a biryani from a nearby takeaway and walked to Broadcasting House.

Once he got there, Billy told the front-desk staff that he had brought a meal for John Peel. John hadn't started his programme yet, so he came down to meet Billy in person. The takeaway was handed over on one condition – that John would try to squeeze Billy's single into that evening's show. John agreed, and Billy had the unique experience of hearing his very own song on national radio. At the wrong speed.

John said later that he thought the record was wonderful, and would have played it even if a mushroom biryani had not been hanging in the balance. In fact, it led to Billy being offered his first Peel Session. At first, he didn't think he could accept, as he couldn't afford the cab over to Maida Vale. Then it was explained to him that the BBC would pay for the taxi. Thus was Billy Bragg initiated into the corrupt and illicit rock 'n' roll lifestyle, of which free transport is only the first rung on the ladder.

The Biryani Incident, as we shall call it, was typical of the kind of stunts that artists would pull to catch John's eye and ear. The backlog of demo tapes that he had to wade through, along with bona fide new releases that required his attention, meant that any band that had some little detail or trick, however whimsical, with which to distinguish itself was likely to leap out from the rest. For some, like Kevin Shields of My Bloody Valentine or David Fielding of the Chameleons, that meant loitering outside Broadcasting House in order to press their tape directly into John's paw.

In the case of the Chameleons, John thought he was the victim of a practical joke after listening to their demo: the recording was so accomplished that he suspected he had been given a cassette of an established band like The Cure in the hope that he would fail to recognise it and look like a twit. The group landed a session despite this, and their success in staking out Broadcasting House inspired David Gedge, then in

John compiling the running order for his programme in his room at home

MOBILE STUDIO AT READING FEST '96

Clockwise from top left: John with Alexandra on the London to Brighton bike race in the late 1980s; with Florence at Reading, 1996; with Thomas at Reading, 1992; with William at Glastonbury, 1993; with Thomas, William and Zahra at Glastonbury, 2000

Left: Leningrad, 1998
Right: Bulgaria, 1992

JOHN PEEL
THE WORLDS MOST BORING MAN

JOHN PEEL
EXQUISITELY DULL

John Peel
"DR. EXCITEMENT"
BBC RADIO ONE
BROADCASTING HOUSE
LONDON W1A 1AA ENGLAND
TEL: LONDON (71) 927 5658

Above: Broadcasting a
programme in Germany
Right: Victoria Falls, 1988

Above: with PJ Harvey broadcasting a live programme from home
Below: with Billy Bragg on the miners' march, 1992

Clockwise from top left: With Robert Wyatt; with Paul Gambaccini; with Andy Kershaw at the Isle of Man TT races; White Stripes playing live at the house; with Biggie Tembo in Zimbabwe; receiving a Sony Award for the programme *Offspring* in 1996 from Feargal Sharkey

Above: Celebrating John's sixtieth birthday at the BBC Maida Vale Studios. The design on the cake was taken from the cover of a compilation album from John's *Top Gear* programme.

Above left: a flyer for the album. The photo is of John and Sheila's feet

Opposite page,
Top: John editing a programme in his studio at home
Bottom: John with his grandson Archie, 2004
Bottom right: A roadside tribute to John

JOHN PEEL
PRESENTS
TOP GEAR

You are now leaving
WIRRAL
.... come back soon

HAIL KING John!
RiP John Peel
KiNG of NEW Music

The family together at John's sixty-fifth birthday party at home in Suffolk.
From left to right: Tom, Florence, Danda, Sheila, John, William.

his pre-Wedding Present band, the Lost Pandas, to do likewise. John enjoyed the Lost Pandas tape enough to grant David an unusual request and allow him to sit in on the recording of that night's programme.

Friends of our children who were in bands would simply drop by the house with a demo tape for John and a bunch of flowers for me. I think John got the rough end of that deal. As did the children, who when asked by their friends what John thought of the tape had to come up with ever more ingenious and polite ways of saying, 'Dad didn't think much of it and won't be giving you a session until dogs walk this earth on two legs.'

Other hopefuls would simply deposit their tapes in the mailbox outside the house, or hand them to John when they saw him in the street. That's something I could never fathom. Wherever we were – on the underground, in a pub, out shopping – someone would always give John a demo. But how did they know they were going to bump into him? Perhaps that's what separated the passionate musicians from the dabblers. The ones who were serious about it would presumably keep a tape or CD about their person at all times, on much the same principle as an organ-donor card – *In the event of my death, I agree for this demo to be passed to John Peel.*

There was no telling what might endear John to a particular demo. He gave three sessions to Terry and Gerry, whose tape had been fished out from hundreds of others simply because they happened to share their name with my former flatmates. That coincidence, John decided, was simply too incredible to overlook. Another resourceful outfit, Que Bono, found a unique way of making their demo tape sparkle alluringly in the morning postbag: they mailed it to Kenny Dalglish, and requested that he pass it on to John.

The young musician Cowcube, known to his loved ones as Paul Stimpson, gave his own demo to William in a pub in Stowmarket. The tape's next stop was William's shelf, where it remained for a year, surprisingly attracting no music-industry interest whatsoever. When John finally got his hands on the tape, he was smitten, and proclaimed it to be the best thing he had heard that year; indeed, Cowcube's 'The Popping Song' went on to reach the number-thirty spot in the 2000 Festive Fifty.

There were always factors that reduced automatically a band's chances of being heard by John. He has already identified in these pages those words that should not be mentioned in a press release, but there were other things that could be just as off-putting as having a saxophonist or citing the New York Dolls as an influence: bass players prone to the wearing of wacky headgear; band members who spelt conventional first names in an unconventional manner ('Jhon', 'Jym'). As the story of Cowcube proves, entrusting a demo to William could be just as hazardous to your prospects.

Cowcube was part of the local music scene, which John was never slow to support. In the eighties, he was an enthusiastic fan of the local grindcore outfit Extreme Noise Terror. He gave three sessions each to them and fellow grindcore specialists Napalm Death between 1987 and 1990, and they delivered some of the shortest but most frenzied songs ever aired on the show. Napalm Death's first session contained twelve numbers, yet still managed to clock in at only five minutes forty seconds. The audience at their shows had a wicked sense of humour. One Napalm Death song that John had played on air, 'You Suffer', was only 0.75 of a second long, and if any of the numbers they played live started to near the one-minute mark, there would be booing and the band would be accused of turning into hippies.

William and I went regularly with John to the gigs that Extreme Noise Terror and Napalm Death played together at the Caribbean Centre in Ipswich. These were grimy, chaotic affairs attended largely by crusties wearing layers of shredded denim and dreadlocks thick as rope. The moshpit was like an initiation ritual – if you could make it out of there in one piece, you knew you could survive anything life had to lob at you. People would stagger out with nosebleeds, clutching their heads, complaining of double vision, drenched in sweat. And yet a good-natured atmosphere prevailed somehow. William, who was around thirteen at the time, took one look at these crusties, who mostly shunned bathing or showering, and decided that this was the musical sub-genre to which he wanted to pledge undying allegiance. His karate teacher attended the reggae nights upstairs at the Caribbean Centre, and would say to William on the way out, 'What are you doing listening to *that*?'

In the last few years, John had a special affection for the Bury St Edmunds music scene. As well as Cowcube, there were bands like Bearsuit, Miss Black America and The Dawn Parade. The latter teamed up with the Exiles to record a special 'Bury scene' joint session for John in March 2003. So keen was John on another local outfit, the Vaults, that he had saved the band's T-shirt to wear at Machu Picchu, which we had planned to visit on our last day in Peru. We were taking our own snaps to accompany the travel feature that John was writing for the *Telegraph*, and he wanted to give the Vaults some helpful publicity.

Whatever music John accommodated on his programmes in the eighties was unlikely to cross over on to daytime playlists. The argument presented by management was that people didn't want to hear John's kind of music while they were at work, or doing the housework, or collecting the children from school. But John's response was always the same. People didn't want it because they weren't made conscious of its existence; their standards had been systematically lowered by having the same glossy pop records piped into their homes by every radio station, commercial or otherwise. It was precisely because of this bland diet, he wrote in *The Listener*, that 'the guys and gals want fishfingers, Tony Blackburn and television serials about, if possible, lavatory assistants whose wives have monstrous breasts'.

In fact, when daytime audiences were served something unusual, they didn't always reach for the 'off' switch. John proved surprisingly popular with listeners when he stepped in as Jakki Brambles' replacement in the lunchtime slot one week in 1993, though one factory owner called to complain that everyone had stopped work to listen while John played Dick Dale. He kicked off his stint with The Fall's version of 'Why Are People Grudgeful?', and responded to the title of Chris Isaak's latest single – 'Can't Do A Thing To Stop Me' – by announcing, 'Yes I can, mate, I can take your awful CD out of the machine and throw it as far away from this studio as is humanly possible.'

The conservative nature of Radio 1 in the eighties meant that listeners got the DJs who best reflected the station's personality and ideology. For example, mornings were dominated by Simon Bates, to whom John had taken a shine when Simon began as a newsreader at Radio 1. On 8 February 1972, John had written in his diary that Simon was 'a nice man . . . the first news guy who hasn't put the fear of God in me'. A decade later, John was plotting with Kid Jensen to beat up Simon in the BBC car-park. Simon never materialised on that occasion, though it was possibly John and Kid who had the lucky escape there.

Kid was one of John's best friends at Radio 1. Their musical tastes didn't always coincide, though Kid would often have artists in session on his programme that John had first introduced – Siouxsie and the Banshees, The Cure, Orange Juice. But they were very relaxed with each other, and shared a daft sense of humour.

For over twenty years now, there has been a box of Kid Jensen postcards in John's room. Every Radio 1 DJ has his or her own cards that are autographed and despatched to desperate fans who then presumably shower them nightly with strings of tender kisses. John was uncomfortable with anything that had about it the stench of celebrity worship, so if ever such a request came his way he would autograph one of Kid's postcards and mail it to the correspondent in question. I hope Kid won't be wounded to learn that, latterly, his postcards were sometimes supplanted by those of Chris Moyles.

John regarded Kid as something of an ally. Throughout his career, there were producers and DJs and occasionally members of management with whom John had a mutually protective relationship. From Bernie Andrews, Teddy Warrick and John Walters through to Paul Gambaccini, Kid Jensen and Andy Kershaw, John was lucky enough to hook up with people who were not only kindred spirits but were prepared also to defend his choices and instincts.

Andy was a particular tonic when he joined Radio 1 in July 1985. A few months later, he was installed in Room 318, the cramped, untidy office shared by Walters and John – just as Paul Gambaccini had been fifteen years earlier. (That makes it sound as though Paul was still there, beneath a pile of old *Melody Maker*s or trapped behind the filing cabinet. He wasn't. He got out.) There, Andy had to make do sitting on an upturned bin. He says he experienced some wariness at first from John, who might well have wondered if Andy was the young gun that the BBC were grooming to be his eventual replacement. But it soon became obvious, as John and Andy spent hours and days talking and laughing and playing records in that nine-foot-square room, that they were allies, not rivals. With Walters as the big avuncular figure who somehow held it all together, Room 318 became like a radio station within a radio station. It was a little fortress of its own.

John and Andy's enthusiasms were mutually nourishing. They would go record shopping together for African music at Stern's on Whitfield Street, and head back to the office with armfuls of discs. It was in that room that their jaws would hit the floor as they clapped their ears on the Bhundu Boys, or the Four Brothers, for the first time.

For a while in the nineties, Andy's programme followed John's, with increasingly surreal handovers that mocked DJ convention, until the phrase 'matey DJ banter' was employed in lieu of any actual conversation. The feeling of being slightly outside the Radio 1 circle, mocking the establishment, was important to both of them. One of their most mischievous adventures was the special journey we all made to catch Simon Bates in pantomime in High Wycombe, where he was performing in *Aladdin* alongside some minor cast member from *The*

Bill. It took some doing – getting to High Wycombe involved a 250-mile round-trip – but it was worth it just for the opportunity to boo Simon. What an experience it was to see Aladdin holding a knife to Simon's throat, and to feel everyone in the theatre baying most authentically for blood. Finally Andy could stand the suspense no longer. 'Oh, for God's sake, do it!' he bellowed to Aladdin from the stalls.

Along with music, football remained John's abiding passion, but the eighties were not the happiest of times to be a Liverpool supporter. Yes, our triumphs included two European Cups, four League Cups and five Charity Shields, among other wins. But by the time the decade was out, these victories had been overshadowed by the tragedies of Heysel and Hillsborough.

When we first moved to Suffolk, John went more regularly to Anfield than he ever did before, setting out at around eight in the morning – usually alone, though sometimes we took the youth club. Upon arrival in Liverpool, he would go through the same ritual in order to ensure, as he saw it, the team's continuing good fortune. He would park in the same place on the same street and pay the same urchins to mind the car. He walked to the same chip shop, bought and consumed a bag of chips before buying two pints of bitter in the same pub just down the road. He drank these, if possible, at the same table while reading the *Daily Mirror*. At the same time each home Saturday, he left the pub and crossed the road to enter the ground and stand, at first, at the Kemlyn Road end. Later he graduated to the Kop. He arrived home between eleven and midnight, usually with tales of yet another triumph.

As the years went by, work commitments often prevented John from getting up to Liverpool, though he made some half-hearted attempts to get a season ticket while William was studying there at the university. During this time, William went from being defiantly unenthusiastic about football to being not far short of obsessed, by which time his feelings about having Anfield as his third name had been similarly transformed.

We are, as a family, devoted to the club, my Ipswich season ticket notwithstanding. In fact, John's present to me on my fiftieth birthday was a genuine Robbie Fowler shirt, worn and signed by the striker, which he bought at Christie's. We debated where in the house this votive object should hang. Over the years, the red-and-white kitchen units have gone, as has the red car, the Liverpool bedside lamp and mat. I don't know what became of the Kenny Dalglish pillowcase but that seems to have gone too. John gave away the cheap scarf, peppered with holes from bonfire night sparks, to a youth in Moscow in a moment of *perestroika*-fuelled madness. And in the end we never agreed on a suitable spot for Robbie's shirt. Consequently it is still gathering dust, like most of the pictures we have ever bought or been given.

John and I both attended the game between Juventus and Liverpool at Heysel Stadium on 29 May 1985. It was one of the most terrifying and disturbing experiences either of us ever had. Kenny had got us our tickets, and we stopped at Heysel on the way back from Germany, where John had been recording a programme. We were positioned directly opposite where the fans had massed, and there was an almighty roar as the wall collapsed under their weight; at that point, John grabbed my arm and steered me out of the stadium, warning me to hide my Liverpool scarf as we hurried away. By the time we emerged, the bodies of fans were being laid out around the stadium. It was a chilling sight that I will never forget.

Four years later, John was invited to the match at Hillsborough. He hadn't attended a game since Heysel, and chose not to go. But in the wake of the tragedy, in which ninety-six Liverpool fans died, he made a pilgrimage to Anfield with our friend Pyotr from Warsaw, who was staying with us at the time. It was utterly spontaneous: John simply announced in the early hours of the morning that he had to go to Anfield. By seven a.m., John and Pyotr had joined the queue, which stretched around the ground, down one side of Kemlyn Road and back up the other, and similarly up and down the parallel Skerries Road and Wylva Road. There was noise and conversation, he reported, but more than anything there was a sense of awe.

You will remember photographs of the tributes left there, the banners and scarves that hung from railings and goal posts, the poems, programmes and souvenirs left on the steps of the Kop. Pyotr was reduced to silence. John was surprised to find in himself the apparently mediaeval instinct that had drawn him to Liverpool.

In 1997, we all went to Anfield for the Hillsborough Justice Concert. There were fifteen of us, what with aunts and uncles, nephews and nieces and our friends Charlie and Alison, so when the only officious official of the day told us we weren't allowed to look at the players, we shuffled about a bit and got to see them anyway. John happened to be making his way to the stage as the team filed off it, and he rather hoped that one or two of them might say, 'Awright there, John?' so that he could gloat afterwards about the chat he'd had with Steve or Jason or Barnesy. But he was becoming increasingly resigned to the fact that the world was overstuffed with tubby little fellers with beards. The only person who did speak was former player Sammy Lee. Sammy had done the same in Paris after the Real Madrid game, and John never forgot that.

The day itself was remarkable. John's function was to play records in between the live bands and he got to be, as far as we knew, the first person to speak from the stage at what may transpire to be the only concert at the ground. That was more than enough for him. 'Good afternoon,' he said, remembering his manners. Then, remembering Bill Shankly, 'This is Anfield.' Then he played Aretha Franklin's gospel recording of 'You'll Never Walk Alone', the same majestically drawn-out record with which he had opened his first programme after Hillsborough.

In 1990, John asked Radio 1 if he could be transferred to weekends in order to enjoy more time with the children. This meant that he spent eight hours a week in the car rather than sixteen, and though the effect on the children was negligible, it made John feel better, even if he believed he deserved something more considered than a distant grunt when he stood at the foot of the stairs and shouted, 'Well, I'm off to work now. See yer later.'

When he heard that a university study had concluded that half of all British fathers spend less than ten minutes per day with their children, he found this hard to believe – after all, ten minutes of quality time seemed to him to be an unattainable dream, though under the heading of 'extenuating circumstances' he would have mentioned that he was scared of Thomas, who as a child appeared to have been intended for another planet, and that Flossie refused to have much to do with him unless he was taking her to a Kylie Minogue gig.

John might have found the anarchy of a family hard to deal with, but he was heartbroken when the children went away to university and it was just him and me left in the house. He missed them so much. He was, by his own admission, an emotional fellow, but I don't think he ever shed quite so many tears as when the children left home. When Flossie headed off to university, he was inconsolable. 'I felt as low as I can remember feeling in all my life as Floss disappeared down the lane,' he wrote in the week she left.

If there was one shortfall for me in our family life, it was that we never went on enough holidays. I used to see my friends setting off in the summer and feel a little pang of jealousy. But John hated flying. He had been advised to take a course to overcome his fear, but reasoned that it would be of little use – should the plane start to take a nosedive, having taken a course would hardly excuse him from the crash. He struggled with this phobia throughout our marriage, knowing that he was limiting our travel options. While we were in Peru, he even said that he wanted to conquer his fear with hypnotherapy once we returned to England.

And there was John's work, which had to take precedence. Summer was festival time for him, and one of the busiest periods in his calendar. Instead of holidays, we had festivals. I never attended Glastonbury, preferring instead to use it as an excuse to have a peaceful weekend on my own. But John adored it. He first went with Marc Bolan in 1970, and later as part of the Radio 1 team. He liked taking the children backstage at Glastonbury so that they could become accustomed to ignoring famous pop stars – disrespect for celebrities being something that he considered an essential trait in any sane human being.

The children didn't always get into the spirit of Glastonbury; some of them, who would prefer to remain anonymous in this context, stayed in the caravan drinking tea rather than venturing out to see Rancid Hell Spawn play a set of ballads on the second stage. William, to his credit, camped outside the media enclosure once, but got attacked by a man with a big candle who thought he was taking the piss out of his hat when in fact he was simply asking, 'Have you seen a big tent that looks like a Cornish pasty?'

Apart from festivals, only BBC-related trips could tempt John away from his show. One of the most recent was our cruise back from New York on the *QE2* accompanied by other *Radio Times* contributors, editorial team members and a horde of readers. John and I flew out to New York a week earlier, with John having been tranquillised into fly mode by wantonly exceeding the dosage prescribed on the box.

This was my first trip to the US, and John's first since leaving San Bernardino in 1967. We had a miraculously good time there, making the obvious tourist stops and snapping away at the Chrysler Building, which John considered possibly the most beautiful man-made object on earth. We stood on a crowded intersection a block off the East River and watched the Fourth of July fireworks, ate and drank in Mexican and Indian restaurants and Irish bars, and spent an evening at Birdland celebrating the venue's importance in the history of music, before discovering that it was actually the third room to be called Birdland and Charlie Parker had never played there at all.

To compensate for this we walked forty-five blocks to Greenwich Village to meet the singer Laura Cantrell, whom John had proclaimed on his programme to be the best artist he had heard in ten years, see the house where Charlie Parker had lived, and seek sanctuary from the heat in a couple of neighbourhood bars – one apparently the last bar in the city to admit women, the other by reputation a former speakeasy. The second of these, John reported proudly, had Liverpool FC graffiti in the Gents: 'Scousers here, Scousers there, Scousers every—' well, you know how it goes.

On the cruise back home, John took his turn to be quizzed by the cruise director, in front of the passengers, on the stage of the Queen's Room. The director had already asked John if he still appeared on *The Archers*, with an aside that he must remember to start watching it again. Delia Smith, Alan Hansen and Barry Norman had all been through a similar process with minimal bruising, although Barry had been addressed at least once as Norman and had to endure being called Norman Norman by the rest of us for the following twenty-four hours. When it was John's turn to talk, he said he regretted eating a minimum of three enormous meals a day since we set sail, and tried to persuade the audience that when we had boarded he had been a svelte eleven stone and not the fat little guy they now saw before them. Some of them may even have believed him. We mingled with the readers afterwards, and left the ship in Southampton wishing that some of them lived within striking distance – the couple whose daughter had got married while they were on board, or that nice man with the white beard from York. The man was from York, that is, not the beard.

Our most memorable and enlightening trips were those promotional jaunts organised by the BBC to promote the World Service. These were wonderful times, and often dramatically illuminating, such as our visit to Sierra Leone, which Dave Tate from the World Service arranged in conjunction with the British Council. John visited the university, and did a question-and-answer session with the students, who were all very charming and shy. The British Council did some splendid work in the country, and John enjoyed engaging with the people there, despite his own shyness. But it was quite an upsetting trip; we witnessed a level of poverty that left us feeling physically shaken. After a while, we realised that we hadn't seen any elderly people on our travels. That's when our guide explained that few people lived beyond forty.

Our favourite trip had been another joint venture between the British Council and the World Service, this time to Zimbabwe in 1988. John's role on this occasion was to open a pop-music exhibition in Harare, though he was careful to remind himself that he had only been asked after Dave Lee Travis had turned it down. 'I'm only here because Dave Lee Travis couldn't be' – that's the kind of thing that will always keep a man from getting ideas above his station.

Dave didn't know what he was missing. The trip was a complete joy from the moment we touched down in Zimbabwe; by the time we left, John was seriously considering moving there. We spent a lot of time travelling into the townships to sample the local music scene. There was dancing everywhere. In one bar that we visited just outside Harare, an elderly man approached John and asked why he wasn't dancing. John replied, 'I don't like to,' to which the man responded by proffering the bottle of beer he was clutching. 'Have this and you'll feel like dancing,' he beamed.

Another night, we went with Biggie Tembo to see a local band, the Four Brothers, who were performing at the Saratoga

Club. John first met Biggie when Andy Kershaw took him to see Biggie's band, the Bhundu Boys, in London. Halfway through the gig, Andy turned to John and realised that he had plump tears cascading down his cheeks, so uplifted was he by the music. Much the same can be said for the Four Brothers. John and I felt so exhilarated by their songs; they could lift you up on the darkest days. I danced with Biggie during three numbers, and when we left the dance floor there was enthusiastic applause; John said afterwards that he felt rather proud.

When the Four Brothers had finished, John said wistfully that he wished they could play at his birthday party. And they did. I arranged for them to perform in our garden, and even as John was entering the marquee on his fiftieth birthday, he had no idea which band he was going to find there. It had been quite an effort keeping it a secret. John and I had been at the Reading Festival a few days before his birthday, where the Bhundu Boys were playing – and where Biggie babysat for Thomas, who insisted on pronouncing his name as Big Ears – and friends kept approaching me and asking me about the party. But when John set eyes on the Four Brothers in the marquee, he was completely surprised, as well as speechless.

That trip to Zimbabwe was also important because we got to visit Victoria Falls, which John had always wanted to see ever since he saw a photograph of it as a child. There were four places, in fact, on this wish list that he had compiled in his youth. As well as Victoria Falls, he got to see the Taj Mahal, and he also visited the Pyramids, where he had his photograph taken riding a camel – a pose that he'd wanted to replicate since seeing a picture of his father doing the same. The fourth place on John's list was Machu Picchu.

Our excursion to Victoria Falls was memorable for more than just the grandeur of the location. Once we were there, we hired bicycles and rode by The Falls; the spray was momentarily cool and refreshing on our faces, but it dried in an instant in the thick heat. We cycled on to what was formerly the Zambian border with the intention of crossing to see The Falls from the other side. The border guards didn't seem too keen to let us pass until John commented that he was hoping to go into Livingstone to buy some records. One of the guards wanted to know which records, and when John mentioned a few names, he seemed suddenly interested. 'Do you know "Samora Michel" by Shalawambe?' he asked. 'Of course!' replied John. And after he'd duetted with the border guard on a few verses of the song, we had our passports stamped and were waved cheerfully through.

The children didn't normally accompany us on these trips, although William came with us on one World Service expedition to Bulgaria, where we spent a week or so on a double-decker bus, stopping off at various places to hand out pens and leaflets and carrier bags. We would get mobbed in market squares by people desperate for anything we were willing to give them. At the end of each day we would clean the bus, then sleep in a hotel and set off the next morning to distribute more pens and leaflets and carrier bags. It was on that trip that William fell dramatically in love with three different girls, two of whom nursed him on a park bench after he had been horribly sick. In recent years he seems to have recovered from this whirlwind non-romance, and also to have severed his emotional attachment to Bulgarian wine.

But apart from that, none of the children came with us on those more far-flung expeditions. Or, as Thomas puts it, they never got invited anywhere exciting. Perhaps he is forgetting the family trip to Finland in 1991. We went because we'd never been there before, and also because John did a show for Radio Mafia in Helsinki. We reached Denmark through Germany but found that, by and large, the country was shut. We drove to Legoland. Shut. We drove to the Tivoli Gardens. Shut. We looked for a hotel.

On the way, we subsisted on service-station food, swiftly ran out of money and ended up staying in the one establishment in Copenhagen that had any vacancies – a venue for gay assignations where I was spat at on the staircase. It may not have been Disneyland, but no-one could say it wasn't character building.

In the morning, we took the ferry to Sweden. Sweden turned out to be even more shut. There were no cafés, no shops, no hotels. After two days of virtually non-stop driving, we decided that the international symbol for cafés, the crossed knife and fork, must, in Sweden at least, mean that if you could find a shop that was open, you would be able to buy a knife and fork. For two days, we lived on chocolate. So depressed were we all by now that we voted to abandon our attempt to reach Finland, settling instead for having our photographs taken outside the factory in Huskvarna where our fridge was made.

Despite the size of the family, John and I still managed to get plenty of time to ourselves. One of the reasons why we lasted so long, and so well, was that we spent half the week apart, but never stopped longing for one another. The worst I can say about him was that he had a terribly annoying habit of sitting in the car with the engine running when he was trying to persuade me to get a move on. Not much of a complaint, I suppose.

And as far as I know John wasn't overly irritated by anything I did, except maybe when I would pop to the garden centre for a plant and return with several acres' worth of foliage crammed into the boot of the car. Or whenever I was late for anything. Yes, come to think of it, that really annoyed him. John was hyper-punctual: he'd arrive for his train so early that he would be there in time for the one *before* the one he had intended to catch. Or when I spent hours on the telephone: that really got on his nerves too. But that's still pretty good for more than thirty-five years together.

Whenever John was asked, as he often was, how we had managed to maintain our marriage, he usually came up with some Wildean quote like, 'The secret of having a long and happy marriage is not trying too hard to have a long and happy marriage.' He didn't like to go into any more detail than that. He declined plenty of invitations to be interviewed about the complete and utter wonderfulness of our marriage because he felt it would be tempting fate to brag about it publicly. Whenever anyone boasts about the rock on which their relationship is founded, you can usually bank on one of them eloping with someone half their age within days.

I had always told people that there were countless differences between John and me, but I feel hard pressed now to think what they were: perhaps we just grew more alike as the years went by. The children have their own ideas about what distinguished us from one another. Having discussed this with them, it seems to come down to the idea that I am level-headed while John was a miniature Mount Etna who might erupt one moment with cascades of love, and the next shower with molten lava any poor souls who happened to be loitering within a ten-mile radius.

Danda tells me that if she had done something stupid – like, say, break a family heirloom, or join a Satanic cult – then she would have an approximate idea of my reaction, whereas John might do anything from banning her from ever setting foot again in Suffolk to congratulating her on her innate good sense. That's why she was so terrified about telling him when she was pregnant with Archie; she genuinely had no idea which way he would go.

Often he would be most incensed by things that seemed insignificant to others. An abandoned coffee mug in the living room could be the catalyst for Armageddon. On the other hand, the spiralling debts incurred by a hedonistic student lifestyle, or the comprehensive destruction of the family car, could summon forth from John a show of parental warmth and affection normally associated with the safe return of a loved one from a long-fought war. There was simply no knowing.

The children learned how to divide up their various wants and needs to maximise their gains. If those needs were material, they'd go to John. If they needed to minimise the consequences of some wrongdoing or other, a quiet word in my ear would be required. It must be like that in every two-parent family: each parent at some point acts as intermediary or diplomat. And John had other uses too. If the children's homework had an imaginative or literary basis, they would take it to John for advice or approval. He would point out how poorly written their assignment was, to which they could only reply, 'I know, Dad, I'm eight.' Invariably he would take over, correcting spelling, restructuring sentences, even rewriting entire paragraphs if he was in an especially domineering mood.

The homework would be handed in, and the child would be duly summoned before the teacher, who would then accuse him or her of enlisting John's help. When John heard about this, he would be furious. 'How can they say you haven't written this?' he would rage. The absurdity of his position was apparently lost on him.

After a while, the children learned not to turn to John for their various sick notes, since he would invariably write them on postcards, or in the over-familiar style in which he composed his columns for *Sounds* or *Radio Times*. 'Mum,' they would say, out of John's earshot, 'I can't hand in this note. It's so . . . *silly*.'

And they learned to exercise discernment too in requesting John's assistance with homework. Danda once came to him asking for help with a story on the theme of suspense. Everyone else in her class handed in generic scary stories. But Danda, following the advice of her father, wrote an account of an ordinary humdrum day that ended abruptly when the specified word-length had been reached. 'Now that's suspense,' reasoned John, 'because you're left wondering what happened next.' What happened next was that Danda got an 'F'.

So as she got older, she would take fewer of his suggestions on board. Once he read one of her essays and decided that she should drop some jokes into it. 'Dad,' she reasoned, 'it's about female genital mutilation. There's not a great deal of scope there for humour.'

While John's own response to the prospect, or rather threat, of university had been one of cheerful indifference, his subsequent years of gigging at higher-education establishments across the country illustrated to him that student life brought with it benefits equal to, if not far beyond, degrees and doctorates. At some point it dawned on him that students were, by and large, having a whale of a time.

That idea appealed to him. He had told Danda that one of his happiest memories was from when she was about fifteen, and he saw her making her way to a meadow in Stowmarket where teenagers generally idled away their days. He watched her walking there with twenty or so of her friends, ready for an evening of getting hammered on cheap cider and Lambrusco, and he was overcome suddenly with pride and contentment. She was, he realised, enjoying her life, and that pleased him no end.

His rather irreverent attitude towards the children's education was clearly influenced by the rigid parameters within which he had been taught as a boy. Imagination and invention were generally frowned upon during John's school years, and he didn't want his own children to feel cramped or oppressed by education, as he had done. The children don't remember their father expressing discontentment when their grades weren't up to scratch. John had a lack of faith in the education system, preferring the children to get as much extra-curricular information and experience as possible.

This could mean something as simple as letting them stay up late with him to watch a television programme that he felt would be more beneficial to their development than their school work, which is how some of them were able to devour *Twin Peaks* in its entirety long before their minds were properly equipped to do so. Or it could mean taking the children out of school to go travelling; William and Danda were both removed from classes in the mid-eighties to accompany John to the studios of Radio Bremen in Germany, where he recorded two regular shows – the British Forces Broadcasting Service programme *Mittagspause* (Midday Break) and *Ritz*. These were done with disapproving engineers who hated the music, and John, and the fact that he was speaking in English. It made for a very hostile environment, but John was much comforted whenever William and Danda came along with him.

The German shows went on for a few years, but John was very shabbily treated, and eventually the station dropped his programmes with no explanation or notice – the first he heard of it was when a listener wrote asking why he was no longer broadcasting. He had begun recording the programmes at home and sending them over, and the station had simply stopped putting them out.

I think John felt particularly aggrieved because he had always enjoyed an affectionate relationship with Germany; he even drove a German car with left-hand drive. So many of the friends we acquired over the years were German. There were always swarms of leather-clad Germans pulling into our drive-way in undersized cars. John would feel very paternal towards them, which was rather funny in the case of our friend Tullus, who is seven foot tall and rather like an excitable child. People in England are prone to remarking, 'You're tall, aren't you?' in a manner that implies they are worried that Tullus might not have noticed how tall he is and should be told before he hurts himself.

Six months after John died, two German brothers did indeed appear in the driveway, wearing leather and spilling out of a Nissan Micra. They had come from Berlin to see the studio where John recorded those programmes. 'Your father is one of the greatest men in my life,' one of them explained to Thomas as he showed them around the house. 'Is there any chance you will keep this room exactly as it is, like a museum?' asked the other fellow as they entered the studio. They were very sweet. They took a photograph of a German dictionary placed beside John's decks. One of them was so taken aback that he started to reel. 'I am feeling slightly dizzy now,' he explained.

The German programmes were a source of pride to John, and a success with listeners. The BFBS programme was intended for the military, but in fact its audience was comprised largely of German teenagers. John thought it was hilarious that as a result of these shows he was voted 'Top DJ in Europe', despite not being able to speak more than a few disparate words of German.

His shows were valuable for many young Germans starting out in their own bands. The Berlin group To Rococo Rot was one of those who named John as the reason why they per-severed with their music, despite the oppressive regime in East Berlin at the time. Bands had to apply officially to the govern-ment for permission to play gigs. If they were approved, they would then be told where and when they could play, for how long, and even what clothes they should wear. In this climate, it was only the music on John's show that gave them a taste of what was happening musically beyond the Wall, and en-couraged them to keep going.

When he curated Meltdown in 1998, John invited another Berliner, Xol Dog 400, to play. It was one of the best and wildest gigs of the fortnight, and possibly the year. Xol Dog 400 is a madman specialising in hardcore techno. Once he'd mixed a record in, he would throw himself into the crowd and start going crazy along with them, dancing with his head-phones on, putting his ear against the thumping speakers, and then clambering back on stage in time to mix in the next record. He was so intimidating during the gig that it was somehow all the more shocking when he breezed into the after-show party looking cheerful and ordinary, inviting William and Thomas to stay with him in Berlin, and generally being more kindly lollipop man than rabid German techno DJ.

It didn't seem to matter how large John's audiences were, or how much acclaim he received for his shows – he was never secure in his job. He liked getting awards, and won the DJ polls most years in *NME* and *Melody Maker*, but if there was ever an occasion when he didn't come out on top, he would automatically think: Oh God, this is the end. He was always waiting for some young gun to swan in and make his or her name by being the DJ who replaced John Peel. Ironically, no single person has filled the job since John died, and Radio 1 plugged the gap instead with three different presenters. I wonder what John would have made of that.

Perhaps John's constant insecurity provided him with the creative tension necessary to stave off complacency. If he had ever considered himself indispensable, the show might have gone downhill. His anxiety was always there, beneath whatever he was doing, only rising to the surface when the time came around for annual contract negotiations. When those talks were over, he was usually so relieved that another year had passed without Radio 1 finding a way to get rid of him that he would quietly stomach whatever new limits had been imposed on his running time. The rest of us, though, were furious at the way his show was being surreptitiously nipped and tucked.

John escaped the Radio 1 clearout in 1993, when Matthew Bannister took over from Johnny Beerling as the station's Controller. Matthew fired those DJs whom he considered to be anchoring the station in the past, but declared that John would always have a place on Radio 1. They got on well, and John approved of the changes, at least initially. For many years, he had got a cheap laugh by claiming that he knew very little about the station because he never listened to it. But under Matthew, Radio 1 became for the first time a station more in tune with some of John's philosophies about broadcasting. By the beginning of 1994, he was approving enough of Matthew's rejuvenation strategy to praise the station in print:

> The new 1FM, built on footings dug by Johnny Beerling, has contrived to sound different without sounding as though it is being different for the sake of being different, if you see what I mean, and the respect, even affection, for the listener which is the best thing that Mark Radcliffe, Mark Tonderai, Andy Kershaw, Claire Sturgess, Pete Tong and others have brought to the station, has been the provider of an atmosphere that has encouraged veterans such as Steve Wright and Nicky Campbell to reinvent themselves.

It took some time, and several blows to John's own airtime, before he realised that he had been premature in his enthusiasm. Matthew assured John that this wasn't a case of death by a thousand cuts, though John found it awfully difficult to see what else it could be. With the announcement in early 1996 of a new drum-and-bass show that would eat into John's airtime, it struck him that he had been made weirdly complicit in his own downsizing. On 25 January 1996, he put his feelings on paper in a letter to the Controller:

Dear Matthew

I wanted to say how disappointed I was to lose yet another hour on air in the recent schedule changes. I had naively imagined when I heard you were attempting to contact me that you were going to tell me that you had, as you had suggested you might a year earlier, managed to claw back some time.

As you may have noticed over the past few years, I have enthusiastically supported, in thought, word and deed, the many changes you and your team have made to Radio 1. I did this, not out of any thought of self-preservation, but because I believed that the changes were very much needed. No-one doubts, I think, that Radio 1 is a much better station now than it was in the last days of Beerling. Last summer, our son William gently pointed out that part of the policy I was endorsing included the gradual reduction of my hours on the radio. (Our other son, Thomas, was more forthright when I told him why you had called the other day. 'They're taking the piss, Dad,' he said.)

When you came to Radio 1, it was with, amongst many other things, ringing endorsements of the type of programming practised by Andy Kershaw and myself. Andy was overjoyed. I advised caution, knowing that such attitudes can change overnight, particularly when there is much critical hostility to the changes that are being made – as there was, of course. There does seem to be a new orthodoxy in the air, one which supports narrowly focused programmes rather than broadly based ones built on the if-you-don't-like-this-record-wait-until-you-hear-the-next-one principle.

Over the years my programmes have often been the first to play music which subsequently found a wider audience and, very occasionally, a niche on Radio 1. This, I know, is what I am employed to do.

For example, I started playing hip-hop when the first records, imported from New York, arrived in this country. I did this despite the fact – perhaps, on reflection, partly because of it – that a producer and presenter both came to me independently and told me I should not be playing what was, in their view, the music of black criminals. Now, of course, we have Westwood – and quite rightly so, although I would suggest that he should have been on Radio 1 seven or eight years ago. This, I know, was the fault of the previous regime.

Since then, I have played jungle – for about three, three and a half years, I think – and we are, again quite rightly, about to have a jungle programme. I have played reggae since 1968 and, apart from two sadly misconceived programmes that ran fitfully for a while in the seventies and eighties, no-one else has. Now there is to be a reggae programme and, again, this is exactly as it should be. What saddens me is the fact that, with the introduction of these programmes, I lose air time. I already have to leave unplayed music which I believe deserves exposure and, with the new hours, this situation can only get worse. I already circulate lists of recommended records that I have not had time to play to an admittedly small number of regular listeners.

I know that no-one has the right to be given radio time and that with the number of new programmes that you are scheduling, something has to give. I appreciate the move to Sunday night, understanding that on Friday night people are out, going out, watching laddish comedy stuff on television and so on. I agree with you that Sunday night is a better time for my/our programmes.

I hope you understand this. There remains in me, I suppose, some of the old hippie and something of an evangelical fervour about the work I do. I think – and I hope this isn't going to read wrong – that the programmes on which I have worked, with a range of enthusiastic people from Bernie Andrews to Alison Howe, have contributed to the enduring health of British music and the capacity of that music to reinvent itself. There are several things going on now which may or may not evolve into something substantial. It would be disappointing, in the event of one or other of these being really popular, to lose yet another hour so that you could schedule time for programmes devoted to it.

Think of my programmes as your research department. Noisy, smelly but occasionally coming up with the formulae which you can subsequently market. Thanks for reading this. John Peel.

*

Since 1992, John had been attending the annual TT Races on the Isle of Man in the company of Andy Kershaw. Andy was, and is, a complete bike nut, and only persuaded John to go by arranging all the transport and accommodation. On that first visit, John professed himself astonished that thousands of people from all over Europe could come together in a confined space, consume absurd quantities of strong drink and not kick each other's heads in. He also found it wonderful, after the prices, predictability and showbiz bullshit of Grand Prix motor racing, to see some proper white-knuckle stuff again.

These annual breaks could be full of surprises. It came as a shock to John, for instance, to discover that those muscles normally assigned the job of preventing him from breaking wind in public were given responsibility for clutching on to what he was horrified to learn was called the 'buddy pad' of Andy's mighty Harley. Being a country boy, John thought the combination of racing, mountain sunshine, amusing companions, fattening food and bottles of beer and wine would make him swoon clear away with pleasure. But the dangers involved were forcefully underlined whenever he looked up to see, say, Steve Hazlett or Martin Ayles cartwheeling through the air and almost receiving unwelcome and high-speed rectal surgery courtesy of a row of fence-posts.

One morning in June 1996, while John was away with Andy and his wife Juliet at the TT, I was gripped by an agonising headache. I had been polishing in the kitchen when I suddenly had to drop everything and stumble outside for some fresh air. Thomas and Flossie, who were sitting at the kitchen table, watched with increasing concern as I began to wander around aimlessly, fighting the terrible nausea and clutching my head. I was completely disoriented. I managed to stagger to the living room, where I collapsed on the sofa and started drifting in and out of consciousness. Danda came down from her bedroom and phoned my sister Gabrielle, who sped over from her house in the village. When she arrived, I was groaning in agony. Danda remembers that I kept saying I wanted to die because the pain was so bad.

My doctor, who was also a family friend, came to the house to check me over. I remember it was his first day back at work after a heart operation. 'What are you trying to do to me?' he demanded. An ambulance was called. Thomas whizzed to the top of the winding lane on his 50cc motorbike, and waited in the village to flag down the ambulance, which arrived bearing more flashing lights than a mobile disco. The driver later said that he was less worried about me than he was about Thomas, whose vision through his visor as he led the ambulance back to the house was obscured by tears.

I was rushed to hospital in Ipswich, and wheeled into a darkened room where a doctor told me to keep as still as I could. 'You've had a brain haemorrhage,' he explained.

'What does that mean?' I asked.

'It means you'll need an operation as soon as possible.'

'What if I don't?'

'You'll die.'

'And what if I do?'

'You still might die.'

Gabrielle received the news in much the same straight-talking fashion. She was called into a room away from Danda, Thomas and Flossie, where a doctor told her, 'I don't want to say this to the children, but you should be aware that she may not make it.' Then Gabrielle had to go back in to face the others with a brave face. One of the nurses had given Danda my sandals and said, 'You might as well take these.' I have this sad image of Danda clutching my sandals disconsolately while trying to reach John on the hospital payphone. In the end, the children returned home, where Danda managed to get through to Juliet on the Isle of Man.

'Is Dad with you?' she asked.

'Of course,' Juliet replied.

'Can you stay with him while I speak to him?'

When John heard what had happened, his immediate reaction was, in hindsight, less than comforting. 'Do you realise that if your mum goes, I go too?' he blurted. 'I don't want to go on living without her.' I don't know exactly what thought sprang to Danda's mind as she heard that, but it can't have been too far from: Gee, Dad, thanks for the moral support.

Once John had calmed down, he got the details from Danda, and Andy arranged heroically to get him back home as soon as possible.

Neither Andy nor John were the kind of people who played the celebrity card for personal gain. But when Andy called the ferry company and discovered that all the crossings were fully booked, he thought this was probably a good time to make an exception. When he explained the circumstances to the representative on the phone, he was told to bring John to the next ferry: they would find room for him and Andy. John said many times since then that he couldn't have wished for someone better in that situation. Thanks to Andy, John was at my bedside in the early hours of the following day.

By the time John reached me, I had been moved to Addenbrookes Hospital in Cambridge for my operation. The children remember that their father was strangely calm when he got there. The nearer he got to me, the calmer he seemed to become. It was a bit like his attitude to watching Liverpool matches. When he wasn't there in the stands, he would sometimes feel impotent and frightened, scarcely able to bear watching on television. But if he could just be at the game in person, cheering them on, then he would have the sense of being somehow able to influence events, to tip the score in Liverpool's favour. Likewise, he could scarcely bear the pressure when he was stuck on the Isle of Man, howling into the night sky, fearing that he would never see me again. Once he was at the hospital, he was somehow in control again.

Before the operation, the doctor told John and Danda that there was only a 30–40 per cent chance that I would survive the operation. Apparently, the type of haemorrhage I had suffered was usually fatal.

When I came round, I remember John sleeping in the chair next to my bed. I had an impressive bandage on my head, as robust as a turban, with a drain emerging from the back. The children were all in my room; William had come down with his partner Zahra on the train from Liverpool, where he was in his first year. It wasn't long before the gravity of my condition was being dispelled with laughter: we're very good in our family at fooling around during the darkest times. I even remembered the advice of John's mother, and got Danda to paint my toenails while I was languishing in my hospital bed. There is nothing worse, you see, than coming round after almost dying from a brain haemorrhage only to be confronted by an ugly row of unpainted toenails.

I was discharged after a couple of weeks, and there was no shortage of friends and relatives to look after me. John also received lots of support while I was ill, especially from his brother Alan, who put his own life on hold temporarily to be with John.

My illness had been reported in the newspapers, and I was inundated with bouquets and messages of support; when I left hospital, the children distributed my flowers around the ward because there were far too many to drag back home. However, there was a downside to this interest in my condition. When I returned to the house, a journalist from one of the Sunday tabloids called John demanding an interview and photographs, and threatened to camp outside the house and harass me if he didn't comply. John agreed reluctantly to talk, but drew the line at pictures. Still, it was reassuring to know that the press was pursuing with fiercely ethical vigour a story so clearly in the public interest.

The doctors had predicted some deterioration in my

eyesight. That aside, I recovered well, though I suffered a fit three years later as a result of scar tissue pressing on nerves in my brain. I had been rushing around organising John's sixtieth-birthday party when I just collapsed; naturally everyone feared it was another haemorrhage. Though I was pretty spaced out – I remember at one point trying to let dogs out of my hospital room because I was convinced I was at home – I was soon back home and arranging the party, against the doctors' wishes. Photos from the day show me smiling serenely, but in truth I don't remember a thing about it.

I know that my illness had a serious impact on John. After I returned from hospital, he was always checking on me. He'd get up in the middle of the night to go to the bathroom, and he would lean over me to make sure I was still breathing. If he couldn't be absolutely certain in the darkness, he would even turn on the light, at the risk of waking me, just to make sure. He later wrote:

> For ten days, I watched with something approaching reverence those tending Sheila on Ward A3. Their generosity and tenderness transcended anything I could have imagined. By now, the nature of nursing and care will have meant that they have forgotten us as they turn to other hurt and frightened patients and their families, but we will never, never forget a single one of them. They did, after all, combine to save Sheila's life.

*

The music industry had changed dramatically in the nineties. What would have been termed 'indie music' a few years earlier was becoming increasingly popular, and more easily accommodated into the daytime schedules. In the eighties, New

Order, Echo and the Bunnymen, the Smiths, Pixies and Mudhoney had found their only British radio exposure on John's show, but their nineties equivalents – Blur, Radiohead, Pulp, Nirvana – were all over the airwaves.

There was no shortage of music that John played but which daytime radio still wouldn't touch with a bargepole. Yet he found that he had to realign himself, or readjust his expectations. Bands that he had been championing might want to record more sessions with him once they had found success. But their management or record company would often choose instead to plump for other shows earlier in the day, such as *The Evening Session*, which had a wider audience. So despite having helped their careers, John would lose out.

He was also incredulous to find that Radio 1 breakfast DJs were continuing the station's tradition of advising listeners about what they could be watching on television in the evenings rather than listening to John's show. Whenever he mentioned this, however, it had no effect other than to make him unpopular with colleagues.

It was perfectly understandable that John felt nervous in this climate – after all, he was approaching sixty in a medium routinely categorised as youth-oriented. He was bound to feel paranoid. And still he didn't want to move to Radio 2, as many of his colleagues had done, because he felt that would bring a different audience. He valued the fact that he was broadcasting to teenagers, and he wanted to be there for them. He saw his role as always offering something new.

While he would never willingly have left Radio 1, John had been working regularly on Radio 4 since 1995, when he began the series *Offspring*. He had always loved doing things for Radio 4: he saw them as the more traditional side of the BBC, and liked being associated with that at the same time as being on Radio 1. Chris Berthoud from *Home Truths* told me that John had a peculiar fondness for bringing together these two sides of his professional life; apparently John was delighted whenever his Radio 1 and Radio 4 teams could be united over a long boozy lunch. He always had something of the match-maker about him.

If forced to choose between the two stations, though, John would have clung passionately to his Radio 1 programme, even if it had been pruned to a single hour. Once a month. Every leap year.

But he needed Radio 4 in his diet too. He was thrilled at being asked to appear on *Desert Island Discs*, and was especially sad that his parents weren't around to hear that. And he could scarcely believe it when he was asked on to *The Archers*. He had been a fan of the programme since before dinosaurs walked the earth, as had Walters, and both men were long-time members of the Eddie Grundy Fan Club. When John met Princess Margaret at a *Desert Island Discs* anniversary party, their conversation was dominated by the coincidence that they had both appeared on *The Archers* as themselves. Not as incredible as if they'd both appeared on *The Archers* as each other, admittedly, but certainly enough to bond over.

The first edition of *Offspring* went out in September 1995. The *Radio Times* announced it as 'a foray into the family' and called John a 'seasoned chronicler of domestic life in his *Radio Times* column'. He'd never been described as a 'seasoned chronicler' before and thought it a measure of the brawling times in which we live that he could be so described after less than two years of chronicling.

He has already written here about his ambivalent feelings

towards the label 'self-deprecating', but he liked spotting other ways in which people would attempt to encapsulate him in a sentence. A pupil interviewed by a local paper after John had visited his school observed that John was 'quite with it for his age'. 'Eccentric recluse' was another of John's favourites. He was overjoyed to be considered eccentric, though he wondered what exactly he did that genuinely merited that adjective, unless you counted occasionally going to the village shop in his bedroom slippers, or refusing sometimes to wear trousers around the house. 'My legs get overheated,' he would protest whenever Danda complained that her friends had been traumatised by accidentally seeing him in his underpants. She would find herself silently praying, '*Please let him have his kecks on*' whenever she was bringing a friend home.

John's eccentricity possibly found its pinnacle in his habit of collecting portions of himself in a plastic container labelled 'Dad's Scrapings'. Toenails, blistered skin, verrucas – if it fell off John, it was in there. Whenever he shed some part of himself, he would bring it in to show everyone. We'd point out that it was disgusting and he'd say, 'Oh, you'll all be fighting over these toenails when I'm dead.'

It wasn't just bits of his body that he hoarded. He couldn't bring himself to throw anything away. He once managed to squeeze an industrial-sized Comic Relief red nose, about two metres in diameter, into his car; he had seen it on the side of Broadcasting House, had formed a close bond with it, and couldn't bear to see it ruthlessly discarded. The decline of my ancient Renault 4 after I had used it to thieve manure for the garden was not, in John's mind, a cue to hasten its passage to the scrap heap, but rather an opportunity to build it into the wall of the house and use it as a door. I saw to it, though, that this never came to pass.

About old biros he was especially sentimental. 'That pen's been good to me these past few weeks,' he would point out. 'It's served me well. How can I discard it?' I had to prise things off him in order to throw them in the bin. Invariably I'd find them back in his room, and would have to chuck them out again. He genuinely felt sympathy for these inanimate objects.

It was the sort of behaviour that would have fitted in neatly on any edition of *Home Truths*, and helps explain why he took so naturally to the programme and made it his own. *Offspring* had been a success dealing with a slightly narrower brief, and *Home Truths* was essentially *Offspring*'s offspring. The trouble was that even its makers weren't entirely sure what it would be about.

John met with the executive producer, Peter Griffiths, in February 1998, and said, 'I just ask one thing of you: that you don't try to turn me into a Radio 4 presenter. I am who I am and I don't particularly want to change now.' Peter agreed, and concurred with John that the show should be a celebrity-free zone. They got working on the pilot, which included an interview with an angler whose prize catch was a legendary carp. The angler described the lengths to which he and his rivals had gone in their pursuit of the fish: believing that it was intelligent enough to know when they were in the area, they had taken to parking their vehicles half a mile away so that the carp would not be alerted to their approach by engines and slamming doors. Then they would creep on all fours up to the lake's edge. After this item, John was hooked.

The programme was still lacking clear definition – 'Everyday life transformed by humour' was the shorthand phrase employed by Radio 4's Controller, James Boyle – but the makers knew that John's sense of humour would be pivotal to its personality.

Home Truths made its début on 11 April 1998. Rarely has any birth been the cause for less celebration. The calls and letters and emails were, to put it mildly, disheartening: the programme was described as 'inconsequential', 'rubbish', 'infantile rubbish', 'puerile rubbish', 'absolute rubbish', 'inane', 'irritating', 'droning nonsense' and 'tasteless, trendy, negative trash'. I could go on. They certainly did. One complainant saw a silver lining: 'Thank you for changing your Saturday-morning programmes because now they are so boring that I go out and see my friends.'

There were a few enthusiastic voices in the wilderness. 'You've got yourself a winner here,' wrote one man. 'Mr Peel is one of the most relaxed and thoughtful broadcasters in your organisation,' said another. 'He is made for this.' Over the next few months, general opinion began to shift gradually. The programme also started to find a neat balance between absurdity and weightiness. The themes and subjects were diverse: an item focusing on people who have a phobia about buttons preceded a piece in which a woman in Northern Ireland spoke matter-of-factly about visiting her parents' graves; the topic of slugs was very popular at one point, but there was also an edition in which John spoke to a couple who had survived a contract-killing attempt.

One sticking point for John was his reluctance to conduct interviews in person. He found the whole business of asking direct personal questions intensely embarrassing and intrusive, and the producers would constantly have to prod him to pose those awkward enquiries: 'But what were you actually feeling when you discovered that your best friend was sleeping with your husband/ your llama had been abducted/ you had hair growing there?'

This problem had been raised back in 1995, before the first edition of *Offspring* had even been recorded. John had told the producer, Fiona Couper, 'I can't interview people.' Fiona had responded to this spanner in the works by refusing to believe him, and saying, in a rather schoolmarmish manner, 'Of course you can, don't worry about it.' For one programme, she accompanied John to interview the poet Benjamin Zephaniah, who had written movingly about the experience of infertility. That was intended to be the focus of the item. But when they got to Benjamin's house, John was too shy to raise the subject. Instead, they talked for what seemed like hours about martial arts, and it was only as they were leaving that John asked about infertility.

John told his producers that he was worried about turning into Ricki Lake; I presume he meant he was concerned about the show becoming sensationalist, rather than that he thought he might start shouting, 'Go, girlfriend!' at strangers. A favourite defence when he was being forced to ask a prying question was for him to say to the interviewee, 'I've been told by my producer that I have to ask you this . . .' What was suspected at first to be a weakness – John's reluctance to dig for personal details – transpired to be a hidden strength, since interviewees realised immediately that John had nothing of the cynical investigative journalist about him, and so felt relaxed in his presence.

There were several series of *Offspring*, and it picked up a mantelpiece full of awards. A year after its début, *Home Truths* was repeating the pattern; John won Radio Broadcaster of the

Year at the Broadcasting Press Guild Awards, while the show took three Sony awards. Some of its harshest critics, though, were persistent in their derision, and close to home. I don't mean the children – they were never up early enough on a Saturday morning to hear it, though William has pointed out to me that he once heard half the programme. John was driving him to the station, and there was a moment of awkwardness as *Home Truths* started and it dawned on John that William had no idea what it was.

Harder for John to stomach was the derision with which *Home Truths* was greeted by Andy Kershaw and John Walters. They were so vocal in their dislike of the programme, deploring John's involvement in it, that it seemed as if they were accusing him of betraying or compromising his principles. But *Home Truths* was no less an accurate reflection of John than his Radio 1 shows had always been. John took the criticisms terribly hard. He invested so much of himself in the programme that the attacks couldn't help but feel personal.

I used to bring John breakfast in bed at quarter to nine most Saturday mornings, and then I would listen to the show in the kitchen while he listened in bed. It was just our ritual; I'm not sure how it evolved. Then he would come downstairs at ten and we'd have an informal little analysis of the programme, discussing what worked and what didn't.

Neither of us considered *Home Truths* to be perfect. He was aware that the material could sometimes be sugary or anodyne, and he tried to steer the show away from excessive whimsicality. But much of it was witty and poignant. And I thought it was lovely that John encouraged Bryan Gallagher, who had originally appeared on *Home Truths* as an interviewee, to write regularly for the programme. He recognised in

Bryan a genuine wit and dexterity with language, and helped him to become published in much the same way that he had previously given a boost to bands like the Undertones.

Not long after *Home Truths* had gained a toehold in the public's affections, John found that he was getting stopped much more. We could be at the supermarket and people would rush up to tell him their funny anecdotes in the hope that he would hear something that tickled his fancy.

A measure of how empathetic and approachable listeners found him came only a few months after the launch of *Home Truths*, when a woman named Dawn Gregory emailed John to ask if he would call round to check on her son Will, who was studying in Newcastle. 'Our son lives in a house with six friends,' she wrote, 'and is keen to convince us that his final year dissertation is underway. We are sure that the lure of pubs, clubs and the student union bar must be strong. How about giving him a ring and checking him out? You might even get tea and cake.' John happened to be up that way one day, so he called in on a suitably astonished Will and asked to see his work. It transpired that he had only written the opening sentence, though on the plus side John said he made a terrific cuppa.

The newfound attention in the wake of *Home Truths* could be disconcerting. We were at an open-air concert in summer 2004, when the man sitting next to me leaned across and said, 'Would you care for a biscuit, Sheila?' I just looked at him, dumbfounded. 'I won't offer John,' he continued, 'because I know he's diabetic, and these have got chocolate on.' I nearly fell off my chair. It felt strange that people knew so much about us without actually knowing us. That was the nature of John; he invited that familiarity.

It was just under three years earlier that John's diabetes had been diagnosed – on 11 September 2001, a day when John could concede that his problems were overshadowed by graver concerns.

He had been feeling sluggish for a long time, and was displaying many of the symptoms of diabetes: tiredness, mood swings that subsided after meals, dizzy spells, insatiable thirst. It hit me just how serious this was becoming when we were on our way back home from a weekend in Betws-y-Coed, where John had been filming something for the Welsh Tourist Board. When that was done, we hung out with Melys, a band that had featured a lot on the programme, and whom John had become good friends with after taking them with him to appear at the Gronigen Festival in Sweden. They're a lovely bunch, and I think John was even more chuffed than they were when their song 'Chinese Whispers' made the top of the Festive Fifty in 2001.

We had a rowdy weekend of boozing with Melys. Paul from the band worked as a chef in the hotel where we were staying, so we would go drinking in the evening with him and his wife and the rest of the group. John really enjoyed himself, but the journey home was hell. His vision became blurry, and he needed to keep stopping for naps.

The napping was nothing unusual. Having gigged across the country since the late sixties, John had developed techniques to prevent himself falling asleep on the drive home. He would keep one arm in the air whilst driving, so that if he dozed off, his arm would fall and startle him. If he had the scent of home in his nostrils, he would keep on going. But if he was excessively tired, he would simply pull over. The children have memories of returning from gigs with John, and having to sit in a lay-by with him while he had a snooze.

Upon returning from Wales, I ordered John to get himself checked out. When the results came in, the doctor told him to get over to the hospital immediately. He was in serious danger.

John was kept there on a drip for a week. We had rarely seen him looking so calm, or so relieved. He had obviously known for some time that something was wrong, and was just glad that it could be treated. As his health had begun to let him down, I'm sure too that his ever-present fears of being jettisoned by Radio 1 had been heightened. What I'm amazed at is how he slogged on regardless. Even before he was diagnosed, his stamina was unbelievable, especially given his age, the amount of hours he worked and the distance he covered each week. He could out-do anyone; whenever a band came to the house to do a live session, you could guarantee he would be up all night with them afterwards, knocking back one glass of red wine after another, orchestrating singalongs and generally holding court. When Laura Cantrell and her band did a session here, John stayed up until around four in the morning, putting on obscure records and challenging the musicians to perform their own versions.

I think the injections of insulin helped him mellow. On one level, they provided him with a new source of pleasure. It is impossible to overestimate just how much he enjoyed injecting himself in public, stabbing the needle through his T-shirt and into his belly in crowded restaurants, attracting startled looks and making himself the centre of attention. But they also tempered his moods. Despite having a work schedule that would have daunted a Trojan, John was happier and more contented in the last few years of his life than I had ever seen him.

It must have raised his self-esteem a few millimetres to have so much validation and approbation coming from every corner, and within such a relatively short space of time. At the end of 1995, John had been chosen to appear on *This Is Your Life*. The plan was to ambush him while he was presenting *Top of the Pops*. The problem was that he hadn't hosted *Top of the Pops* for around eight years, and was slightly puzzled, if pleased, to be asked after so long. The technology had changed since 1987, though, and John had some trouble adapting. 'Can you try to remember to look at the camera?' a weary voice would ask as acolytes were despatched to retrieve Boyzone or Björk from their dressing rooms with the glad tidings that they would be required to do their numbers once more because John had got it wrong again.

As if this was not unsettling enough, John had written a frankly hostile review of Björk's performance at that year's Reading Festival and found it most alarming to be standing a few feet from her. When she smiled unexpectedly at him, he assumed this was a prelude to sudden violence. 'POP GODDESS MAULS VETERAN DJ: POLICE NOT TO ACT, SAYS SPOKESMAN'-type headlines sprang into his thoughts.

Eventually John delivered his final link. Having said his goodbyes surrounded by fifteen-year-olds, he turned to remonstrate with someone who had been shoving particularly aggressively at his right elbow, only to find Michael Aspel standing there with a large red book in his hand. John was quick-witted enough not to express joy and gratitude immediately. He could imagine Michael saying, 'No, it's not for you, I'm afraid, John. Björk, This Is *Your* Life.' When he realised Michael had come for him, he said, 'I was actually quite looking forward to going home.'

To the astonishment of everyone who knew John, he didn't cry. Well, not much. But he loved every minute of it. As Danny Baker pointed out to him later, how could you fail to enjoy the only time in your life when your friends and family are obliged to applaud when you walk in the room?

In summer 1998, John was offered the OBE. I remember he hesitated momentarily and sought the family's advice. But William pointed out to him that if he turned it down, he would be one of those people who went around telling everyone that he had declined an OBE, so he should just go ahead and accept it. John agreed that this made perfect sense, so we trooped off to Buckingham Palace with Alan and Francis. The children, barred by sheer weight of numbers from attending the investiture, walked to the Palace gates with us before returning to our hotel.

The drill, once inside the Palace, was stiff and precise. Those being invested were separated almost at once from their guests and ushered into the gigantic Picture Gallery. After a bit of standing around, during which John earnestly hoped to see someone he could talk to (he was rescued from solitude by the companionable Terry Pratchett), he was called to attention to observe a demonstration of the processes he was about to go through. Once this splendidly patronising demonstration was over, names were called in groups of twelve. They were then led in single file through to an immense ballroom, before queuing to receive a medal and a few seconds of royal chat. This latter involved standing to attention, executing a smart left turn and humbly inclining the head; meat and drink to a former military man such as John.

The Prince of Wales spoke to each of the 150 recipients for around forty-five seconds. It would be a betrayal of trust to repeat what he said to John, but he was surprisingly forthright on the subject of the BBC. A princely handshake, firm but not oppressive, was the signal that John's moment was over. He retreated, bowed again and was dismissed to the right, re-entering the ballroom at the rear to sit and amuse himself by trying to locate friends and family in the bleachers that surrounded the room. John never spotted us; having explained to an usher that my eyesight was poor, and that I wouldn't be able to see if seated at the back, I was promptly seated at the back. Even ushers have to take their fun where they can.

Then there was the music – two hours or more of 'These You Have Loved', played with intermittent accuracy by a military ensemble. When we were finally discharged into the community again, we went with the children for a slap-up meal during which we all took photos of each other as the other patrons looked on and muttered, '*Provincials*.' It was a fantastic day, and John's only regret was that none of our parents had been alive to witness it, though happily my father had been with us when John received the letter the previous summer.

The honorary degrees and doctorates were tremendously gratifying for John, though there were other accolades that demanded to be taken with a fistful of salt. He was voted forty-seventh in the 1998 *Cosmopolitan* readers' poll, which translated as prettier than Woody Harrelson but not quite as fetching as Tony Blair. Being placed forty-third in the national poll of Great Britons was even more peculiar. We were surprised enough when we heard he was going to be in the list at all. Once we realised that he was going to make the top fifty we started thinking he could win it.

But most of the pleasure came from discovering whom he

had beaten rather than where he ranked. John was so pleased that he was thinking of some way of shoehorning the number forty-three into the title of this book. He did acknowledge, however, that the whole thing was a trifle silly. After all, he was placed above King Arthur, Chaucer and Sir Walter Raleigh, but below Guy Fawkes, Margaret Thatcher and, perhaps cruellest of all, David Beckham. One member of The Dawn Parade took it rather worse than John, complaining, 'Can't believe they gave that Greatest Briton shit to Churchill when there's a man among us who still plays Half Man Half Biscuit records on the taxpayer's buck.'

John's hospitalisation with diabetes had coincided with yet another celebration – a party to celebrate his fortieth year in broadcasting. When the party did finally go ahead a month later than planned, it featured small but perfectly formed sets by Billy Bragg, Nick Cave and Pulp. The last-named dedicated their song 'Help The Aged' to John, for which he was grudgingly grateful.

After the bands had finished, John played records for an hour and we all shuffled about loyally on the dance floor. Back at the hotel, I endeavoured to persuade John to sleep in the hotel bed rather than under it. He wasn't having any of it; he was too wrapped up in singing, as Johnnie Ray had done nearly fifty years earlier, 'It was a night. Oooh, what a night it was. Such a night.'

In the last few years, John seemed to acquire new motivation and energy. He was thrilled about the kind of artists who were doing sessions for him, first at Maida Vale, beginning in May 1998 with 60ft Dolls, and subsequently here at home. John enjoyed the Maida Vale ritual immensely. The evening would begin with him and the production team having dinner at a nearby Thai restaurant; sometimes the musicians – such as Loudon Wainwright III, Underworld or the Immortal Lee County Killers – would come too. When the meal was finished, John would be brought a hot towel, despite the fact that the restaurant didn't provide hot towels for its clientele; this was a special treat just for John. He would usually leave ten minutes before everyone else, at which point the others would smoke the cigarettes they had been holding back in his presence. John then went and sat in the booth in Maida Vale on his own and listened to records until his colleagues arrived with beer for the audience, and the band got ready to perform.

There were some incredible sessions there: Melys played a storming set the night Liverpool won the UEFA Cup; Melt Banana, Herman Dune, T. Raumschmiere and DJ Rupture were also among John's favourites. The White Stripes did a Maida Vale show in July 2001, the day before their gig at the 100 Club. John had been playing the seven-inches that Jack White had sent him, and had got his mitts on *White Blood Cells* just before Jack and Meg arrived in the UK.

When John and his producer Anita turned up at Maida Vale, the band were soundchecking, so John grabbed the chance for a nap. Anita told me she remembers Jack and Meg waiting expectantly for John to wake up. When he did, they all went to the Thai restaurant and talked about the blues. Jack quizzed John about the gigs he'd attended, and John told him all about having seen Gene Vincent. It seems strange in hindsight, but John had little sense of how the White Stripes were poised to explode in Britain. On the way back to the studio, he said to Anita, 'They're very sweet, aren't they? We must make sure we mention their tour dates so they get a good audience.'

The White Stripes rattled through three sets of three songs, and the faces in the audience told the whole story: no-one could believe, from that fearsome sound, that there were only two of them in the band. Anita asked if they could do one more song as a finale. In the event, they did three. The last number was Gene Vincent's 'Baby Blues'. John just welled up. You couldn't have prised the smile from his face with a crowbar.

Another session that was very dear to John was the one by Jeff Mills. In fact, John was so excited when he heard that Jeff was booked for the show in May 1998 that he asked the producer to check that it was *the* Jeff Mills. When he arrived, John nervously watched him through the glass, eventually plucking up the courage to go in and say hello. He had thought Jeff looked like the silent type, but he couldn't have been more wrong. Within seconds, Jeff was asking John questions about records he had played and artists he'd met. Jeff had fifty records with him, and John gently suggested that he had probably brought too many for the thirty-minute set. Jeff just smiled to himself. The set was amazing, with Jeff flitting effort-lessly between the three decks, spinning around, dancing – *and* he played all fifty tracks. John was buzzing about it for weeks.

In the same year, he turned over an entire show to the techno label Tresor Records to celebrate their hundredth release. Until that point, techno acts hadn't been invited on the show, for the simple reason that John and his producer Anita thought they would be too cool to accept. But the likes of Pacou, Tony Surgeon, Carl Regis, Tobias Schmidt and Neil Landstrumn were overjoyed to perform, and the session was revelatory. Tony used the opportunity to try out some new, moodier mixes; Neil claimed it was better than a gig; Carl provided a pounding, teeth-rattling finale. John, for his part, was simply bowled over.

It was lovely to see him so swept up in the music. He was the same when he devoted the programme to the then-emerging grime scene in May 2004. John had started playing grime three months earlier after listening to the pirate station Rinse FM and had picked up some of the twelve-inches – including the first grime track he played on air, 'Battle' by Jon E. Cash – from Black Market Records in Soho. On John's initial visit there with his assistant Hermeet, the guy behind the counter, Nicky, had handed them a pile of grime records and said, 'Pioneer.' John asked if that was the name of a grime act, but Nicky explained, 'No, you're a pioneer, sir, and I just had to say it!' John laughed it off but it clearly made him happy.

Whenever John and Hermeet went record shopping after that, Nicky would present them with new grime twelve-inches. Invariably, John would flick through them and say, 'Got this one. And this. And this one,' like a boy swapping football cards in the playground. He'd bought so many that there wasn't enough new stuff coming in to satisfy him.

The grime night arose because John and Hermeet realised there wasn't anyone playing this music on Radio 1; that made it even more exciting. The studio was overflowing with young DJs whom Hermeet had spotted at a club night in Brixton – there was DJ Eastwood and the Renegade Crew, which comprised MCs Purple, G Double E, IQ and IE. Those among them who had started shaving weren't old enough to drive; those who could drive weren't old enough to vote. Most had previously been used to mixing in their bedrooms or among friends, and now they were going out live on Radio 1. It was quite a gamble putting on these relative unknowns; the music was so under-represented on radio that it felt doubly important that the show was a success. John was just pleased to have showcased grime when no-one else was playing it; he found the rawness and vitality of the scene rejuvenating.

In 1999, John had started broadcasting his Thursday-night programme from a small home studio that had been set up in his study. He would be in London for the Tuesday and Wednesday shows, staying in a hotel; Thursday daytime would be spent working on *Home Truths* from eight in the morning until tea-time, when he would set off for home in time to do that night's programme at ten.

The technicalities of broadcasting from home were a mystery to him. All he knew was that if he pressed a button marked 'BH Feed' on his studio desk he could do the show right here. Every Thursday, then, the show came from the room at the far end of the hall, from behind the old football machine and the pool table that he bought for the children when their grandparents died. In the course of the programme, one or more of the children, depending on who was at home, might interrupt him to discuss such urgent topics as the upcoming weekend's complex travel arrangements. Typical phrases that would emanate from the study while the records were playing included such unforgettable all-time classics as 'Daddy's working,' 'I'm on the air,' '*Please*, I really am working' and 'Floss, fruit of my loins, don't sit on the edge of the pool table,' each delivered in a distinctive pleading whine.

It was around this time that we also began to invite bands to the house to do live sessions. John's producer Anita was the instigator, and the BBC was very happy for the sessions to go ahead since they cost less than the Maida Vale equivalents. The first acts to be afforded the honour of performing in our home were Blur, PJ Harvey and Cinerama, and these went so well that the home sessions became a regular fixture.

From our point of view, they were like little parties. On a typical Thursday, the band would arrive at the house towards the end of the afternoon to set up their equipment and do a soundcheck. When Belle and Sebastian arrived here, they all filed in – I think there were nine in the band at that point – and very generously presented me with gifts: flowers and food, toys for the dogs.

Later, I would prepare dinner for everyone. This could mean cooking for up to thirty people once you took into account the musicians, their entourage and the various friends and family whom we asked along. Then John arrived back from London at around seven, along with whoever was producing that night – Alison, Anita or Louise – and our lovely engineers, George Thomas and Andy Rogers. John would sometimes give the musicians a tour of his record collection, pulling out things he thought would interest them. On the first of Blur's two visits here, Damon asked John if he had heard of the Silver Apples, and John went straight to the appropriate shelf, pulled out a record and played it for him. John was pleased when he was putting together the programme for the Meltdown Festival and he managed to get Blur and the Silver Apples together on the same bill. The Silver Apples even did a version of Blur's 'Song 2' in their own unique style.

Blur played in a marquee in our garden, but most of the sessions were recorded in John's studio. It can get quite cramped in there, and in the case of Belle and Sebastian, the keyboard player had to set up in the bathroom on his own. When PJ Harvey played here, we had so many people round to watch that most of them ended up standing in the lane that runs beside the house, peering into the studio. I love that image: I can see everyone crowded outside the window on that warm summer evening.

We had some terrific people here over the years – Ash, Laura Cantrell, Super Furry Animals, Supergrass, the White Stripes. Nina Nastasia from New York did a few sessions. She stayed in touch after; John always noted that she was the only musician who would stop by to see us even if she wasn't in the area. She'd arrive in England, call John and come up from London on the train for lunch.

Inevitably, those evenings when bands were here would descend into drunken chaos once the show was over. I don't mean to single out Belle and Sebastian, but it has to be said in their favour that as well as bringing gifts for me, they turned up with their own ingredients to make White Russians for everyone. When they asked if they could use the fridge, I thought, 'Why have they brought their own milk?' But then the vodka and Kahlua came out of the bag and the penny dropped. By the time they left, we were incapable of speech or properly coordinated movement.

John had also resumed gigging in the late nineties, though instead of returning to the university circuit, he was restricting himself largely to more ambitious and prestigious events – what would have been called 'happenings' if they had taken place in the sixties. Anything at which he seemed like an unlikely choice, such as the Tribal Gathering or Big Chill extravaganzas, or the Sónar festival in Barcelona, held a special allure.

His first Tribal Gathering was in 1997, and John was surprised to be asked, given that mixing wasn't really his thing. At the site, he drove around to the Pacific tent. He had wanted to scamper up the steel metal ramp to the DJ platform to demonstrate that there was life in the old brute yet, but had selected the wrong footwear for the task, wearing the boots with worn soles rather than the only alternative, the black trainers coated in mud. Consequently, he had to haul himself up the ramp by snatching at tent supports. It can't have looked good.

On stage, Cornershop were playing. A man came over to check the turntables. The tent was full. When the applause for Cornershop's final number began to fade, John launched into his set and succeeded manfully in his ambition not to play the first record at the wrong speed. The second record was another matter.

He had determined beforehand to play different kinds of music at Tribal. Not just dance music, but music people could dance to. That was his motto for the festival, and he thought that was quite clever, though it did mean ending a sentence with a preposition. So he played The Fall, some guitar-driven soukous from the country formerly known as Zaire, a few reggae tunes, Status Quo. Yes, Status Quo. John had told several people that he wanted to go down – or, as he put it, down, down, deeper 'n down – in history as the man who played Quo at Tribal, so he was obliged, really. It was well received, too. Then he did the only bit of mixing he could do, running the BBC commentary of Dalglish's European-Cup-winning goal against Bruges – 'It'll break to Souness ... Souness forward ... Dalglish is not offside ... and Dalglish has scored for Liverpool – one-nil!' – over a techno track.

Thomas and his friends told John afterwards that he'd been good, and that was enough for him. Pete Tong played twenty minutes of it on Radio 1, possibly the only time The Fall has been heard on a dance programme. And John was home just after midnight.

The experience of gigging just got better and better, though John's increasing success, and the rapturous receptions he received, did nothing to quell our anxiety. Whatever gig it was, John and I were sure to spend the preceding hours worrying that it was going to be a disaster. Instead, each one was more magnificent than the last. The club gigs were outstanding. Chibuku, in Liverpool, was a particular highlight because we felt there was more than just John's reputation at stake: Flossie was attending Liverpool University at the time, so she and all her friends were going to be there. If John had messed up, it could have been to the detriment of Flossie's social life. She had been mortified six months earlier when she discovered John was booked to do the gig, but to her credit she never let on to him that she was praying he wouldn't do it.

John and I both felt wretched beforehand; we hardly touched our dinner because our stomachs were churning. He wanted to make Flossie proud. The children had always been reluctant to let on to their university friends that John was their father. All their lives, people had known John's identity, and I think they just wanted to see if they could establish themselves without recourse to their famous parent. This could land them in some uncomfortable situations. When William was at university, one evening he was in the kitchen in halls having that 'Which famous person do you fancy?' conversation with a bunch of fellow students. One named John as her choice and launched into a paean to his charms. This was more than William could take. 'That's my dad you're talking about,' he spluttered eventually.

Flossie was a nervous wreck before Chibuku. Only when the

first record kicked in, and everyone started dancing and cheering and chanting John's name, did she think that this might not be the end of the world after all. Her dad went down a storm, and she was terribly proud of him.

The first Sónar that John played, in 2001, had really given him a boost. We both fretted that it had been a dreadful mistake for him to accept, but once again the crowd were ecstatic. That gave him confidence, and he began to enjoy gigging again, even taking to the turntables for Radio 1 parties, where his sets were always a highlight of the evening.

He varied the records that he took along to gigs in his transparent box, though there were stalwarts – 'In The Midnight Hour', 'You'll Never Walk Alone', a blast of Quo. And what he played wasn't esoteric; he just put on whatever he thought would make people get up and dance. He was probably the first DJ on the circuit who didn't mix records together. He used to try to mix occasionally, but he couldn't really do it. I was sometimes worried that John would scupper the crowd's goodwill at any moment. He would play a happy hardcore track, then kill it and throw in a jig out of nowhere, and you'd think: He's blown it. But everyone would still be dancing.

He enjoyed the two Big Chill festivals that he played, especially the one in July 2004. We stayed in a little bed-and-breakfast nearby in the Malvern Hills, and as we made our way on to the site, the reaction to John's arrival was amazing. People were cheering and applauding him before he'd even got into the tent where he was playing. It was sweltering in there, and crammed to bursting point. When John started DJing, the crowd became hysterical.

It always amazed me to see him holding sway over a young club or festival crowd, especially as I was always on at him to stop acting older than he was. 'You don't need that bloody stick,' I'd complain when John insisted on hobbling around with the mop handle that he has already celebrated near the start of this book. He had this obsession with turning into an old man; it was like he was trying to accelerate the process. It was strange, because in his taste and stamina he was so youthful. But he found the idea of being elderly and senile quite appealing. He was hoping eventually to become Sir Henry at Rawlinson End, and was looking forward to causing the children and me untold embarrassment and torment in his senility. He often threatened, for instance, to wake up believing himself to be in the year 1847 or a four-mile tailback on the M6.

Before his Big Chill set was finished, a woman approached the stage and handed John her baby, which she asked him to kiss. He was quite overcome, but he obliged merrily, then handed back the infant and advised the mother to remove it from the tent for the sake of its little eardrums. It was a marvellous, euphoric event. It was also the last gig John played.

Shortly before we set off for Peru in October 2004, the children had asked me to persuade their father to change his hours. In July, the schedule had been revamped once again, and John's Radio 1 programme had been moved back an hour so that it now ran from eleven p.m. until one a.m., Tuesday to Thursday. As a result, the Maida Vale sessions could no longer go out live because audiences were not allowed in the building after midnight. When the sessions were pre-recorded, the atmosphere simply wasn't the same. And so an intrinsic part of John's programme had been scheduled out of existence.

John was happy in himself, and there was no good reason

why he shouldn't have gone to Peru; he had been given a clean bill of health before we left. But we could all see that he was getting exhausted more easily. He was even considering pre-recording one show per week. Fitting *Home Truths* into his schedule could also be stressful. Chris Berthoud had felt for some time that the show needed a summer break. John had often said that he needed to be able to 'have' the funny experiences so he could refresh his repertoire of stories. Fifty-two weeks a year on *Home Truths* didn't allow that. But Chris's suggestion never found much favour at Radio 4. When Chris and Fiona had first approached John with the idea of turning *Offspring* into *Home Truths* and giving him an hour every Saturday, he had responded to their concerns about his other commitments with a remark that seems, in hindsight, rather sad. 'Don't worry,' he told them, 'I never take holidays.'

That's one reason I am pleased that we fitted in a proper family holiday the year before John died. It had been a decade or so since we had all gone away together, and it was clear that any sizeable break would be precluded by John's work schedule. Unless, that is, he was forcibly wrenched away from his turntables and microphones. In the end, he didn't need to be press-ganged – the fact that his children actually wanted to go on holiday with him was persuasive enough on its own.

The idea had come one day from Danda and Zahra, William's partner. Between them, and with only a month's notice, they organised for twelve of us – John and me, the four children and their respective significant others, Gabrielle and her son Little John – to stay in a beautiful chateau in the Dordogne. The holiday followed on directly from the Big Chill festival in July 2003. After John had finished DJing there, we drove with William and Zahra across France, meeting up with

the others at the chateau. It wasn't an especially eventful fortnight, but you could tell that John was sorely in need of some
rest. He spent most of the time floating in the swimming pool
in a rubber ring, sporting a straw Stetson cocked at a jaunty
angle and proclaiming himself to be a jellyfish. Well, it made
him happy.

We also went canoeing and kayaking in a nearby river that
was virtually dry, so that it was more a case of scraping ourselves along the riverbed. And we had an extended badminton
tournament every night. It was almost too hot to move in the
daytime, so once darkness fell we lined the cars up, switched on
the headlights to illuminate the court and played our hearts
out. Despite being eight months pregnant at the time, Danda
emerged the champion, though that may have something to do
with the fact that she was the only player who wasn't drinking,
and therefore the only person still in possession of functioning
hand–eye coordination. When we weren't stumbling drunkenly
around the badminton court in the glare of the headlights, we
could usually be found slumped at the long wooden table outside, drinking to forget how much we had eaten, then eating
again because we had forgotten we were full.

It was a perfect holiday; I can't recall having seen John
looking happier. Towards the end of the fortnight, everyone left
at different times to return to England, until it was just John,
Thomas and me in the chateau. The three of us had planned to
enjoy a few more days there, but that idea didn't last long. The
first morning after the others had left, Thomas came down to
breakfast to tell us that he had been awake all night, having
realised how old and spooky the place was now that everyone
else had gone. He found his father packing the car: John had
had exactly the same experience. I was outnumbered. I

agreed reluctantly to head home with these two lily-livered, yellow-bellied big girl's blouses.

When the children had voiced their concerns before John and I left for Peru, I could only agree. I assured them that I would speak to John. His punishing schedule wasn't helped by his continuing inability to organise himself. There were many instances over the years when he'd find himself hopelessly up against it: I lost count of the number of times in the seventies when he was so tardy with his *Sounds* column that we would be forced to drive into London to deliver it straight to the printers, the ink still wet on the paper.

He was always incredibly busy, even over-committed, but he tried not to let on. If Chris asked him to do an interview or go on a trip for *Home Truths*, he would say, 'I think so, but I must check with Sheila.' We had a calendar on the kitchen wall that held all his appointments, and the system was that John couldn't agree to anything until we had checked it on that calendar. If I wasn't in the kitchen then no arrangements could be made. Apparently this drove producers mad. But it was as close as we ever came to containing John's workload.

In recent times, he was frustrated by the fact that he had time on his hands when he was in the West End on a Wednesday, but none at all when he was here at home during the rest of the week. With nothing much to do in London before his evening programme, he would trawl the Soho record shops or call Thomas at work and say, 'Tom, I'm downstairs, come and have a drink with me.'

If it's possible to be overworked and boundlessly happy, that was John. Everyone who attended his sixty-fifth birthday party in August 2004 had marvelled at how contented he seemed. He loved his life; it really was that simple. He was never happier than when he was doing his programme, or spending time with his family.

One of the things that most pleased John was when he chanced upon a demo that excited him. He must have spent hundreds of hours of his life standing in the kitchen, calling a number that had been scribbled on some cassette inlay card and announcing down the phone, 'Hi, this is John Peel from wonderful Radio 1.' He loved calling up bands and shooting the breeze, inviting them to record a session, or asking them to get in touch when they had finished their next tape.

Even now, there are piles of CDs, tapes and records in his room that he never played, many of them still secure in their Jiffy bags, some having arrived since John died. The letters that accompany them display the typical mixture of audacity, optimism and spirit:

> Dear John,
> Recently I've found myself listening to your show more and more often as exams have loomed and I've been playing catch up. If only I'd studied during the year rather than attempting to form the world's greatest rock 'n' roll band. Anyway, as I stare down the barrel of a fail coupled with an ultimately shambolic band, it's reassuring to find someone else who can have a myriad of technical problems during a show and keep smiling (I assume you're smiling, it is radio). So as we have some common ground I thought I'd send you a copy of our EP. It's a little rough but what can you expect from a 4 Track?
> Best Wishes,
> David Marrs (from Cumbria)

Dear Mr Peel

Hello, my name is Tom Corneill and like many others I am a singer songwriter trying to make it in the industry. I am a big fan of yours and simply wondered if you might have a quick listen to my CD as I think I have a lot to offer, and you might like it! I appreciate that you must get demos all the time, but if you get five minutes please have a peek – all feedback is more than welcome.

Thanks again

Tom Corneill

Dear Mr Peel,

I send you this record in the knowledge that you are the only major DJ who would even consider listening to us, let alone playing our songs. Therefore if you do not play us we shall cry until we finish our next record then hassle you with that. If you are pressed for time I recommend track 4.

Lots of love,

Sexy Butchers

Any one of those might have provided John with the same buzz he got from the Undertones and The Fall, Ragga Twins and Big Black, the Dwarves and the Butthole Surfers, Captain Beefheart and Cocteau Twins, the Faces and Carcass.

One of his brightest moments on radio in the last few years was playing the Delgados' first session, originally recorded for Radio Scotland, on his programme. You could hear the astonishment mounting in his voice after every track. Eventually, he announced on air that he would have to get the band down to Maida Vale to do a proper session for the show.

Shortly after the Delgados' session, John was presenting a

documentary series called *Sounds of the Suburbs* for Channel 4. The idea was to focus on those bands that had emerged from Britain's outlying suburbs. During one episode, John met the band Comatose and interviewed the singer. Afterwards, he told her that he wanted the band to record a session for his programme. It quickly transpired that not only had she never heard the show, she really had no idea who he was or what he was trying to encourage her to do. John thought that this was wonderful.

Another episode in the series highlighted Lanarkshire, and bands like BMX Bandits, The Jesus and Mary Chain, the Soup Dragons and Teenage Fanclub. As part of the programme, John went to meet Stewart Henderson from the Delgados. After they had conducted the interview Stewart asked John if he would care to stop by the Electric Bar the following night to participate in the quiz night. John agreed, on the proviso that it wouldn't turn into a gawp-fest, which is what had tended to happen in the past.

Before the quiz, Stewart made sure to call in at the bar to announce the identity of his special guest. 'Get tae fuck,' was the general consensus of opinion. 'No, honest, it's John Peel,' said Stewart. 'And do me a favour. When he's in, don't act like fucking idiots. I promised it would be all right and no-one would bother him too much.' He left the pub excited by the prospect of one of his heroes patronising his local watering hole, and terrified that the punters would embarrass him, start a fight, throw up over John.

When the big day arrived, Stewart got to the pub half an hour before John was due to arrive. It was only when he walked into the packed room that he realised the power of the grapevine. Apparently everyone within a five-mile radius who had a pulse, and some who didn't, was in that pub, clutching a jar and eyeing Stewart expectantly. Their faces tightened when they saw that he had arrived unaccompanied. 'We fuckin' knew he wisnae comin',' was the first response to reach Stewart's ears, and only when he struggled above the din to reassure them did the clamour die down. Stewart stationed himself at a corner table, slouched behind his pint and began imagining all the worst-case scenarios that could transpire over the coming hours.

John walked in twenty minutes later to a deafening roar. With a nervous, bemused smile, he settled at the table while Stewart got the drinks in. The crowd was brilliant: people came up to say hello, shook John's hand and then left him in peace.

When the quiz started, Stewart discovered that his companion wasn't much of an asset. The introduction to 'Voodoo Chile' was played, and John swore it was 'Purple Haze'. 'Jesus,' laughed Stewart, 'did you not do some sessions with Jimi Hendrix? Maybe you should have listened to him a bit more.'

The night went on in that vein, with John and Stewart getting increasingly drunk and increasingly jolly. John told Stewart he thought it was the kind of evening John Lennon would have loved, since he was into sitting in pubs and talking crap.

At the end of the evening, a shadow fell across John and Stewart's table. Gus Allan, a towering Electric Bar local with a fearsome crewcut, approached them and introduced himself to John. 'Awright John, fuck sake John, you're ma fuckin' hero – see when ah wis at school, nae cunt gave a fuck aboot me but ah used tae listen tae yer show aw the time. Fuckin' brilliant, big man.' One shake of the hand and Gus had gone.

Half an hour later, John departed to unanimous applause, bringing to an end an unforgettable night. When he did his show a few days later, he said on air that he had had the privilege of visiting the Electric Bar in Motherwell for the quiz night and that he'd had a wonderful time. 'A great place,' he said, 'and one that I sincerely hope I'll visit again.' Then he dedicated a song to Gus.

John broadcast his last Radio 1 programme at eleven p.m. on Thursday 14 October 2004, from his room at the end of the hall. It was business as usual. He kicked off the show with 'I Wanna Holler (But This Town's Too Small)' by the Detroit Cobras, and informed listeners, 'We've got a full house tonight, which means everyone else is watching television while I'm at the end of the house doing the programme.' He mentioned a song that he had planned to play to 'our Tom' – 'The Box It Came In' by Anna Firmin and the Trigger Gospel – 'But he's gone to bed now so he won't hear it. You won't either 'cos it's not going to be on tonight.'

Trencher was in session with songs including 'Row Upon Row Of Leper Skulls', 'Attack Of The Sex Attackers', 'I Lost All My Hair In A Skiing Accident' and 'Trapped Under A Train Alive'. The Fall turned up, of course, with 'Powder Keg', while I presented Pig's Big 78 – on this occasion, Conway Twitty's 'It's Only Make Believe'. John and I sang along to every word as the stylus crackled and spat and hissed its way along the groove.

There were, as usual, plenty of the listeners' emails that had made the live broadcast so enjoyable for John. A man studying at the University of Oklahoma wrote to say how interested he had been to hear John mention, on the previous night's programme, that he had worked at KOMA in the sixties. Dan from Steveless emailed with details of a new website address. Someone wrote in to say how much he enjoyed the recent Maida Vale sessions by Super Furry Animals and Phillip Roebuck. Someone else wanted to know the name of a song John had played a few years back, which included the line, 'Hi, I'm Chucky, wanna play?' Gary emailed to say he thought it was by 150 Volts, and John promised to investigate and play the record again in a few weeks' time. Another listener had written asking if he could have a dedication for his ninety-seven-year-old grandfather 'who probably won't be listening'. John obliged with the Aphrodisiacs' 'Backbone Of Society'.

He also played a Japanese thrash track called 'Flummox' by Swarrrm. 'That's "swarm" with three r's,' he explained. 'I mean it's S-w-a-r-r-r-m. They're not actually called Swarm With Three R's. That would be mere silliness.' The record had been sent to him by Dean out of Extreme Noise Terror. 'What a hero that man is,' sighed John. There was 'What's The Matter Blues' by Frank Stokes, 'Hushhh' by Andrew Thomas and 'Shangri-La Tiger' by Dollhouse ('What *do* they think they're doing?' wondered John as the song ended in a hail of feedback).

The last record on the show was Klute's 'Time 4 Change' from the album *No One's Listening Anymore*. Then John signed off. 'I'll be back in your midst at the beginning of November, refreshed, I hope, and with loads of your requests to play too. Thanks, as always, for listening.'

Epilogue

John died of a heart attack in Peru on 26 October 2004. Over the subsequent weeks and months, the children and I were genuinely taken aback by the response from the public and the media. We drew from them an enormous amount of comfort.

We were in a rare situation. Wherever we looked, people were mourning John. We knew the tributes weren't for our benefit, and that they were done spontaneously. But knowing other people out there were sharing our sadness helped tremendously.

When John's death was announced on Radio 1, I was still stuck out in Peru, but the children were at home. They had received the phone call from me in the early hours of the morning, and were bracing themselves for the on-air announcement that they knew was scheduled for the afternoon. After that the BBC aired pieces on radio and TV that included affectionate tributes from colleagues and musicians John had worked alongside throughout the years.

In the weeks that followed, the emails and correspondence flooded in. People who had never even met John sent flowers and letters of condolence. Some were addressed simply to 'Family of John Peel. Somewhere in Suffolk'.

Graffiti appeared in Liverpool, Brighton and Belfast. On Charing Cross Bridge in Glasgow, someone had spray-painted the words 'John Peel RIP' alongside two love-hearts. In Leeds, graffiti artists collaborated on a tribute wall featuring a picture of John with the message: 'John Peel, a major inspiration and a key player in the British independent music scene . . . 1939 to 2004 . . . We will never forget you!!!' A friend of mine came out of a meeting in London and started crying at the sight of a huge banner hanging from a window in a block of flats. 'Goodbye John,' it read. 'We love you.' The HMV chain had a minute's silence in its stores on the afternoon that the news was made public; 'Teenage Kicks' chimed out of the PA system in Virgin Megastores across the country.

It seemed only natural, given the extraordinary public out-pouring, and the support it had given us, to make John's funeral service a public affair. We arranged for speakers to broadcast the service to anyone who wanted to gather outside the cathedral in Bury St Edmunds.

The reaction to John's death was nothing less than over-whelming, but the most intense moment must have been when we arrived at the cathedral and the crowds there were clapping and cheering. We caught messages that were being shouted – 'We love you, John!' and 'Thank you, John!' We were grateful for that. And we were grateful too that when the public service was over, everyone respected our privacy and allowed us to proceed alone to a private service at our village church.

His friends are doing a good job of keeping his memory alive. It feels like Andy Kershaw has a story to tell about John each week on his Radio 3 programme; he even received a mini-disc from a listener who had compiled twenty or so of John's funniest links from his Radio 1 show. Andy keeps dropping these into his programme between songs; sometimes it's as though John is co-hosting with Andy. We have been to gigs recently where Loudon Wainwright and Nina Nastasia remembered John and dedicated songs to him. Danda and Flossie went to a Laura Cantrell gig in London recently. For the encore, Laura came back on and introduced a song that she said was 'for my good friend, John Peel'. We know that bands at gigs up and down the country in the months following John's death also paid their respects.

I wonder if it will ever stop feeling peculiar that John isn't here. When we have a big family get-together, you just naturally expect him to be there. He was always at the centre of things before. Now you can feel his absence. I wish so much that he could have been with us to see Liverpool win the European Cup on 26 May 2005. Danda and Flossie had made red cocktails before the match, and prepared a spread of red food. The living-room walls were covered with Liverpool flags. Archie was in his full kit. At half time, when we were three–nil down against AC Milan, we were praying to John, begging him to do something, then it turned – Gerrard, Smicer, Alonso: three goals in six minutes. Then we won the penalty shoot-out, three–two. It was a terrific night, but for us and those close to John tinged with regret that he wasn't around to celebrate with us. The next day, Johnnie Walker remarked on his radio show, 'John Peel must have been dancing in heaven when Liverpool won last night.' I bet he was. The Westbourne Grove Walk, no doubt.

The morning after the match, we went into town and bought every red flower we could find, then went over to the churchyard. John's grave has seen its share of gentle celebration. We poured champagne on it on our first Christmas Day without him. Not long before that, someone had placed a glass of red wine on the grave. The glass is still there, in fact, though the wine is much diluted. We don't know who made that gesture, but whoever it was, we just want to say thanks.

We placed all the flowers on the grave, and tied a Liverpool scarf around the headstone. We thanked John again for helping Liverpool win the Cup. Then we ambled back through the churchyard, and headed home.

Appendix

In 1992, John began thinking seriously for the first time about writing his autobiography. In preparation, he sent these two letters to his literary agent, Cat Ledger:

```
Dear Cat,
I thought I would write to you before the level
of guilt triggered by your 'phone call of three
minutes ago subsided.
Of course I remain more than eager to write The
Book, the death of my mum giving me, as I
explained, a greater incentive yet. The problems
remain those of finding time amid my hysterical
schedule of unpopular radio programmes. I suspect
only the lure of gold will, as it usually does,
find a way through these problems.
Roughly speaking, the book will include — in
addition to a surfeit of commas — my birth at the
age of four in a woodcutter's cottage in the
Black Forest. But seriously . . . birth three days
before the outbreak of the war (Second World),
memories of listening to the BBC in the Anderson
shelter at the top of the garden, German planes
flying overhead, POWs working in the fields next
to our garden, Liverpool and Birkenhead burning.
Then kindergarten, Father returning from the war
— the first time I had ever seen him — and his
```

almost immediate departure to what was Rhodesia
to give it the once over before shipping us all
out there. His decision not to do this and his
rather wonderful '46 Mercury. My departure to
Woodlands School, Deganwy, as a boarder at the
age of seven.
Four years of blood, sadism, disinformation,
perverted vicars, football and more blood. Also
smoking blotting paper, the banning of the Just
William books, sex education (the Early Years),
incredibly sophisticated bullying and The World's
Strongest Boy.
Transfer to Shrewsbury School at the age of 13,
having failed Common Entrance by 1% but being
nodded through because proud generations of
Ravenscrofts had been to the school before me.
Being bottom of the school my first term, having
landed in what would have been the remedial
class in a state school. My father's lack of
enthusiasm for this small distinction. Setting a
house record for the number of (officially-
sanctioned) beatings in this same term. The
problems associated with being, barely credibly,
rather good-looking at this stage of life i.e.
sexual harassment, up to and including buggery
(I know what the public wants). Musings on the
long-term effects of above. The loneliness of
the solitary footballer and the laziness of the
long-distance runner. Confirmation, disappointment and the start of a lifelong fear of a
religious experience. More beatings, highly
ritualised and very painful. Having a crush on a
boy who eventually became the successful Tory
candidate in the by-election that followed John
Stonehouse's 'disappearance'. Lack of success in
the classroom but J.R.P.R. (me) saved by an
astonishingly wise, funny and generous housemaster (to whom any book would most likely be
dedicated).
Serious attitude change brought about by trip
to boys club in Everton funded by school and

patronised, in the worst way, by my contempo-
raries. Decided Scouse 'oiks' were better human
beings than those with whom I was being educated. Enthusiasm for early work of Bill Haley
and, worse, for Frankie Laine and Johnny Ray,
set aside upon hearing Little Richard.
Rebuffed by Flashman-styled chiefs of school jazz
society — the High Society, inevitably — when I
tried to find kindred spirit. Loneliness of the
lone Lonnie Donegan fan.
Continued academic failure becomes brief period
of excellence in housemaster's class. Reasons
for being grateful that I was too stupid to go
to University. Leave Shrewsbury seriously malad-
justed and with 4 'O' levels.
Work as office boy in Liverpool's Cotton
Exchange. Seeing Duane Eddy at Liverpool Empire
(amongst others). Apply for early call-up for
National Service.
Posted to Oswestry for basic training (Royal
Artillery). Battery commander is silly little
shit who is going out with my step-sister.
Paragraphs on breakdown of marriage of parents
and Father's subsequent marriage to raddled har-
ridan to whom he had been engaged aeons before,
before meeting Mother on skiing holiday in
Wengen in romantic 1930s. My own experience on
skiing holidays, including the Vickers Viscount
and yodelling.
Failure — yes, another one — to become Officer
Training Candidate (possibly the first public
school boy to so fail). Reaction of NCOs to
failed Public School Boy in their midst — further unpleasantness followed by surprising
response of fellow squaddies.
Transfer to Salisbury Plain for further gratu-
itous violence. Unexpected role of Salvation Army
in life of young soldier JRPR. Application for
entirely fraudulent compassionate posting to
Anglesey granted. Removal to Trials Establishment
Guided Weapons Royal Artillery for chapters of

hilarious stuff about life in the army.
Sentimental stuff about taking brother Alan (11)
and his best pal Anthony Holden (Royal biogra-
pher and card player) out for meals and
subsequently watching them play on the rocks at
Tre-Arddur Bay. Formation of skiffle group with
fellow squaddie who threatened me with legal
action last time I named him publicly. Work on
highly secret radar and farcical demonstrations
of same in front of high-ranking NATO officers.
The ritual burning of the QuarterMaster's Stores.
Motor-cycle racing. Trip to Liverpool to see
Gene Vincent and Eddie Cochran. Trips to
Liverpool to see Liverpool. Pages on the wonders
of Billy Liddell (left-wing).
Demob after two really rather happy years.
Hostile report from Battery Commander. Father's
hostile reception of same. Removal to heavy
industrial work in Rochdale cotton-mill. Romantic
sub-Alan Bennett stuff about life in gritty,
Northern setting. Father's threat to send me to
USA. James Dean-like response to same followed
by panic upon finding self aboard SS 'Eugene
Lykes' bound for Houston.
Atlantic crossing.
Arrival in Houston. Death of newsvendor. Hurried
departure for Dallas. Victim of attempted rape
in YMCA. (There has been disappointingly little
sex so far — unless you count masturbation and
lots of it.)
Hurried removal to picturesque boarding house on
Gaston Avenue with shifting population of ne'er-
do-wells, drunks, racists, cowpokes etc. Own
slide into life of drunkenness. Nights spent
chatting up barmaids in dangerous bars and
clubs. First exposure to magic of Roy Orbison.
Second and third ditto. Fourth ditto. Knifefights
in club toilets. Falling in love with red-headed
gal named Judy. First sexual experience (not,
alas, with Judy). Trip to Fort Worth Jail for
medical examination upon application for perma-

nent US residence. Round of concerts — Big D
Jamboree etc. First radio programme (1961).
Bitten by bug and subsequent foolish behaviour.
Fall in love again, this time with Braniff
Airlines stewardess, also called Judy. Trips —
not with Judy — to New Orleans to follow for-
tunes of stripper called Chris Colt, the Girl
With The 45s. Founder member of Dallas County
Cricket Club. Playing cricket in Houston, Austin,
San Antonio, Abilene. Hostile reactions of local
populations. Meeting — and this is all true —
with John Kennedy, Richard Nixon and Lyndon B.
Johnson during 1961 campaign.
Second sexual experience.
First car. Trips to dragstrip. 'American
Graffiti' style life. Continuing role as office
boy. Transmogrified into crop insurance salesman
and trips as such into West Texas, complete with
visits to Mexican brothels (in strictly non-
participatory role).
Further concerts. Meeting Lightnin' Hopkins
and Memphis Slim. Seeing Jimmy Reed. Arrival in
life of Beatles and cheap exploitation of lack
of American grasp of European geography and
belief that if I came from Liverpool I must
know the Fab 4. Exploitation (shameful) of
female fans with similar misconceptions. Mobbed
in downtown Dallas by over 2,000 screaming
teenagers. Several months of bizarre sexual
activity that transcended most fervent
masturbation fantasies. Dangers of above.
Flight from shed in which I was living to home
of one of my regulars. Death of her father
and mother and our subsequent marriage.
She was 15, I was 26.
(Before this: assassination of Kennedy (not me)
and my presence in press-conference at which Lee
Harvey Oswald was charged — later confirmed (to
my astonishment) by Granada TV film.)
Details of own brief incarceration in County
Jail.

Removal — just ahead of police — to Oklahoma
City and first full-time radio job. Massive pop-
ularity of Paul 'n' John Show. Feted at High
School Home-Coming Game. Purchase of Corvette.
Failure of above. Purchase of Chevrolet 409. Use
of above to drive Dan Yankee and the
Carpetbaggers and Jay Walker & the Pedestrians
to gig on Indian reservations. Importance of
'Hang On Sloopy', 'Gloria', and 'Louie Louie'.
Dangers of stopping at 3 in the morning at rural
truckstops for breakfast. Danger of being drafted
and sent to Viet Nam averted when I pointed out
I had already served with allied army. Damage
down to psyche of pal who did go to 'nam.
Trip to Minneapolis to meet Beatles. Failure to
meet Beatles. Manhandled by police.
Further trips into rural Oklahoma. Beginning of
breakdown of marriage.
Domestic violence and a stone frog. Loss of job.
Removal to San Bernardino, California. Eighteen
months on KMEN. Further deterioration of marriage. Trips to Los Angeles to see Capt.
Beefheart and range of other trendy bands. Met
Jefferson Airplane. Didn't like them. Working
with local bands. Sent Misunderstood to live
with Mother in London. Mother's displeasure.
Trips to Watts after riots. Involvement of
Sheriff's Department in continuing deterioration
of marriage. Left California. Arrival home.
(Above padded out with more stuff i.e. Rolling
Stones concert in San Bernardino during which
fan emptied police revolver into stage. Dangerous
proximity of above. Astonishing strength of female
fans. Herman's Hermits, Animals, Hollies concerts.)
Conned my way onto pirate ship Radio London.
Wife joined me in London. Life opposite Royal
Fulham laundry. Further deterioration of marriage
leading to final collapse, removal to flat near
Regent's Park with androgynous photographer (my
removal) and wife's melancholy descent into life
of crime which resulted eventually in prison

sentence and her early death — don't plan to
dwell too much on this though.
Life in Upper Harley St. Snooty neighbours.
Closure of pirates. (Pages of amusing stuff
about life on ship.) Meeting under remarkable
circumstances with John Lennon. Meeting with
Yoko. General musings on life as minor princeling
amongst the hippies. Further sexual experiences.
Trips to VD clinics. Bizarre treatment for crabs
in Birmingham hotel with future wife. Writing
serious crap for range of hippy papers. Writing
awful sleeve notes. Quotes from above. Festivals.
Acid experiences. Meeting Brian Jones. His death.
Hendrix. Radio 1 sessions. Recording Who, Cream,
Hendrix, Pink Floyd. Life as minor television
personality. Oz trials and attitude (continuing)
of Richard Neville to JRPR (including recent
humiliating evening at Groucho Club).
Succession of gigs. Sequence of disasters
associated with same. Meetings with almost every
interesting band of the time. Doors concert in
London. Further sexual experiences incl. same
with hitch-hikers. Meeting with Marc Bolan and
stuff about the three or four years during which
he was my best pal. Life as a dippy hippy in
London incorporating the Velvet Trouser
Experience and unhappy experiences as a dope
fiend. Sex on a train.
Meeting with Sheila Gilhooly (aka the Pig) and
gradual transformation of life for infinitely
better and hope that same will continue to ripe
old age.
Death of Father.

This brings us up to about 1970. I'll send
you more later but I have to go and help the
children put up a tent.

Dear Cat,
As advertised, part 2 of the recollections of An
English Gentleman.

Dandelion Records — the dream crumbles.
Establishment of record label on highly
impractical but idealistic grounds. Curious
relationship(s) with artistes leading to epiphany
on tiled floor of a men's toilet in Portsmouth.
Musings on the great DJs (a contradiction in
terms? viz. the Weird Beard, John R., Wolfman
Jack and the selling of autographed pictures of
the Last Supper, and the only British-based
Great DJ, Alan Freeman).
Humiliating failure on Top Of The Pops and subsequent death of producer. Friendship with
Liverpool Poets, interspersed — as the whole
thing will be — with reflections on Liverpool FC
i.e. Kenny Dalglish, Simply The Best. Letters
from David Bowie scrounging money for building
of wait for it, wait for it . . . the Beckenham
Arts Lab. Reflections on Arts Labs generally,
the limitless quantities of bullshit engendered
therein and the effect of same — the deadening
effect of same — on Eastern European music
(incorporating the Silly Hat theory of advanced
pop criticism).
Settling in Suffolk, starting Youth Club (called,
for reasons long since forgotten, Great
Finborough International Airport). Holidays with
same in Wales, Cornwall and what used to be
Yugoslavia. Save lives (seriously) of minibus
load of young folk when brakes fail coming down
the Alps. Sex. Taking Youth Club to gigs —
Status Quo in Stafford, Tangerine Dream in
Aldershot the week after the pub bombings — and
to matches in Liverpool. Starting a family with
William. Father (me) cries on air. Stories about
Dandelion artists Stackwaddy — punx before punk
— including tales of drunkenness and cruelty and
vengeance on the M6.

Festivals in Holland, PinkPop (near Maastricht —
book guaranteed free of thoughts on Maastricht
Treaty). Other festivals at home and abroad with
anecdotes about the Buxton Festival, Hells
Angels, mud, drunkenness, knives and a retreat
home.
Homebuilding, a beginner's guide, incl. house-
hunting and living in a van, visits of Famous
Friends — well, quite famous i.e. Richard
Neville. The Carol concert with Rod Stewart,
Ivor Cutler, the Faces, Robert Wyatt and others.
John Walters and his influence on our lives.
Bizarre Saturday nights based around late-night
films on TV.
Journalism, starting with crap pieces (opportunity for hilarious quotes from same i.e. 'clouds
are poems written in the sky') in International
Times, Oz, Gandalf's Garden. Progress — of a
sort — to Disc and Music Echo (including centre-
page spread dressed as school girl plus sundry
other photos with naked women and clumsy justification for same, leading to School Girl Of The
Year competitions on Radio 1 which, to be fair
to myself, was won one year by half a rhinoceros
and another by a typewriter) then Sounds, the
Observer, the Independent (briefly) and role as
correspondent for Bike Magazine).
Interviewing Frank Zappa, Canned Heat and Dr
John the Night-Tripper at/in Clympings.
Friendship with Captain Beefheart, arguably the
only real genius yet to work in field of popular
music. Anecdotes (affectionate) about the great
man (now alas seriously ill).
Bay City Rollers at Mallory Park during motor-
racing incorporating Tony Blackburn in a speed
boat driven by a Womble and the eclipse of
Slade.
Meeting with demented man who claimed to be not
one but all of the Small Faces. Thoughts on wide
range of unhinged folk encountered during showbiz
career.

Radio 1 Fun Days and Fun Weeks. Tony Blackburn
entertaining resentful businessmen in Birmingham
and rapid reassessment of Blackburn. Disco dancing competition in Livingston.
Surprise weekend for Pig in Niagara Falls and
bizarre meeting with Dire Straits. Trips with
BBC World Service to Zimbabwe (including singing
our way into Zambia), Sierra Leone (including
profound shock at lives lived by residents),
Bulgaria (including William Falls In Love) and
Baltic states. Radio 1 trips to Russia (pre
glasnost) and to Hungary, Czechoslovakia.
Holidays in St. Lucia and the influence of a Sex
Pistols song.
Heysel stadium and our presence in the crowd,
narrow escape and subsequent trauma. The effect
of Hillsborough — both short-term and long-term.
Tiswas and friendship with John Gorman ex-
Scaffold, including village celebrations of Royal
Weddings and Jubilee.
Short period on Radio Luxemburg (with anarchic
show called Stenhousemuir 2, Cowdenbeath 2 which
was voted, barely credibly, Top Show In All Of
Europe in some publication). (Was only person to
work on Radio 1 and 208 simultaneously, I
think.)
Ruminations on effects of Luxemburg and AFN on
life. Admiration for Kid Jensen. As The Rhythm
Pals we adorned Top Of The Pops and Radio 1 —
deep regret when he left for Capital.
Programmes for British Forces Broadcasting. Lack
of interest in these shown by our brave boys and
girls in the trenches but extraordinary popularity with German civilians which has resulted in
most of my very best friends being German. In
fact, was voted Radio DJ in Germany for past two
years. Complete inability to speak German.
Programmes for radio stations in Bremen and
Berlin (recorded in corner of our sitting room)
both lost in past year in the face of resurgent
nationalism. Programmes (continuing as of this

morning) in Austria and on astonishingly named
Radio Mafia in Finland.

Punk revolution and continuing effects of same
on personal life and globally. The flirtation of
punks with reggae, astonishing reaction of
audience in late 1960s when I started playing
reggae on the radio, brutish hostility of
Reading crowds to reggae, mail and threats from
racist groups incl. campaign of sending turds to
me through the post (including one from the
British Movement cell in Walsall which came with
a letter starting 'Dear John'). Reflections on
racism.

Attempts to syndicate radio programmes in USA,
initial enthusiasm of Yank entrepreneurs
evaporates when they actually get to hear programmes. Present attempt which has at least got
as far as programmes being circulated under
sponsorship of Nana company. Absurdly over-
optimistic forecasts of American publicity
machine and general opportunity to snigger.

Important realisation that retention of sanity
depends on avoiding showbiz — above triggered by
appearance with Clive James and André Previn on
awful TV programme, thought that if I really
hustled I could spend most of time with glamorous folk such as these followed by thought
that would rather have painful and humiliating
rectal surgery — and immersing myself in village
life. Benefits of above and joy of being
described (in Guardian) as 'eccentric recluse'.
This seems to give me licence to behave exactly
as I please. Followed by as many pages as you
like of saccharine stuff about babies, hopeless
love for children, Pig's near death experience
after birth of 4th child (Flossie) and reluctant
decision to Stop There, the buying of a second
hand Morgan which we still own but haven't seen
for 12 years. Experiences in a lay-by on the way
to Bury St. Edmunds.

Wrist broken by John Birt in 5-a-side match in

Holborn. Awful experiences as token Radio 1
person at various heavy duty BBC events including richly patronising behaviour of an
Attenborough.
The effect of a pisstaking review of a Dylan
concert printed in Guardian.
Friendship with Andy Kershaw.
Trips to Eurovision Song Contests in Brussels —
return to Heysel and hilarious meeting with King
and Queen of Belgium in small party including
the late Ray Moore leading to reflections on the
really great broadcasters Moore, Lyttleton,
Clayton, Arlott (including only meeting with last
named and 25 minute monologue from same) — and
Lausanne. Enthusiasm for Eurovision, its
simplicity and daft purity. Regret that it is no
longer important.
Experiences on 'Down Your Way' and 'Desert
Island Discs'. Moving effects of almost any
appearance on Radio 4 including letters from
great and good, appearance of long lost relatives etc. Terror at attending Desert Island
Disc anniversary do in ill-fitting suit. Bizarre
meeting with Princess Margaret and sympathy for
same. Find common ground in admiration for her
father and the Archers, both of us having
appeared as ourselves on same. (Book guaranteed
free of any further Royal nonsense.)
There will also be yarns about being on 'Quote
Unquote', something called 'The Law Game', and
trips to the cinema, theatre and an exhibition
of awful Japanese paintings with Samantha Fox
and Shirley Williams for Gloria Hunniford TV.
Enthusiasm for these and other surreal
juxtapositions.
Visit to address lifers' group at Gartree
(including 3 of Guildford 4) 4 days before
Guildford 4 are released.
Reflections on other Radio 1 DJs including (if
legally possible) the most hated man in the
world, an evening with Noel Edmonds leading to

near death at his hands in front of nationwide
TV audience, and musings on fame and people's
need for trappings of fame.
Meetings with Kylie Minogue and admiration for
same. Her kindness to Flossie and Flossie's
friend Chloe. Explanation of preference for
Kylie, Sheena and the rest over Springsteen, U2,
Dire Straits etc.
There will be anecdotes (unflattering) about
visits to Peel Acres by Sue Cook (who broke our
electric blanket) and Bob Geldof.

That's about all I can think of this morning,
Cat. Obviously as I go through all the boxes of
junk that I have kept other things will emerge —
a preliminary hunt yielded about 10 letters and
cards from Elton John, for example — and I have
just realised that I overlooked a wonderfully
funny trip to Japan in the above. There will be
loads of homespun stuff about cars, dogs, cats,
children, children's friends, cars, neighbours
and parties.

There another thing — my 50th birthday party
featured Zimbabwe's Four Brothers playing in the
garden, something the Pig orchestrated 3 years
after a casual remark in a club in Harare and
the mix at that and at our wedding of sympa-
thetic showbiz folk and our friends from
Stowmarket.

There will be a very real danger of the book
degenerating into a hymn of praise to Sheila but
without her there would be no book worth writing
anyway.

Good hunting . . .

407

Index

1975 May

Thur Fri Sat **Sun** Mon Tue Wed Thur Fri Sat Sun Mon Tue Wed Thur Fri Sat **Sun** Mon Tue Wed Thur Fri Sat **Sun** Mon Tue Wed Thur Fri Sat

May 1 2 3 **4** 5 6 7 8 9 10**11** 12 13 14 15 16 17 **18** 19 20 21 22 23 24 **25** 26 27 28 29 30 31

26 Monday

Week 22 (146-219)

HOLIDAY IN ENGLAND, N. IRELAND AND WALES

Another glorious day and in the morning Paul and Cam did some gardening and I listened to records and made a rather hasty and unsatisfactory list for Petals for Thursday so that I wouldn't have to rush in at the crack of dawn on Thursday. Left around 1:00 for London. It was yet another glorious day and I felt very melancholy about leaving Pig behind — she seemed upset too. Picked up a hitcher beyond Stow who was seen before Delvaux at our Village Hall. Took him near Ipswich, picked up two girls, children's nurses or something, and drove them both into Colchester and to the Clacton roundabout. Rather less traffic than I imagined and I reached London around 3:15. Sat in the car for a bit and then went and sat in Petals office and made 'phone calls. The whole place quite deserted because it was a Bank Holiday and I was feeling very lonely and very forlorn. Ambled over to the studio and the monitor screen in the control room was showing Evel Knievel's attempt at Wembley Stadium to jump his motor-cycle over 13 single-decker buses. Incredible American hokum with Evel telling us all that he is still kinda fond of that old red, white and blue, cheer-leaders high-stepping round the ground, well out of time and duffing their batons as they went. Then Evel did a few rather unshowy wheelies and then stood on top of the buses to tell us, in his home-spun way, that he is no kind of a politician but he reckons, y'all, that our wunnerful country sure should stay in the Common Market and that Amyrica would be real happy if we did. Unfortunately Bill Schimmo ex-Beefheart man, arrived with the tape of the LP of Mallard which is the band which was the Magic Band. I was a bit disappointed with their new vocalist Sam but the first half of the LP, which was all I had a chance to hear, sounded pretty good. Then Greg Nash arrived and stayed for the first thirty minutes of the programme and really distracted me with a series of silly questions while I was trying to get on with the programme. Eventually chased him out and tried to salvage something of the programme. Hate doing these golarn bit holiday shows. When it was over I ruled out and drove fairly swiftly round to Hadleigh and the White Lion arrived exactly at the same time as Pig and the others. Had a drink there — as usual the place was almost empty. Had another drink at a crowded pub outside Hadleigh and a third at one in Elderton. Looked fair from the outside but it was filled w. scruffs around a duff jukebox.